THE RENEWAL
OF EDUCATION

[IX]

THE FOUNDATIONS OF WALDORF EDUCATION

RUDOLF STEINER

THE RENEWAL
OF EDUCATION

LECTURES DELIVERED IN BASEL, SWITZERLAND,
APRIL 20–MAY 16, 1920

FOREWORD BY
EUGENE SCHWARTZ

Anthroposophic Press

BP 45

Published by Anthroposophic Press
P.O. Box 799
Great Barrington, MA 01230
www.anthropress.org

Translated with permission from Rudolf Steiner, *Die Erneuerung der pädagogisch-didaktischen Kunst durch Geisteswissenschaft* (GA 301), copyright © 1977 Rudolf Steiner–Nachlassverwaltung.

Translation copyright © 2001 Anthroposophic Press
Foreword copyright © 2001 Eugene Schwartz

Publication of this work was made possible by a grant from the Waldorf Curriculum Fund.

ISBN 0-88010-455-4

Library of Congress Cataloging-in-Publication Data

Steiner, Rudolf, 1861-1925.
  [Erneuerung der pädagogisch-didaktischen Kunst durch
Geisteswissenschaft. English]
  The renewal of education / by Rudolf Steiner ; introduction by Eugene Schwartz.
     p. cm.—(Foundations of Waldorf education ; 9)
  Includes bibliographical references.
  ISBN 0-88010-455-4
  1. Waldorf method of education. 2. Anthroposophy. I. Title. II.
Series.
  LB1029.W34 S7212 2001
  370'.1—dc21
                                                          2001001608

i

Printed in the United States of America

10 9 8 7 6 5 4 3 2 1

5/10/04

TABLE OF CONTENTS

FOREWORD

Eugene Schwartz

In 1920, when these lectures were given, the Waldorf School in Stuttgart was barely eight months old, and the educational theories and methods developed by Rudolf Steiner were hardly known outside of Central Europe. Far more influential at that time—and still exerting a powerful effect on educational theories and methods to this day—were the educational philosophies of John Dewey and Maria Montessori.

John Dewey's work in education arose out of his original immersion in philosophy and psychology, and thus manifested a strong concern for the development of thinking in the child. In formulating educational criteria and aims, he drew heavily on the insights into learning offered by contemporary psychology as applied to children. He viewed thought and learning as a process of inquiry starting from doubt or uncertainty—the so-called "Problem Approach"—and spurred by the desire to resolve practical frictions or relieve strain and tension. For Dewey, the scientist's mental attitudes and habits of thoughts represented the zenith of intellectual life, and the cognitive side of education should guide children toward this goal: "The native and unspoiled attitude of childhood, marked by ardent curiosity, fertile imagination, and love of experimental inquiry is near, very near, to the attitude of the scientific mind."

Education must therefore begin with experience, which has as its aim the discipline and systemization of these natural tendencies until they are congealed into the attitudes and procedures of the scientifically minded person. The "Problem Approach," developed further by William Kilpatrick of Columbia University's Teachers College into the "Project Method," became the *modus operandi* of the progressive education movement, which controlled many of America's school systems for two generations.

Maria Montessori, who had been the first woman medical student in Italy, approached education with a passionate interest in the biophysical basis of the child's will. Soon after her graduation the young physician worked at the Psychiatric Clinic in Rome, where retarded and emotionally disturbed children were herded together like prisoners. She observed that after their meals the children would throw themselves on the floor to search for crumbs:

> Montessori looked around the room and saw that the children had no toys or materials of any kind—that the room was in fact absolutely bare. There were literally no objects in their environment which the children could hold and manipulate in their fingers. Montessori saw in the children's behavior a craving of a very different and higher kind than for mere food. There existed for these poor creatures, she realized, one path and one only towards intelligence, and that was through their hands. . . . It became increasingly apparent to her that mental deficiency was a pedagogical problem rather than a medical one.

In her renowned school for slum children in Rome's San Lorenzo quarter, Montessori discovered that certain simple materials aroused in young children an interest and attention not previously thought possible. These materials included beads arranged in graduated-number units for pre-mathematics instruction; small slabs of wood designed to train the eye in left-to-right reading movements; and graduated series of cylinders for small-muscle training. Children between three and six years old would work spontaneously with these materials, indifferent to distraction, for from a quarter of an hour to an hour. At the end of such a period, they would not seem tired, as after an enforced effort, but refreshed and calm. Undisciplined children became settled through such voluntary work. One of Montessori's early revelations was that, although wealthy benefactors of the school had given the children costly dolls and a doll kitchen, her students "never made such toys the object of their spontaneous choice. " Healthy children, she discovered, prefer work to play.

The spring of 1920 found John Dewey serving as a visiting professor at the National University in Peking, where he lectured extensively on the philosophy of education and met with such influential Asian leaders as Sun Yat-sen. Dewey's educational ideas were to dominate Chinese pedagogy until the Communist Revolution. At this time Maria Montessori had risen to a similar peak of predominance. Just before the outbreak of the First World War, a Montessori school had been established adjacent to the White House, under the sponsorship of Woodrow Wilson's daughter, and by 1920 Montessori had given training courses for teachers in Italy, France, Holland, Germany, Spain, England, Austria, India, and Ceylon. Paying her first official visit to England, she was accorded a degree of adulation usually reserved for royalty.

In the years following World War I, Rudolf Steiner's influence spread less visibly, but no less profoundly, than that of his more prominent contemporaries. By 1920, a host of practical endeavors were undergoing transformation or renewal through Steiner's anthroposophical insights. Every profession or vocation requiring renewal compelled Steiner to provide new imaginations and inspirations for its practitioners so that they in turn could act with new intuitions as challenges arose. Steiner's role as an *educator*, serving not only the renewal of education per se, but the renewal of human culture as a whole, was an essential theme of the year 1920.

One example of this comprehensive work: A small but insistent group of medical students prevailed on Steiner to help them bridge the gap between a worldview that takes the spiritual nature of the human being into account and the growing materialism of modern medicine. From March to April of 1920 Steiner gave twenty wide-ranging lectures, later compiled under the title *Spiritual Science and Medicine.* To the healer, Steiner stressed, illness may be understood as the battle between the polarized forces of thinking and willing, as these opposites manifest in the physical body. In speaking of the development of the child's teeth, Steiner takes a characteristic leap:

> A considerable part of what is included in the educational methods of our Waldorf school, besides other things promoting health, is the prevention of early dental decay in those who attend the school. For it is indeed remarkable that just in relation to the peripheral structures and processes very much depends upon the right education in childhood. . . . If a child of from four to six years is clumsy and awkward with arms, hands, legs, and feet—or cannot adapt himself to a skillful use of his arms and legs and especially of his hands and feet, we shall find that he is inclined to an abnormal process of dental formation. . . .
>
> Go into our needlework classes and handicraft classes at the Waldorf School, and you will find the boys knit and crochet as well as the girls, and that they share these lessons together. . . . This is not the result of any fad or whim, but happens deliberately in order to make the fingers skilful and supple, in order to permeate the fingers with soul. And to drive the soul into the fingers means to promote all the forces that go to build up sound teeth.

Here handwork and medicine become complementary professions, and the physician recognizes the teacher's proactive healing activity. The interplay of dentition and limb activity, center and periphery, inner and outer, which permeates Steiner's approach to medicine, is no less evident in the education lectures given just eleven days after his talks to the medical students and brought together in this volume as *The Renewal of Education*. Another concern is that teachers understand the physiological consequences of pedagogy in much the same way as the physician must understand that he is often continuing the therapeutic process begun in the classroom. For example, speaking to teachers about the child's experience of music, he says:

> We must try to be aware of what a complicated process is happening when we are listening. Picture to yourself the nerves and sense organism which is centered in the human brain. As you know, the brain is constructed in such a way that only its smallest part is functioning like a solid, for the largest part of the brain is floating in the cerebro-spinal fluid....This cerebrospinal fluid is no less involved as far as human consciousness is concerned, than the solid part of the brain, for with every breath we take, it is continually rising and falling . . . . Now, while we are listening to a sequence of tones, we are breathing, and the cerebrospinal fluid is rising and falling.

Such a passage is especially striking when we consider that in this particular lecture cycle Steiner was not preaching to the choir. These lectures were given *not* to teachers who were already versed in Anthroposophy and using the Waldorf method, but rather to a group of public educators in Basel, Switzerland, in a forum organized by the Basel Department of Education. In spite of his clear and unconditional opposition to state governance of education,

Steiner was never reluctant to cast seeds of regeneration onto any field he felt was fertile, nor was he timid about crossing the modern wall that neatly divides pedagogy from physiology. Indeed *The Renewal of Education* ranks among the most "physiological" of Steiner's educational lecture cycles.

Although John Dewey's contribution to the development of thinking through the "problem approach" is significant, it can easily lapse into dry pedantry that honors cognitive activity in only the most utilitarian ways. And while Maria Montessori's genius perceived the many ways in which the child's will can serve its maturation, her methods can stress practicality to the point that child's relationship to play is impoverished. In *The Renewal of Education,* Steiner charts a course that incorporates the development of cognitive powers without sacrificing the unfolding of the will, in much the same way that his indications to physicians emphasized the importance of harmonious balance on the physiological level. The key to this balance lies in his emphasis on the unfolding of the life of *feeling.*

In charting this course, Steiner approaches the child's nature from four perspectives. On the level of *soul,* he describes the human being as a threefold being, one who thinks, feels, and wills. On the level of *consciousness,* these three forces manifest as wakefulness (thinking), dreaming (feeling), and deep sleep (willing). On the level of *physiology,* they utilize the three "systems" of nerve-senses (thinking), rhythmic-circulatory (feeling), and limb-metabolic (willing). On the level of *human development,* these forces unfold in discrete seven-year periods: willing dominates the first seven years of life, feelings become accessible to the child in the second seven-year period, and independent thinking blossoms after age fourteen. Having laid out these twelve interpenetrating spheres, Steiner serves as a navigator, piloting his pedagogue passengers through shoals and narrows that grow increasingly familiar and even congenial as the lectures proceed.

As we accompany Steiner on this journey, we can understand the appeal of Dewey's "Problem Approach" and the Montessori method—as well as their limitations. By emphasizing the education of the cognitive forces at any age, Dewey's methods can heighten a child's sense of independence and wakefulness, while Montessori's stress on the will can strengthen the life of habit and inner discipline. In Steiner's terms, the "Problem Approach" would not be appropriate until adolescence, and using it exclusively from the kindergarten years on up could result in "accelerated adolescence," a premature wakefulness that would undercut the childlike wonder and playfulness that are the foundations of a healthy adulthood. When viewed from the vantage point of these lectures, the Montessori approach could be valid in the will-filled kindergarten years, but might hold the child back from the development of independent imaginative and creative forces as he or she matured. With her emphasis on the teacher's need to "hold back" and allow the child to discover things for herself, Montessori also weakens the strong bonds of feeling that can grow between a teacher and student.

Cultivating the balancing forces of feeling, which are unfolding most strongly between the ages of seven and fourteen, is the particular task of the Waldorf "class teacher," who remains with his or her class from first through eighth grade—the longest and most enduring relationship between a pupil and teacher to be found in any educational system. The eighty-year history of the Waldorf movement has time and again validated the importance of this time commitment and the difference that it has made in the lives of tens of thousands of children. When these lectures were given, however, the school's first class teachers had been teaching for a mere eight months—and Steiner was obviously well aware of the daunting assignment that he had given them! His audience was filled with teachers, and the more deeply the lecturer guided them into the Waldorf method, the more they wondered how anyone could be trained to fulfill this responsibility. Rudolf Steiner's response to this unspoken question is worth repeating at length:

> If I were asked what my main aims had been in preparing the present Waldorf School teachers for their tasks, I should have to answer that first of all I tried to free them from following the conventional ways of teaching. According to these, they would have to remember all kinds of things that would subsequently have to be taught in the classrooms. However, a typical feature of spiritual science consists of one's forgetting, almost every moment, what one has absorbed, so that one has to relearn and recreate it all the time. In order to gain knowledge of the Science of the Spirit, one has to lose it all the time.
>
> I hope that you will forgive me if I tell you something personal. When lecturing on the same subject for the thirtieth, fortieth, or even fiftieth time, I can never repeat the same lecture twice. I could do this just as little as I could eat again what I have already eaten yesterday (if you will pardon the somewhat grotesque comparison). In eating, one is right in the midst of living processes. And the same applies to one's absorbing spiritual-scientific content. One always has to acquire it anew. And when preparing the Waldorf teachers, I wanted them to feel that every morning they would have to enter their class rooms with fresh, untrammeled souls, ready to face ever new situations and ever new riddles. The Science of the Spirit teaches us the art of forgetting, which, after all, is only the other side of digesting what one has taken in. This is part of the self-education demanded by spiritual science. Now you may remark: But we know some spiritual scientists or anthroposophists who can reel off from memory what they have learned. This is quite correct but it represents a state of immaturity among anthroposophists. I

have not been able to keep some of them away from these meetings and they will have to bear hearing such a statement about themselves. To carry anthroposophical knowledge in one's memory is a sign of imperfection, for Anthroposophy must be a living spring which constantly renews itself within the soul. And this is the very mood in which one should face one's pupils. Therefore the real task of spiritual science is to revitalize the human soul in a similar way to that in which our digestion gives new life to the physical body every day. All memorized matter should disappear from the mind to make room for an actively receptive spirit. Allowing spiritual science to flow into one's sphere of ideation will fructify the art of education.

Even when speaking to a public audience, Steiner did not hesitate to point to the inextricable ties between Waldorf education and Anthroposophy; even when addressing people highly trained in the teaching profession, he did not back away from emphasizing self-education, that is, self-development, as the most important element in pedagogical preparation. To Rudolf Steiner, the "renewal of education" can be brought about only by men and women who, with courage and initiative, will be willing to undertake their own renewal. These lectures are clearly dedicated to such individuals, and it is to be hoped that this new edition will find its way to their minds, hearts, and deeds.

Sunbridge College

Eugene Schwartz, author of Millennial Child *(Anthroposophic Press), has been a Waldorf educator for twenty-five years. He is a class teacher at Green Meadow Waldorf School in Chestnut Ridge, New York, and he lectures on educational topics throughout North America. His essays and commentaries may be accessed at MillennialChild.com.*

1

SPIRITUAL SCIENCE AND MODERN EDUCATION

Basel, April 20, 1920

Today I want to present a preview of the direction I will take in the following lectures. I ask you not to conclude from the way my topic is phrased that I, like some radical, am implying that the way education has developed during the nineteenth century until now is worthless. Please do not think I believe that education has been waiting for spiritual science to give it life. That is not my intent. On the contrary, I am starting from a very different position.

I am thoroughly convinced that education as it developed during the nineteenth century, with so many exemplary representatives, and as it influences the activities of the present, can now achieve a particular level of perfection. I believe that those who today, for one reason or another, need to look about and understand the various sciences in theory and practice, who need to comprehend the effects they have upon life, and who are also concerned with education will need to compare education to the other sciences. Through that comparison we may arrive at an unusual conclusion, but I want to express my own experience. We could conclude that modern education contains many valuable principles that should be a part of today's education. When we look upon the desires and practice required by education today, we get only the most favorable impression. It is with just that impression that I wish to begin by stating that I do not at all underestimate a great man such as Herbart.[1] I have learned a great deal about Herbart's perspective on education. I spent the first half of my life, until I was about thirty, in Austria. During that period Herbart's pedagogy was the underlying principle for all public schools, as they were then under the direction of Exner.[2] Professors at the Austrian universities also taught Herbart's pedagogy, so during the course of my life I have encountered his educational model in all its details. However, if I extend my considerations beyond the pedagogy proposed by Herbart to those of other perspectives, many of which affect the most modern education, then I would also have to say that there is much we can joyfully receive in the realm of pedagogical thought and feeling. This is a stream of thought we encounter when we look at education as a very important part of our modern civilization.

On the other hand, pedagogy, the whole art of teaching and educational thinking, has never been under such broad criticism as it is today, though criticism has always existed. Both lay people and professionals criticize education in a rather blunt manner, yet it is often defended itself in clumsy ways. Listen to everything said by people who, for instance, establish country boarding schools[3] and speak of a complete renewal of education. Then follow the way a broad portion of the population takes up such discussions. Pedagogues try to defend how their practices developed and how they are generally sustained. When we do this, we must also admit that, despite the marvelous achievements of our modern science of education, when we look at what is actually done in the schools, this criticism is not completely unfounded.

We find ourselves caught between these two perspectives, but there is a third that is much more comprehensive. I do not believe

I will go beyond the limits of an introductory lecture on education if I draw your attention to this particular viewpoint.

Though it may have been less noticeable here in Switzerland, throughout Europe we have gone through a very difficult time during the past five or six years. Yet even here in Switzerland you have to admit that this was a time that would have been unimaginable ten years ago. We need only ask ourselves whether ten years ago people could have dreamed that what was to spread over Europe was even possible. We should also not forget the damage that resulted from the terrible experiences during the war: chaos in social relationships throughout a major portion of Europe. Those who believe that this chaos is improving and that life will be better in the near future are only deceiving themselves. We are only at the beginning of these chaotic relationships. We need to ask whether it is only external situations that have caused this social chaos in Europe. If we look at the situation dispassionately, we will realize that social relationships cannot be the cause, since these relationships were created by human beings. The cause must lie with the people.

The problem is that today, although everywhere we hear demands for more "social relationships"[4] within our society, people have so little social and so much antisocial feeling. We cannot help but admit that this has arisen in spite of all the marvelous pedagogical principles, in spite of all the achievements that deserve recognition, in spite of everything that has been done with the best intent. In spite of all that, we have not managed to bring people to a point where today they can encounter one another with genuine understanding. We see before us a period where people are certainly not stingy with their praise for how much we have achieved; but during this same time, we also see that things have developed to a point of absurdity. A desire must arise in the hearts of at least some people to find out whether our education has created that group that is so annoying in Europe today.

If we look more closely, we discover we can do nothing other than honor those great figures of nineteenth-century pedagogy: Herbart, Ziller,[5] Diesterweg,[6] Pestalozzi,[7] and so forth—I don't need to name them all for you. On the other hand, we must admit that although we have an exemplary science of education, there is more to teaching than simply exemplary science. In teaching, what is particularly important is the ability to transform that science into a genuine art; then education becomes an art.

To be clearer, if we compare education with art, we could have wonderful aesthetics or a marvelous understanding of how to do something in music, sculpture, or painting. That is, the science of painting, sculpting, or composition could be marvelous, but it is something different to be able to practice that science. We might even say that those who practice the arts—sculptors, painters, or musicians—often have real antipathy toward the "scientific" principles people have thought up. It is not important for these people that such principles enter their conceptual life. For them, it is important that such principles live in their deeds, in their entire beings, and that those principles become living entities within them. In education, the situation is not quite the same as in other artistic sciences. To educate, we must be much more conscious, much more filled with concepts than, for instance, those concerned solely with the practices of painting, music, or sculpture. Nevertheless what we understand to be correct in education must still go on to fill our entire being if we are to be genuine pedagogical artists.

In this course, I want to speak about the help spiritual science can give to education. It is not that I think every principle of pedagogical science needs to be reformed. Rather I believe that in order to use these principles in a truly practical way, whether individually or in a large class, we need to enliven and permeate them with what only spiritual science can provide. Spiritual science wants to be included into all areas of modern scientific understanding. Spiritual science can refresh everything for which our modern culture strives. Although many people believe that it is now in the process of returning to idealism, our modern culture arose out of materialism. It arose out of the materialism of the last half of the nineteenth century, and it is still imbedded in it. All areas of human mental activity—we can almost say all areas of human culture—have taken shape through the materialistic attitude of that time. This materialistic attitude has not been visible in the same degree in every area, but it has had the most damaging effects upon education.

That is what I wanted to say today as an introduction. It is the basic perspective of my lectures. Spiritual science is often misunderstood, and I find it necessary to indicate, at least in a few words, how we can correct that misunderstanding. Before I can show you what spiritual science can contribute to the proper use of pedagogical science, how it can transform pedagogical knowledge into pedagogical activity, I first need to speak in detail about some of the misunderstandings about spiritual science. I do not want to speak in abstractions and will therefore begin as concretely as possible.

Many of you may have heard that it is not as easy to consider the human being through spiritual science as it is through modern anthropology. Modern anthropology has greatly simplified the questions about the human being that confront us. People easily believe it is a kind of superstition when they hear that spiritual science believes we can view the human being as consisting of supersensible aspects. They consider it superstition when we look at growing children and see not only the general development of human beings, but also, broadly speaking, the development of four aspects of the human being.

With a modern worldview based upon our progressive understanding of nature, it is easy to laugh when we hear that spiritual science says the human being consists of a physical, etheric, and astral body, and a special I-being. I can well understand this laughter. People laugh about such things because they misunderstand. Nevertheless they laugh at the cost of genuine further development of humanity and at the cost of an art of education that truly sees the human being. I need to say you are right when you hear that here and there, in some cultlike way, Theosophists sit together while someone who has read something in a book or heard something in a lecture talks about the human being consisting of a physical, etheric, and astral body, and an I. That would be a highly unfruitful activity, and you have a certain right to laugh about it. If such people spread such things out of a religious conviction, they will achieve nothing real for human culture or human life. We can achieve something positive only when we consider such things as guidelines for enriching life, and not as abstract concepts of the human being or the growing child.

If we remain with the most abstract concepts, we can say that it is a good principle of education to help children develop according to their individuality. In that case, we should study the forces that arise and develop in the human being during childhood, and we should use education to develop that which desires to be expressed through human nature. This is certainly a wonderful principle, but we must not allow it to remain abstract. It is significant only when we genuinely bring it into life, when we consider the human being from the first years until adulthood in such a way that we can actually see those forces develop.

If we take only the concept of the human being offered by modern anthropology, the one you can learn from science, we simply will not notice what becomes visible in a human being, what wants to develop. I am only suggesting some guidelines when I say that the human being consists of a physical body, an etheric body, an astral body, and an I. What I am saying is that you can use the method of observation common in modern materialistic natural sciences only for the physical body. You also need another approach for observing human beings. You need to see them as much more complicated and develop an eye for how human nature develops. Human nature is not completely contained within purely natural laws, and we can comprehend it only through its higher aspects.

What does it mean when I say the human being consists of four aspects? I am pointing to something that is pretty obvious to every teacher who has learned about psychology. It is very well known, and yet a genuinely deep view of the entire human being does not flow from that understanding. Everyone knows how many psychologists, including educational psychologists, speak about the fact that we have to look at the human soul—I need to be cautious here—as consisting of three aspects, thinking, feeling, and willing. You certainly know how much discussion there was in the nineteenth century about whether the will came first and thinking developed out of it, or whether thinking or imagining was the basis. For example, you know that in Herbart's pedagogy there is a certain predominance of intellectualism; from that perspective, the will results only from the desires of imagination, and so forth. However, when you stand back from the whole discussion about thinking, feeling, and willing, you will notice that something is missing: a true picture of human nature. Spiritual science wants to provide the way to obtain that genuine view of human nature. Spiritual science wants people to acquire the capacity to view human nature in its totality.

If we are not totally crass materialists, we often speak about the fact that the human being is not only a physical body but also a soul. To this soul we ascribe thinking, feeling, and willing. Perhaps you are familiar with the current discussions that ultimately lead to the statement that it is impossible to comprehend how the soul is connected with the physical body and how the soul affects the body, and the body, the soul. Nearly everyone who takes this question seriously undergoes a form of suffering, but they do not realize that the way the question is normally presented is simply not correct. They do not realize that perhaps we need to change the entire viewpoint.

When we look at the developing child, we can understand how the soul develops out of the physical body. Those who have a sense of outer form see how the child develops in such wonderful and mysterious ways. They can also see that when we follow the child's growth from day to day in the first weeks of life, and then from week to week, month to month, year to year throughout the child's life, that development speaks strongly to our sense of humanity. Those who watch this transformation and have a sense of how the soul is progressing must pose the question, "How is what develops as the soul connected with the physical body as we see it revealed externally?" It is clear that the soul is active within the body, particularly in children. Modern science, however, is not strong enough, we might say. Its weapons are dull and cannot properly approach the question of how the soul works within the physical. Certain phenomena are simply not objectively observed by modern science; yet when we observe a child's first years of life, we see things that give us a new riddle each day. We need only to look.

The child cuts its first baby teeth about the age of one or sometimes a little later; these baby teeth fall out and are replaced by the permanent teeth around the age of seven. But what do they really mean, these facts modern science describes in detail everywhere? What do they suggest about the development of the human being? Modern science cannot research that. If we go on, we see that growing children develop until the age of puberty. We see that puberty causes a complete revolution in the child's body and soul. If we think about elementary school, we realize that public education in elementary school encompasses the most important human developmental period, which begins with the change of teeth and ends with puberty. However, science and modern life in general cannot penetrate what actually occurs in this realm, which we do not separate into "body" and "soul," but instead call the soul-body aspect.

In the end it is important to learn a more exact and intimate way of observing human nature. Try looking a little more closely. A year or so after birth, the human organism forms the first teeth, not out of just the upper or lower jaw, but out of the entire organism. This is also repeated around the age of seven. Here we can see that the human organism needs a much longer time to express its hardest structure, the teeth, than it needed to produce the baby teeth in early childhood.

You can see that you should use more than modern natural science to look at something connected with the body. At the same time, you need to see how the entire nature of the human being, including its soul aspects, changes with every week from the eruption of the baby teeth to that of the permanent teeth. You can see that other forces contained within human nature affect the soul during the period from the change of teeth until puberty than those that affect it later. We need to consider human beings in their entirety, and then we will find that the life of the soul exists in an entirely different way before the change of teeth than it does afterward. If we have some sense of what actually happens following the change of teeth, it follows that if we look at thinking, at the intellectual nature of the human being, we will need to understand what happens to human intellectual nature, to our imaginative nature, before and during the change of teeth! If we consider this without prejudice, we have to admit that a great deal happens. Jean Paul,[8] who thought a great deal about education, properly noted that the first years of life have more impact upon a human being than three years at the university. (At that time, there were only three.) It is certainly true that when we look at the configuration of the intellect, the most important years for forming the human intellect, for forming the capacity to reason, are those first years of life before the change of teeth.

We should also try to gain a genuine sense of what changes in the soul. Try remembering, and see how far back clear memories reach.

Then think about how little we remember prior to the change of teeth; that is, how little people can collect concepts to retain in their memory before the change of teeth. We can thus conclude that the less the organism has to use those strong forces to create the adult teeth, the more a human being will be able to form its thoughts into firm pictures that can remain in the memory.

Today I only want to sketch the situation. From what I just said, you can see that there is something that runs parallel with those forces in the body that in a certain sense culminate in producing the second set of teeth. In tandem with this process, there is a firming of those forces in the soul that transform the pictures we would otherwise lose into firmly contoured concepts, that remain as a treasure in the human soul. I would like to simply suggest an idea today that you will see to be true in the next days. We need to ask ourselves: Can those forces that give rise to the teeth be in some way connected to the pictorial aspects of thinking? Isn't it as though the soul needs to give the child's body the use of certain bodily forces during the first seven years, until the change of teeth, so that the teeth can form? When they are complete, a metamorphosis occurs and the child transforms these forces so that they become forces for conceptualization in the soul. Can we not see how the soul, the conceptualizing soul, works to form the teeth? When the formation of teeth, that is, when the use of certain soul forces in the conceptualizing soul is finished, that is, after the teeth have erupted, these same forces begin to affect the soul.

Think for a moment how little modern science tends to look at such metamorphoses. People rack their brains trying to determine the connection between body and soul. What we need to do first, though, is to look at the area where the soul acts upon the body. We may ask if it is conceptualization within the soul that expresses itself by forming teeth. Can we not see how the soul affects the body and recognize that it is then spared expressing that activity in another way, in a way that relates purely to the soul? It is important that we arrive at truly healthy ideas, ideas people had before materialism became so widespread. It is important that we return to actually seeing how the spirit-soul affects the physical body.

It is strange but true: materialism is slowly losing the capacity to understand matter and its phenomena. It is not simply that materialists are losing connection with the spirit; the true tragedy is that they are condemned to not understanding matter. Materialism is unable to look at the physical body as relating to the same forces that later enable us to remember, that are active later in our thoughts, that are the same forces active in the physical formation of the teeth. It is not simply that materialism has lost sight of the spiritual; it has lost sight of the physical to an even greater extent in that it cannot see how the spirit-soul works upon the body.

Spiritual science wants to contribute a proper understanding of what works upon human beings. Materialism is in truth condemned to not understanding matter. Matter is what the spirit continuously works upon, and the materialistic perspective cannot follow that work in the human spirit-soul. All of us can certainly believe that it would cause enormous damage if materialism completely lost the spiritual world of thought and human beings had to cease thinking, if human beings had to become animals. No one can admit that when we think, we are actually engaged in some form of spirituality. That, however, is the fate of materialists, to not understand the physical.

The same forces that are active in conceptualizing, in picturing our world, work to form our teeth. If you know that, then you can observe children in a much different way. Most of all, you can observe them differently—not only intellectually; you encounter children with your feelings, with your perception, and with your will in a very different way. In the following lectures you will see how these things that really arise from the spirit-soul are not simply abstract principles, but elements we can directly apply in the present.

During elementary school, we see that important period in the life of growing children where memory is active, where we can count upon memory, where it is so endlessly important to children that they have a teacher in whom they can sense an authority, yet an authority freely chosen by the children. To not admit that one of the basic forces and basic needs of children from the ages of six or seven until fourteen or fifteen is the desire to have an authority in their lives is to completely misunderstand human nature. We will show here how this kind of authority, freely chosen through the children's perception, an authority outside but alongside the children, is one of the most important aspects of human life.

Someone who has sharpened their vision to see a certain connection between the soul-spirit and the physical body until the change of teeth will also notice something extraordinarily important for the following period. We, of course, need a certain amount of time to grow our first baby teeth. That is a relatively short time. We then need a longer period to exchange those first teeth for permanent teeth. In the course of these lectures, we will hear how the permanent teeth have a much closer connection with the individual than the baby teeth, which are based more upon heredity. This is true not only with teeth; there is another place where we, in a certain way, reproduce those things we have received through heredity out of our own nature. This principle is also true for human speech.

At this point I would like to introduce something that I will describe more fully in the following lectures: the secret of the development of human speech is hidden in its most important aspects from the entirety of modern science. People are unaware that just as we receive our first teeth through a kind of inheritance from our parents, we receive language through the influences of our external surroundings. That is, we receive language through the principle of imitation, which, however, becomes an organic principle.

In the first years of our lives, we learn to speak from our surroundings. However, the language we learn then, that we speak until the age of four, five, or six, has the same relationship to the entire human being as baby teeth have to the entire human being. What people speak after they have reached the age of puberty, that is, after the age of fourteen or fifteen, what is active within them as they speak is something they achieve for a second time. It is something they very recently achieved, something they accomplished for themselves in just the same way that they grew their second set of teeth. In boys, we can see this externally in their change of voice. In girls, the development is more inward. It is nevertheless present. Since these forces act differently upon the larynx of a boy, they are externally visible. This is a revelation of what occurs in the entire human being during these important elementary-school years, not simply in the human body nor in the human soul, but in the entire soul-body, in the body-soul. It occurs continuously from year to year, from month to month, and is connected with the inner development of what we already learned as language from our environment during our early childhood. Those who understand how the spirit-soul acts upon the human being until the age of fourteen or fifteen, those who can, through a direct, instinctive intuition, observe elementary school children, will see this directly. Such a person might say that here we have a student; he makes throaty sounds in this way, sounds with his lips in this way, and with the gums in this way. This student can make sounds with his gums more easily than lip sounds and so forth. This can become a very intensive science; however, it is a science that points in all its details to what develops as a soul-body or body-soul in the child.

Those capable of observing them can see the transformations that speech undergoes between the ages of seven and fifteen, which people normally do not notice, as accomplished by the soul acting upon language. This is something that is lost if you have learned to observe without the help of spiritual science. Those who can observe this will then find that in the first years of life until the change of teeth, conceptualization was completely occupied with the forming our teeth; after the change of teeth, it can then act to form itself. At that time conceptualization, our ability to picture our thoughts, in a sense pulls back from the physical body and becomes something independent in the soul. Later, from the change of teeth until puberty, although this can sometimes be seen earlier, it is what we call the will that withdraws from the entirety of the child and becomes localized in the larynx, in the organs of speech. Just as the imaginative life withdraws and becomes an independent part of the soul, in the same way around the age of fourteen or fifteen the element of will localizes and concentrates in what becomes speech and its associated organs. The transformation a boy's larynx undergoes is where the will culminates. We will speak more about the corresponding phenomenon in girls.

In other words, if we look at things from a spiritual-scientific perspective, conceptualization and will cease to be so abstract. We cannot, of course, form a connection between these abstractions and a quite differently formed body. If, however, we learn to observe and recognize how very different the nature of a child is, where we see how the child speaks quite differently with the lips than with the gums and the throaty sounds are quite different also, we can recognize how the forces of conceptualization work in the physical body during the first seven years of life. We can recognize the external, physical revelation of a spirit-soul aspect and to recognize that the will is localized in the larynx. We can learn to observe how will enters human speech. The will is thus developed and conceptualization is no longer abstract, but something we can observe in the real processes of life. In much the same way, we observe gravity in water falling from the mountains and see the speed of the flowing water in the weight of the water meeting its resistances. Thus we can learn to recognize how the body develops from the spirit-soul week by week when we first learn to observe that spirit-soul in its work upon the body.

In what I have just said, you can see guidelines for observing the development of the human being. Spiritual science speaks of human nature in a somewhat difficult and complicated way. You can contrast that with modern science, which simply does not take into account the fact that the human being is a wonderful being that draws into itself the rhythms of the entire world, that is an entire world in itself, that holds within itself a microcosm corresponding to a macrocosm. If I say the human being consists of a physical body and also an etheric body, that means you should learn to observe how the physical body develops during the first seven years of childhood. But you should learn this not only on corpses—not only anatomically or physiologically. You should learn to observe how human beings are soul-spirit and how this soul-spirit, whether we call it an etheric body or something else, acts upon the physical body. In that way you can learn to recognize how it forms the physical body by forming the teeth that arise out of the entire body, and then how it works upon its conceptualizations so that they can remain. Thus we can say that at the time of the change of teeth, the etheric body is born. Until the change of teeth, it is still active in the physical body and forms what culminates in the change of teeth. Then it becomes free and works upon the formation of concepts that can remain in memory. Later we speak of an independent I primarily concentrated in the will but which we can perceive in the development of speech when we look in the proper way. We can recognize the will if we do not simply compare it with conceptualization, but instead see it in its activities in the development of speech, that is, in a concrete form. In that development of will, we recognize the development of the I, which needs to be followed further. But we see something lying between the etheric body and the I that is expressed through speech. This is particularly important to observe educationally in the early years of elementary school.

There we see the actual soul aspect of the human being. When the child begins elementary school and is still under the influences of the forces involved in the change of teeth, the intellectual aspect is not yet present. However, by becoming more localized, the will aspect becomes from week to week and from month to month more enclosed in the body during the period of elementary school. If you know that, you will include in the elementary school curriculum those things lying in the proper direction to support the development of the will in the intellect. If you understand what will and intellect are, and can observe how from month to month and from year to year the will becomes localized in the child's speech, and the intellect that has withdrawn into the spirit-soul; if you understand how these interact, you will understand what you must do in teaching the children for their physical and soul upbringing. Then you will consider education an art and will recognize that you first need to understand the material, human nature. Just as a sculptor has clay and works with it the way a painter works with colors, so must an artist in education understand how to work the will into the intellect. A pedagogical artist must understand how to act in order to create the proper interpenetration, the proper artistic form, of the intellect that was born at the age of seven, and how to approach the will that is to develop through the hands of the elementary school teacher until puberty.

Discussion Following Lecture One

It is not possible to say everything in the first lecture, and I mentioned many things only as a sort of introduction; later I will present them in more detail. Therefore there may be some questions that I will answer in their full context in subsequent lectures. Nevertheless I would like to ask if you have any questions today. Perhaps you can write your questions down, and I will attempt to answer them in later lectures. That way I can answer them within the full context. It is not at all superfluous to pose such questions today, or perhaps, even better, tomorrow, after you have had some time to think.

I have a written question here asking how to handle a boy in the third developmental stage of childhood, that is, after puberty, who is one-sidedly gifted in mathematics and the natural sciences, but who has absolutely no talent for foreign languages.

That question is related to a great deal that I will discuss in detail later. In the next lectures, I will discuss these special but one-sided talents and show how you can place them in the service of developing the entire human being. I will also show how you can harmonize them by proceeding in a particular way pedagogically. Nevertheless I would like to say something about it now.

There are some girls who have this kind of talent, but it happens so seldom that you can often find complete biographies of these women because they then became famous mathematicians. The one-sided talent for mathematics and natural sciences that we find in boys is generally based upon the fact that an organ that appears quite unimportant is very subtly developed in these young men. Perhaps some of you are aware of such families as the Bernoulli family,[1] in which individual members of the family were particularly gifted in mathematics over a period of eight generations. In another famous case, we have the Bach family,[2] which produced a large number of "little Bachs" who were extremely talented with regard to music. I should also mention that there are many boys who are highly talented with regard to the physical and mathematical sciences, but whom we cannot observe so well because their talents lie more in the direction of botany and zoology. At the same time, they are also highly talented in the area of mineralogy, but are not particularly gifted in observing the physical characteristics of minerals.

Such things can take on many different nuances. In these boys, the three semicircular canals in the human ear are particularly well developed. It may be that these three tiny vertical bones within the human ear are so arranged that they bring with them a highly developed sense of space and numbers. In other cases, they are much less well developed. These talents are connected with that development. If the human organism is particularly well developed in that way, a special talent arises out of the ear.

Within the organ of hearing are all the organs necessary for hearing, but these are further connected with the organs for speaking, for balance, and for a sense of numbers. In a certain sense, they all meld together. If these small bones that appear as three semicircular canals within the ear are one-sidedly developed within a person, then that development occurs at the cost of the development for hearing the sounds in speech and so forth, namely, for hearing the proper structure of language. This weakens the talent for hearing language, with the result that particularly those children who are very gifted in mathematics have less talent in language. The only thing we can do with such children is to begin teaching them language as soon as we notice that they are particularly gifted in mathematics. We teach them language without placing a strong value upon the intellectual aspect, that is, upon grammar. Rather we teach them language through the rhythm of the language itself. If you have the children memorize things without going into the actual content, but so that they simply enjoy the rhythm of the foreign language in short poems, then teach them the content through the sounds and what the sounds carry within them, you will see, if you begin this early enough, that these children will overcome this one-sidedness.

As we have shown in practice at the Waldorf School in Stuttgart, it is absolutely necessary to avoid beginning with an intellectually oriented education when children are seven or eight. Instead we need to work from the more artistic aspect. We do not teach writing in an intellectual way, by working with the forms of the letters. Instead we teach it by beginning with a kind of primitive drawing. In that way, we develop the will more than the intellect, whereas the common way of teaching writing today speaks too strongly to the intellect. Thus we attempt to engage the entire human being. In that way, the individual one-sided talents balance out.

If you ask how to awaken the memory for correct spelling, my answer would be that you need to observe the differences in human strengths during the three periods of human life, that is, until the change of teeth, until puberty, and then after puberty until the age of twenty. You need to develop a sense for observing these three periods of life and the differences in the specific forces of life that develop. Then you will notice that people who, until the age of fifteen, have absolutely no sense of correct spelling or correct grammar will develop it if they are treated in the way I just mentioned. If you draw their attention to the rhythm of the language, they will develop this sense out of the depths of their souls after the age of fifteen.

This is why it would be totally inappropriate to keep children who have well-developed talents from progressing through the grades simply because they do not demonstrate any particular talent for grammar. If you look at what Goethe wrote as a young boy and then see that when he was older, he stood in a very exclusive group with regard to grammar, you will think about him very differently than the way people usually think about a boy or girl who cannot spell properly at the age of thirteen or so. Instead of wringing our hands about how poorly such children spell and continually asking what we should do to teach them to spell, it would be much better to think about what capacities the children actually have, seek out those special talents, and then find a way to teach the children what they need to learn from those talents.

You will see that if you emphasize the artistic element when teaching children who are one-sidedly gifted in mathematics, you will always achieve a balance.

2

THREE ASPECTS
OF THE HUMAN BEING

Basel, April 21, 1920

To our modern way of thinking, it can be difficult to describe the particular characteristics of spiritual science. It is natural to judge something new according to what we already know. Spiritual science, in the way I mean it here, differs from what we normally call science. It does not give things another content or put forth other ideas, but it speaks about a very different human being. It is because of this other perspective that spiritual science can be fruitful for education. If I were asked to explain this difference, I would give the following preliminary description.

When we study something these days, we think we gain some ideas about this or that. Then, depending upon the strength of our memory, we carry those ideas with us for the rest of our lives. We remember things; therefore we know them. Spiritual science is not to be practiced in that way. Certainly people often see it that way, out of habit, but those who take it up like a collection of notes do not value it properly. They approach reality in a way that is just as foreign to life as our sensory, material manner of consideration is.

For instance, if someone were to say that she ate and drank yesterday and having done that, she would not need to eat or drink again the rest of her life, you would think that is nonsense. The human organism must continually renew its connection with those things it needs from external nature. It can do nothing other than enter this process of receiving and working with what it takes in time and again.

In a way, it is the same with spiritual science. Spiritual science gives something that enlivens the inner human being and must be renewed for it to remain alive within the human being. For that reason, spiritual science is much closer to the creative powers of the human being than normal knowledge, and that is why it can actually stimulate us from many directions to work as with this most precious material, the developing human being.

It is not immediately obvious that spiritual science is alive in that regard. However, if you patiently consider those things that our modern habits say must be presented more abstractly, you will notice that they slowly become genuinely alive. We then not only have knowledge of facts, but also something that at each moment, in each hour, we can use to give life to the school. If you are patient, you will see that spiritual science goes in quite a different direction, and that those people who treat it like any other knowledge, like a collection of notes, damage it the most.

I wanted to offer these preliminary thoughts, as you will need to consider the things I need to say today in that light. Yesterday I mentioned that we can genuinely understand the human being from various perspectives, and that these lead us to a unified view of the body, soul, and spirit. I said that in spiritual science we speak of the physical human being, the etheric human being, the astral human being, and the I. Each of these aspects of human nature has three aspects of its own.

Let us first look at the human being from the physical perspective. Here the modern physiological perspective is often inaccurate and does not arrive at a truly mobile view of the nature of the human being. After a thirty-year study, I mentioned these things in my book *Riddles of the Soul*,[1] published two or three years ago. At the beginning, I spoke of the natural division of the physical human being into three parts. Now I will present these at this point in our course more as a report to substantiate what I say.

If we consider the human being first from the physical perspective, it is important to first look at the fact that it perceives the external world through its senses. The senses, which are, in a way, localized at the periphery of the human organism, are brought further into the human being by the nerves. Anyone who simply includes the senses and nerves with the rest really does not observe the human being in a way that leads to clear understanding of its nature. There is a high degree of independence, of individuality, in what I would call the nerve-sense human being. Because modern people consider the whole human being as some nebulous unity, science cannot comprehend the fundamental independence of the nerve-sense human being. You will understand me better when I describe this further.

A second independent aspect of the physical human being lies within our organism. I call it the rhythmic organism. It is the part of our respiratory, circulatory, and lymphatic systems that is rhythmic. Everything that has rhythmic activity within the human being is part of the second system, which is relatively independent from the nerve-sense system. It is as though these two systems exist alongside one another, independently, yet in communication with one another. Modern science's vague concept of a unified human being does not exist.

The third aspect is also relatively independent of the whole human being. I call it the metabolic organism. If you look at the activities of these three aspects of the human being, the nerve-sense being, the human being that lives in certain rhythmic activities, and the human being who lives in the metabolism, you have everything that exists in human nature to the extent that it is an active organism. At the same time, you have an indication of three independent systems within the human organism. Modern science creates quite false concepts about these three independent systems when it states that the life of the soul is connected with the nerves. This is a habit of thought that has established itself since about the end of the eighteenth century.

In order to develop a feeling for these three aspects of the body, I would like to discuss their relationship to the soul. Allow me to state first that everything that is concentrated in the human metabolic system, that is an activity of the metabolic system, is directly connected with human willing. The part of the human being represented by the circulatory system is directly connected with feeling, while the nerve-sense system is connected with thinking.

You can see that modern science has created some incorrect concepts here. It says that the human soul life is strongly connected with the life of the nerves, or with the nerves and senses, and that thinking, feeling, and willing are directly connected with the nerves; through the nerves the soul indirectly transfers its activity to the circulatory, the rhythmic, and metabolic systems. This brings considerable confusion into our understanding of the human being. People become more removed from their own nature instead of being brought nearer to it.

Just as thinking is connected with nerve-sense life, feeling is directly connected with the human rhythmic system. Feeling, as soul life, pulsates in our breathing, blood circulation, and lymphatic system and is connected with these systems just as directly as thinking is with the nerve system. The will is directly connected with the metabolism. Something always happens in the human metabolism when a will activity is present. The nerves are not at all connected to willing, as is usually stated. The will has a direct relationship to the metabolism, and the person perceives this relationship through the nerves. That is the genuine relationship. The nerve system has no task other than thinking. Whether we think of some external object, or whether what we think about occurs in our metabolism in relation to the will, the nerves always have the same task.

Modern science speaks of sense nerves, which it presumes exist in order to provide impressions of the external world from the periphery of the body to the central organ. We also hear that motor nerves exist to carry will impulses from the central system to the periphery of the body. I will speak more of this later. People have created very clever theories to prove that this difference between the sense and motor nerves exists. But this difference does not exist. More important than these clever theories is the fact that you can cut a motor nerve and then connect one end to the end of a sense nerve that you have also cut. This then becomes a nerve of one kind. It shows that we can find no real differences in function between the motor and sense nerves, even in an anatomical or physiological sense. The so-called motor nerves do not carry will impulses from the central organ to the human periphery.

In reality motor nerves are also sense nerves. They exist so that if I, for example, moved a finger, there is a direct relationship between the decision and the metabolism of the finger, so my will can exercise a direct influence upon the metabolism of the finger. The so-called motor nerves perceive this change in the metabolic process. Without this perception of a metabolic process, no decision of the will can follow, since the human being depends upon perceiving what occurs within himself. This is just like our needing to perceive something in the external world if we are to know things and participate in them.

The differentiation between sense and motor nerves is a most willing servant of materialism. It is a servant that could have arisen in materialistic science only because a cheap comparison could be found for it in modern times, namely, the telegraph. We telegraph from one station to another and then telegraph back. It is approximately a picture of the process of telegraphy that people use to describe how the sense and motor nerves communicate between the periphery and the central organ. Of course, this whole picture was possible only in an age like the nineteenth century, when telegraphy played such an important role. Had telegraphy not existed, perhaps people would not have formed that picture. Instead they might have developed a more natural view of the corresponding processes.

It may seem as though I want to trample all these theories into the ground simply for the sake of being radical. It is not that easy. I began to study nerves as a very young man, and it was very earthshaking for me when I noticed that this theory served materialism. It did this by transforming what is a direct influence of the will upon the metabolism into something merely physical, into an imagined physical strand of nerves carrying the will impulse from the central organ to the periphery of the human being to the muscles. People simply imposed material processes upon the human organism.

In an act of will, there is in truth a direct connection between the will impulse of the soul and some process in the metabolism. The nerve exists only to transmit the *perception* of this process. To the same extent, the nerve also exists to transmit the perception necessary when there is a relationship between the person's feeling and a process expressed in circulation. That is always the case when we feel. Essentially, the basis is not some nerve process; it is a modification of our circulation. With any feeling, there is a process that does not exist in the metabolism, but in the rhythm of circulation. What happens in the blood, in the lymphatic system, or in the nonmetabolic aspects of the exchange of oxygen (the exchange of oxygen is actually metabolic, and to that extent it is a part of the transfer of will)—to the extent that we are dealing with the rhythmic processes of breathing—belongs to feeling. All feeling is directly connected with the rhythmic processes. Again, the nerves exist only to directly perceive what occurs between the feeling in the soul and the rhythmic processes in the organism. Nerves are only organs of perception. In a sense, spiritual science allows us to first see what it really means when time and again we find in textbooks on physiology or psychology: "We can make the hypothetical assumption that human beings have sense and motor nerves." However, anatomically they are differentiated at most by small differences in thickness; certainly not by anything else. I will return to the speculations made by Tabes and others. Today I wanted only to give some indication of what is shown by an objective observation of the human organism as consisting of three aspects: namely, that the nerve-sense organism is related to the imaginative, thinking life of the soul. We have the rhythmic organism, which relates to the feeling life of the soul, and finally, the metabolic organism, which, in its broadest sense, is related to the willing life in the soul.

To clarify this, we can look at some part of life, say, music. The musical part of life is the best evidence (but only one among many we will encounter) of the particular relationship of feeling to the rhythmic life of the organism. The imaginative, thinking life connected with the nerve-sense organism perceives the rhythmic life connected with feeling. When we hear something musical, when we give ourselves over to a picture presented in tones, we quite obviously perceive through our senses. Those physiologists, however, who can observe in more subtle ways, notice that our breathing inwardly participates in the musical picture; how much our breathing has to do with what we experience; and how that musical picture appears as something to be aesthetically judged, something placed in the realm of art.

We need to be clear about the complicated process continuously going on within us. Let us look at our own organism. The nerve-sense organism is centralized in the human brain in such a way that the brain is in a firm state only to a small extent. The whole brain swims in cerebrospinal fluid. We can clearly understand what occurs by noticing that if our brain did not swim in cerebrospinal fluid, it would rest upon the blood vessels at the base of our skull and continuously exert pressure upon them. Because our brain *does* swim in cerebrospinal fluid, it is subject to continuous upward pressure—we know this from Archimedes' principle—so that of the 1300–1500-gram weight of the brain, only about 20 grams press upon the base of the skull. The brain is subject to a significant pressure from below, so that it presses only a little upon the base of the skull. This cerebrospinal fluid participates in the entirety of our human experience no less than the firm part of the brain. The cerebrospinal fluid continually moves up and down. The fluid moves up and down rhythmically from the brain through the spinal column. Then it radiates out into the abdominal cavity, where inhalation forces it back into the cerebral cavity, from whence it flows back out with exhaling. Our cerebrospinal fluid moves up and down in a continuous process that extends throughout the remainder of the organism; a continuous vibrating movement essentially fills the whole human being and is connected with breathing.

When we hear a series of tones, we encounter them as breathing human beings. The cerebrospinal fluid is continuously moving up and down. When we listen to music, the inner rhythm of the liquid moving up and down encounters what occurs within our hearing organs as a result of the tones. Thus there is a continuous clash of the inner vibrating music of our breathing with what happens in the ear when listening to music. Our experience of music exists in the balance between our hearing and our rhythmic breathing. Someone who tries to connect our nerve processes directly with what occurs in our musical perception, which is filled with feeling, is on the wrong path. The nerve processes exist in musical perception only to connect it with what takes place deeper in our I, so that we can actually perceive the music and transform it into imagination.

I have attempted to follow these questions in all possible directions. There was a time when people in Europe were more interested in such questions. As you probably know, there was quite an argument about the understanding of beauty in music between Richard Wagner and his students and the Viennese musicologist Hanslick.[2] There you can find the question of musical perception discussed in all possible nuances. You will also find mention of some experiments we can do to more fully comprehend musical perception. It is particularly in the perception of music that we can find the direct relationship between our circulatory processes and human feeling; at the same time there is a direct relationship between the nervous system and imagination or thinking. However, we find no direct relationship between the nerves and feeling or between the nerves and willing.

I am convinced that the incorrect hypotheses about sense and motor nerves that modern science has incorporated as a servant of materialism (and incorporated more strongly than we may think) have already taken over human thinking. In the next, or perhaps the following generation, it will become the general attitude. I am convinced that this materialistic theory about the nerves has already become the general mentality and that what we find today as theory in physiology or psychology has entered so deeply into our thinking that this attitude actually separates people. If you have the feeling—and many people do—that when we meet another human being, we make only sense impressions upon that person, and the other person upon us; that the other person is a closed entity with its own feeling life, separate from us; and that this person's feelings can be transmitted only through her own nerves, we create a wall of separation between people. This wall leads to the most peculiar views. Today we hear people say that when they look at another human being, they see only that the other being has a nose in the middle of her face, or that she has two eyes in the same location where I know that I have two eyes.

The other human being has a face formed just like my own. Thus, when I see all this, I draw an unconscious conclusion that there is an I just like my own in that organism. There are people today who accept that theory exactly and who understand the relationship between two human beings in such an external way that they think they must come to an unconscious conclusion based upon the form of the human being in order to determine that another human being has an I similar to their own. The perspective that connects the life of the nerves with our ability to creatively picture our thoughts, that connects our living circulation and respiration with feeling, and connects our entire metabolism with willing, will bring people together again once it becomes the general attitude, once it finally becomes actual experience. For now, I can only use a picture to describe this reunion.

We really would be separated in spirit and soul from one another if, when we met, all our feeling and willing developed within our nerves, enclosing us completely within our skin. Modern people have that feeling, and the increasingly antisocial condition prevalent in modern Europe is a true representative of that feeling.

There is, however, another possibility. We are all sitting together in this hall. We all breathe the same air; we cannot say that each of us is going around enclosed in our own box of air. We breathe the air together. If we limit our soul life to the nervous system, then we are isolated. Someone who, for example, connects breathing with the soul makes the soul into something we have in common. Just as we have the air in common, we also have our soul life in common when we reconnect it with the rhythmic organism. Even though in today's society some people can purchase better things and others must purchase poorer things, a rich person still cannot get his food from the moon, from a different heavenly body, just so he won't have to eat the same things as a poor person does.

Thus we have a commonality in our metabolism, and our willing takes on a commonality when we recognize the original and direct relationship of our will to our metabolism. You can see the endless effects of recognizing the connection of our feeling life with the rhythm within human nature when you also recognize that the rhythms of our being are connected to the external world. You can see the same thing in regard to our will when we recognize its connection with our metabolism. From this, you can see how well-equipped spiritual science is to understand matter and its processes. Materialism, on the other hand, is destined to not understand anything about matter.

Here you have a preliminary view of the three aspects of human life: the nerve-sense life, life in the rhythmic organism, and life in the metabolism. I will explain this in more detail later. In connection with the life of the soul, we have discussed only physical life. We can consider the simple division of our soul life into what people normally consider as its three aspects: thinking, feeling, and willing. However, we will not understand it well if we make that division, however justified, our primary viewpoint. As you probably know, many psychologists separate the life of the human soul into imagining, thinking, feeling, and willing. For an objective observer of human nature, however, it should become clear that this perspective cannot offer a good picture of soul life.

Now there is a phenomenon, or rather a whole complex of phenomena, that is more characteristic of our soul life than these abstractions. To understand the life of our soul in a living way, it is better not to begin with thinking, feeling, and willing. If we instead concentrate on something that permeates our entire soul life, we can recognize it as a primary characteristic of our living soul. We can see that the soul lives alternately in sympathies and antipathies, in loves and hates. Normally we do not notice how the soul swings between loves and hates, between sympathies and antipathies. We do not notice it because we do not properly evaluate certain processes of the soul.

People make judgments, and these judgments are either positive

or negative. I could say that a tree is green, and in doing so I connect the two ideas of "tree" and "green" in a positive way. I could
say you did not visit me yesterday, and in doing that I connect two
ideas or complexes of ideas in a negative way. Something of sympathy or antipathy forms the basis of such judgments in our souls.
Positive judgments are always experienced with sympathy and negative judgments with antipathy. The accuracy of the judgment is
not based upon sympathy or antipathy; rather the accuracy is experienced through sympathy or antipathy. We could also say that a
third situation lies clearly between sympathy and antipathy. That
is the situation when someone has to choose between the two. In
our souls, we do not merely have sympathy and antipathy; we also
clearly have alternation between the two, which is also a positive
state. Though this is not as clearly differentiated as in the physical
body, since we are dealing with a process and not with clearly
defined organs, we can divide our soul life into sympathies,
antipathies, and something in between.

We can see these different aspects much more clearly when we
look at what is spiritual in the human being. Modern psychology
just tosses this in with the soul. We will see that we can gain a genuinely flexible view of human nature only when we can keep these
three aspects separate. The physical consists of the nerve-sense
processes, the circulatory processes, and the metabolism. The soul
aspect of the human being consists of experiencing antipathy, sympathy, and the alternation between those two.

The spiritual aspect of the human being also exists in three parts.
When we want to understand the human being spiritually, we
must in the first place take note of waking experience, which we all
know as a state of spiritual life and which is a part of us from waking until sleeping. Another spiritual state, sleeping life, exists from
the time we fall asleep until we awaken. Finally, we have a third
state between those two, which we encounter at the moment of
awakening, namely, dream life. Waking, dreaming, and sleeping

are the three aspects of spiritual life. But we should not associate trivial ideas about these things with a genuine understanding of spiritual life. Instead we need to acquire a sense of how that sleeping spirit actually exists. We can speak of sleep as a state when a human being becomes motionless, when he or she no longer perceives sense impressions, and so forth. But we can also try to see things from a different perspective.

We can acquire some understanding of the meaning of sleep for our life by approaching it in the following way. When we look back upon our life, we usually believe that we are looking at an uninterrupted stream. We collect all our memories into a continuum. However, that is an error. You remember what happened to you today since you awoke, but before that there was a time when your consciousness was asleep. The period of sleep thus interrupts the stream of your memory. Daily life comes again and is then again followed by a period of sleep. What we carry in our consciousness as a uniform stream toward the past is actually always interrupted by periods of sleep. You can see this has a certain significance, even for consciousness. We could say that we are trained to perceive periods when something is missing in just the same way as periods that are filled, but we do not always make that clear to ourselves. If I were to draw a white area here on the board, so that I leave out black circles, you would look at the white area, but actually pay less attention to the white area than to where nothing is, that is, to the black circles. If we have a bottle of seltzer water, in a sense we do not see the water; what we mostly see is the little bubbles of carbon dioxide. We see what is *not* in the water. In the same way, when we look backward, we do not actually see our experiences. We overlook them much as we overlook the white area here on the board. We directly perceive something else, something that we must understand much more exactly. We realize this when we really try to understand the basis of our actual sense of I. I will discuss the reasons in later lectures, but slowly we come to realize that our perception of these periods of sleep gives us our sense of I. Thus we destroy our feeling of I when we do not properly sleep. The interruptions of sleep must be strewn in among our memories for us to achieve a proper sense of I. If you study those disturbances that can arise in your sense of I through an improper sleep life, you will be able to grasp the idea that an I-sense is based upon these holes in consciousness. Please note that I am not referring to the *concept* of I, but to the *sensing* of I.

It is not only what we could call the content of waking consciousness that lives in human beings. Sleep also directly affects what exists in the human being, perhaps to an even greater extent. Those who can genuinely observe human subjectivity will find that when they are accurately aware of the waking state, it is present only in thinking. It would be impossible for us to have the same level of wakefulness in our feeling. Feeling is not directly present in our consciousness in the same way as thinking is. In fact, feeling has the same relationship to our consciousness as dreaming. As strange as it may sound, those who can gain clarity about the differences between thinking and feeling as pure phenomena of consciousness will conclude that the same kind of experience occurs when we perceive our dreams as occurs in our feeling.

We also find the same kind of experience in willing that we find in the unconscious state of sleeping, in dreamless sleep. You need only consider for a moment that, when you raise your hand or your arm, you perceive the *result* of willing. The impulse of willing, that is, the direct spiritual impulse, is connected with the metabolism. You do not perceive the inner process that occurs between the will impulse and the metabolism any more than you consciously experience what occurs within you during dreamless sleep. The conscious experience of the actual processes of will and of dreamless sleep are equivalent. The processes of your feeling life and of dreaming are also the same. True wakefulness exists only in thinking. We do not sleep only between falling asleep and awakening; we also partially sleep when we are awake. We are awake only in regard to thinking, we dream in regard to feeling, and we sleep in regard to willing.

Now please do not assume that willing should remain unconscious. It is *not* always unconscious. If I had here a white area with four black circles within it, then where there is nothing, where I left something out, I would perceive something just as I consciously perceive the left-out content, the content of the will that I sleep through in my normal waking life.

If we look at the human being in a more flexible way, we will see the inner activity of clearly separated aspects of three spiritual states. In thinking, the waking spirit is active; in feeling, it is the dreaming spirit, and in willing, the sleeping spirit. We need to be able to differentiate wakefulness and sleeping as more than alternating states in day and night. We need to be able to observe how these states interact in a human being who is awake.

This has an extremely practical implication for education. We need to ask how we can learn to understand the interactions between willing and thinking and how can we learn to best teach a child at the age of six or seven, when we especially need to take this interaction between thinking and willing into account. The answer is to learn to observe the interaction between willing and thinking in other phenomena, the ways it occurs in a concrete form, in a way we can see, namely, in waking and sleeping. If I study waking and sleeping, I will have something I can compare with thinking and willing.

We needed to discuss this at the beginning of this course because it is through spiritual science that our psychology first acquires some genuine content. If you pick up any modern psychology textbook, you will find definitions of willing and definitions of thinking, but they more or less remain mere definitions of words. We need to understand such things in a real way, but we can do that only if we can relate them to things that exist in the world, for example, to study them through the relationship of wakefulness to sleeping. That is something we will do, and in so doing we can also throw some light upon the relationship of thinking to willing. Thus we can penetrate the real world, and that is just what spiritual science tries to do.

Spiritual science does not consider spiritual life out of some purely subjective need, simply because it is nice for people who have nothing else to do, and who, rather than making small talk about some other subject, prefer to chat about the fact that human beings consist of a physical body, an etheric body, an astral body, and an I. Many people have such a superficial attitude. What is important in spiritual science is not to offer material for small talk. What spiritual science can contribute to our understanding of the spirit is, in fact, necessary to illuminate human life so that we can work with it as a practical reality, something we have forgotten how to do. The chaos we now find in Europe, the absurd events of the last five or six years, is the result of that forgetfulness. There is a direct connection between our collective denial of the real content of the world and the distress within our civilization. Those who believe we can keep our old attitudes make a serious error. We are working with the adults of the future, and we must think first and foremost about the future of humanity. It is particularly here, in the area of education, that we should first think about those forces that enable us to give something to the future generation that is more than what we received, and which has brought about the terrible conditions of our society. In this way we open our eyes beyond the somewhat confined realm of education, as wholesome as it may be, onto the entire development of humanity.

3

UNDERSTANDING THE HUMAN BEING:

A Foundation for Education

Basel, April 22, 1920

I have tried to give you some insight into the nature of the human being and thereby into the nature of the developing child. For pedagogical artists, such insights are quite practical in that they enable us to guide this human material into life in a fruitful way. From what I have already indicated, you can see that the question I posed in the first lecture can be at least partially answered. I believe that question is particularly important for today's teachers. The question is: How is it that we have, on the one hand, such a wonderful science of teaching, with all its well-thought-out principles and, on the other hand, so much justifiable public criticism of education and current teaching methods?

The reason is that although pedagogical geniuses developed our principles through a kind of instinctive intuition, although we have many theories about how to teach, this recently assembled collection of principles that has permeated our entire worldview is not related to a genuine understanding of human nature. We cannot develop an art of education from the sciences as they are practiced today. I certainly do not want to trivialize the great progress and triumphs of modern science. Nevertheless we must understand the developing human being from a very different perspective. The sciences have remained theoretical and have created a contradiction between external physical existence and the spirit-soul. We can therefore say that they offer no support or help to our pedagogical principles. Putting those pedagogical principles into practice depends upon teachers who are highly skilled at practicing them instinctively.

Pestalozzi, Diesterweg, and others obviously had a marvelous pedagogical instinct and developed an instinctive understanding of the human being. However, we live in a time when we can go no further on instinct alone. In older patriarchal societies, we could survive more or less instinctually. However, we live in a time when we must become more and more conscious of everything, and we therefore need to consciously understand human beings. We can do that only by bringing the practical perspective needed for teaching into a closer connection, a systematized understanding of human nature. What science tells us about human physiology or biology offers us no basis for the development of pedagogical principles. What modern science tells us gives us no direct help in seeing how we can best use a child's talents when they are unequally developed.

For that to be possible, our understanding of the human being must be different than that of modern science. I have already mentioned some basic goals for such an understanding. We still need to learn what can create a bridge to a genuine art of education. I would like to stress that in this age of materialism, we are less and less in a position of genuinely understanding the physical human organism. On the other hand, we have hardly anything other than language as a means of approaching other human beings.

Although illustrative materials can be very useful in certain areas of education, the method of teaching through illustration should not be the only one used. We need to ask whether language, when used as the primary means of communication with growing children, can really bring us closer to the nature of the child. We cannot answer that question without penetrating a little deeper into the nature of the human being.

Everyone who attempts to form a picture of the human being from normal pedagogical texts or texts on psychology, who attempts to fill education with principles from natural science or psychology, ends up with the idea that a human being is just a collection of various forms. Such people would have the perspective that here we have a human organism, and within the skull there is a firm brain (or at least a semi-solid one). They would also think here are the other organs, the liver, the lungs, and so forth. If we look at things superficially or clinically, the drawings we see would convey the idea that these firmly delineated organs are the only things that exist within a human being. But remember that people consist of at least 80 percent fluid, that they are actually a column of fluid; therefore they consist of only a very small amount of something solid. Is it really possible to assume that a human being really consists only of sharply delineated individual organs? The human being is a column of fluid and is moreover filled with gases. Yet these texts describe the nervous system as more or less solid strands, or possibly as a somewhat softer solid. They have no awareness that these are in fact imbedded in liquid or even in gas, a gas that exists in the human organism in the form of vibrations or rhythmic movements.

Aside from the gaseous aspect, the human being is actually a liquid column and the brain is imbedded in cerebrospinal fluid; indeed much of the life of our organs is connected with the up-and-down motion of the cerebrospinal fluid as we inhale and exhale. If we become aware of these things, we will not ascribe parallel organic processes to spiritual and soul facts; we will not assume they are firmly delineated. Instead we will form a picture that describes how while I am thinking, while I am feeling or willing, the moving fluid portions of my organism take on certain liquid structures which again dissolve.

We need to ask ourselves why, for example, we should connect the process of thinking with some vibrations or similar processes in the nerves. Of course they are not. Why shouldn't they be connected with the vibrations within the liquid portion of the human being? This is a question natural science, under the influence of our materialistic period, have not even asked. We can be satisfied with what science discovers when we accept its common goals. Modern science has brought about numerous practical results in the area of solid or liquid technology where the liquid exists in an external form in space. It has also been very successful in working with gases, such as in steam technology, where the steam exists in space and can be worked with there.

When we are working with the results of conventional science in a technology, working with inorganic substances, we need to take into account how things operate. For that reason, conventional science in this era of materialism has had such great success, since it has had to closely follow advances in technology. Consider this example: if someone constructed a railway bridge using the principles of mechanics incorrectly, we would very soon see how such a bridge would collapse when one or two locomotives went over it. Such a catastrophe would occur because the proven results of conventional scientific testing were not applied; this is how incorrect principles are corrected in practice.

The further we go into areas where inorganic technology can no longer have a correcting effect, the less we can base our practice upon theory. We need think only of how slowly medicine has advanced in comparison with modern technology. You can very quickly see the significance of incorrect principles in the process of building a railway bridge or similar things. However, when a physician treats someone, it is not at all common to try to determine whether the physician has done everything necessary to restore the person's health, simply because that is impossible to determine. Here the situation is very different; it is simply not possible to correct theories through practice. You will forgive me if I make a comment here, but I think it is important for teachers, since everything in life is important for teachers. In the areas of jurisprudence or economics, for instance, if we followed the way people's principles were applied, we would very quickly see how lame the concept of control through practice is. What is officially determined in legal matters is then made correct through laws. This is true in all countries. Whether we can justify such things from the perspective of a genuine understanding of human beings is a question that is just as neglected today as it was when Goethe gave Faust the question of which rights we are born with.

Furthermore people have not the slightest interest in finding out how our use of externally superb pedagogical principles relates to what then transpires with the developing generation. That, however, is just what I want to draw your attention to. We hear a great deal about the terrible social things now occurring in the eastern part of Europe and in Russia. The things being done in Eastern Europe under the influence of Lenin's[1] and Trotsky's[2] theories are horrible. However, people today give no thought to what is actually happening. People today have no idea of what the results of those things being done today will be in twenty or twenty-five years, what kind of barbarism will fall upon Europe. It is, however, the task of teachers to observe what will happen to human development.

Now here is something unusual. You see, in Zurich, Avenarius,[3] an honest and upright citizen, once taught philosophy. Somewhat later, Vogt,[4] a student of Ernst Mach,[5] taught together with the philosopher Adler,[6] who was the same Adler who shot the Austrian

Minister Stürgkh.[7] We can certainly not say of Adler that he was as
honest a man as Avenarius, but Avenarius was an honest, upright
man. Nevertheless he taught a philosophy that was possible to
teach only because of the materialism at that time. If you now look
into the "state philosophy" of Bolshevism, you will find it is none
other than that taught by Avenarius.[8] After two generations, what
was once taught in Zurich as an appropriate philosophy has
become the theory the Bolsheviks put into direct practice.

   People pay no attention to the relationships of different periods
because they are not at all clear about what happens when the
views of one generation are inherited by the following generation.
Of course, I do not mean just physical inheritance. The honest and
upright Avenarius taught a philosophy which, after a relatively
short time, led to the barbarization of Europe. It is important not
to simply accept abstract judgments when we want to see what
value a viewpoint has for human development. Instead we must
look into the way that viewpoint takes effect. An important responsibility of all education is to look at what will become of what we
do in the classroom in twenty or thirty years. All education has the
task of placing itself consciously in human development, but we
cannot do that without a thorough understanding of the human
being, an understanding that spiritual science can give to a renewed
natural science. A natural science renewed through spiritual science
will not be some fantasy or figment of the imagination. Rather it
will provide a good understanding of the material human organism
as the physical vehicle for the soul and spirit.

   Today I want to mention an important aspect of our soul life
that you all know well and that will prove particularly important
as we move on to the actual pedagogical subject. The phenomenon
I refer to is how what we think about as children eventually
becomes memory. You all know that to maintain a healthy soul, we
must properly transform the ideas we develop from our sense
impressions, that result from our judging and so forth—we can

discuss the details of this later—and that we must take the results of this thinking into our memory. When we then describe something, we recall from within our souls what we previously experienced in the external world or in our interactions with other human beings. We bring it back into our consciousness. But what actually takes place here?

The general view has moved more and more toward looking at this process in a one-sided, abstract way, as simply a process within the soul. People ask, what becomes of our thoughts once we take them into our soul? What have they become, once they are taken in and returned to us as memory? How does this process take place? We cannot study this process if we have not first looked into the relationship between the spirit-soul and the physical body in some detail. There are some so-called idealists who might say spiritual science is basically materialistic, since it is always referring to physical organs. To believe that, however, would be an enormous error. Spiritual science recognizes the great effects of the soul on the formation of the organs. It sees the soul as having a greater influence than simply working on abstractions, and in fact sees the soul as actually having the power to form the organs. Spiritual science primarily seeks to understand the soul during childhood, when the spirit-soul continues to work upon the formation of the organs after birth.

In my opinion, Goethe's color theory[9] offers the first beginning of a really reasonable consideration of the soul and physical life, something that has been previously unrecognized. Yet today all one needs to do to be immediately branded a dilettante is speak about it in a positive way. I believe, however, that physicists will soon see it much differently from the way it is seen at present. I do not intend to go on praising Goethe's theory of color today, I only want to direct your attention to the wonderful chapter where Goethe begins to speak about physiological colors, and to another chapter toward the end, where he speaks about the sensory and moral effects of colors. Physicists have attempted to refute the portion in between. The beginning and the end have been of more interest to people with an artistic nature, and they can more easily understand them. However, for us to develop a scientific foundation of education, we need to accept some of the help offered by Goethe's considerations of the world of colors.

In the beginning, Goethe draws our attention to the lively interaction between the eye and the external world. That lively interaction exists not only while we are exposing the eye to some color process in the external world, but also afterward. Goethe specifically discusses the afterimages that result from the direct impression. You all know these afterimages, which occur in the eye itself. You need only expose your eye to, say, a green surface and then turn away from this sharply delineated green area. You will see the same area as an aftereffect that is subjectively red. The organ is still influenced for a time by what it experienced in the external world.

This is the basic process as it occurs in the sense organs. Something happens in the sense organs while they are exposed to a process or to things in the external world, and something else happens afterward, which then slowly subsides. From an external perspective, we also can see a certain similarity between what briefly takes place in a sense organ and what happens in the human organism in regard to memory. Just as the green surface continues for a short time as red, a thought with its associated images resulting from a direct experience exists in our organism, only the time periods are quite different.

There is another difference that brings us closer to an understanding of the difference in duration. If we expose the eye to a color impression and then see an afterimage, it is something partial, an individual organ on the periphery of the human organism that brings forth that aftereffect. When a memory arises from within the human being, it reproduces something that existed years before. This is something we can feel, that is apparent, that participates in this reproducing—thus it is the entire human being that participates in this aftereffect.

What actually occurs within the human being? We can understand this only when we have a detailed understanding of certain interactions within the human being. Here I want to draw your attention to a fact that our modern scientific way of thinking has put into an incorrect light, namely, the function of our heart in connection with the whole human organism. You now find the heart described everywhere as a kind of pump that pumps blood throughout the organism. Actually, the blood circulation is forced upon the heart. The fact that embryology contradicts the standard view and more detailed observations of the heartbeat and such things also offer contradictions is something modern people still do not want to hear. Only a few people have noticed this: for example, the physician Schmid,[10] who wrote a treatise about it in the 1880s, and the criminologist Moritz Benedikt.[11] That was not enough, though. There are only a few who have realized that the movements in the heart are a result of the movement of the blood, and that the blood circulation itself is what is fundamentally alive. Thus the heart does not pump; rather its movement is due to the influence of the living movement of the blood. The heart is nothing more than the organ that creates a balance between the two blood circulatory systems, that is, between that of the upper human being, the head, and that of the limbs. These two movements of blood form a pool in the heart. The blood, however, is not something dead; it is not simply pumped like a stream of water. The blood itself has an inner life and is subject to its own movement. It passes that movement on to the heart, which simply reflects the movement of the blood in its own movements. Just as we can say that there is a parallel between the more or less solid organs and processes in the soul, there is also a parallel, which I mentioned yesterday, between the movements of the blood and soul processes.

61

What is the task of an organ such as the heart in relationship to the soul? I would like to ask that question in the following way. If, under the influence of a genuinely correct science, we say that the blood itself has life and the movements of the heart, the entire activity of that organ results from the blood circulation and are only inserted into the living blood circulation, then what is the task of the heart?

Unprejudiced observation shows that if we expose the eye to the external world, the eye's experiences create an afterimage that soon disappears. When we develop the world of feeling, that world has a close connection with the circulation of the blood. It has a connection with other things also, but here I am speaking only of the blood circulation. Recall for only a moment that when we feel shame, we turn red. Everyone knows this is because the blood comes to the surface. If we are fearful, we turn pale as the blood moves toward the inside. The physiologist Lange[12] from Copenhagen has done a number of good studies about the connection between blood circulation, and other organic processes, and processes in the soul. Just as in the extreme cases where the soul's experience of fear or shame has an effect upon blood circulation, the normal life of the soul also continuously affects our circulation. Our feeling life is always active, but it influences normal circulation toward one direction or another only when our feelings move toward one extreme or another. Just as we are continuously breathing, we also continuously feel. Just as our blood circulation is uninterrupted, our feeling is uninterrupted. If we were to follow these processes further, you would see that we even feel during sleep.

What circulates in the blood is the external physical expression of our feeling. Furthermore, our feeling is connected with our thinking. What we imprint upon the circulation also vibrates within the heart. Goethe used the word "eye" to mean an inner, living organ, and the heart is just as much a living organ. It does not just move the blood. It has an enormous significance within the entire organism. Whereas the eye is affected for only a short time by light outside it, the heart continuously responds to feeling and thinking as it relates to feeling with small vibrations that are then carried into the blood. After a time, the heart's vibrations include what lives specifically in feeling and in feeling-related thinking. The heart is a part of the body that influences us when we remember experiences. All human organs that partake of the currents of organic human fluids, that are included in the liquid currents—whether it is the kidneys imbedded in this flow or the liver connected to it in the digestive stream—all these organs vibrate in unison, vibrate with our feeling and willing in circulation and metabolism. Just as an afterimage arises in the eye, in the same way a memory arises within the entire human being, though in differentiated and specific ways; it is a memory of experiences in the outer world. The whole human being is an organ that vibrates, and the organs people normally say are placed next to each other are there in reality so that human beings can process and retain spiritual-soul experience in a certain way. We will see that this only appears to be a materialistic perspective. We will see that it is precisely this that allows us to properly recognize the human being as a spiritual being. Today, however, now that I have mentioned this, you can see how we can grasp the entire human being through such a perspective. We can comprehend the human being not only in the way materialistic science does, by placing the individual organs alongside each other, even assuming that they interact mechanically. The spiritual-scientific perspective shows that the entire human being is unified as body, soul, and spirit, but our thinking separates these three perspectives. In reality, body, soul, and spirit are always interconnected within the human being.

You need learn only a little embryology to learn that the heart slowly develops in the organs of the blood circulatory system, in the system of vessels. You can see that the heart is not there first, with the circulatory system developing from it, but that the circulatory system develops slowly, with the heart as the final result. You can see directly from embryology that the situation is just as I have described it. Therefore, when we consider things from a spiritual-scientific perspective, we need to think of the human liver not simply as a liver, the human spleen not simply as a spleen in the way these things appear when we dissect a corpse in the laboratory. Instead we need to try to investigate the significance of these organs in the spirit-soul life. We do not see the eye, or any of the other organs, as merely some physical tool. Although it is commonly believed that the liver is only an organ in the digestive system, it has a great deal to do with human spiritual life.

We can often learn much from language itself. Ancient peoples, who still had a kind of primal, instinctive knowledge, did not always consider things as abstractly as we do. Take, for instance, *hypochondria*, which in Greek means "below the cartilage of the breast bone," an anomaly of the soul that has its origins in the human abdomen, which is indicated in the word itself. In the English language, which in comparison to the languages of Central Europe is still at an early stage of development, the word *spleen*, as an emotional state, has something to do with the soul. However, *spleen* also refers to an organ, and for good reason, since the *spleen* of the soul has much to do with the *spleen* organ. Such things are nearly all lost. Materialism has nearly lost an understanding of the physical organs, particularly those of the human being. How can we work with a human being if we are not in a position to understand what the human being is physically? We must first understand that the human being is built up piece by piece out of the spirit-soul, so that there is nothing physical that is not a revelation of the spirit-soul.

We need to be able to see the physical properly if we are to have a solid foundation for education. When I say such things, some people may think I want to throw out everything in the world that has been learned through hard scientific work. I certainly do not do that lightheartedly, you can be certain of that. In general, it is much more comfortable to play the same tune as everyone else than to counter prevalent views from genuine understanding and from the realization that a true cultural renewal in our decadent times requires such an understanding in the area of spiritual life. Personally, I would much prefer to present all the scientifically recognized perspectives rather than argue against many of them, particularly where the concern is an understanding of the human being.

We also need to resist the standard scientific perspective when we consider human interactions in practice. Instruction and education are essentially a special case of human interaction. We need to differentiate human life before the change of teeth and then again until puberty. I have attempted to characterize how different the forces are during the first period of human life in comparison to the second. It requires a very different kind of soul experience for these two periods, for the simple reason that the forces connected with imaginative thinking are directed toward an inner hardening of the human body during the first period of life. This activity culminates in the change of teeth at about the age of seven. The most important means of communicating with human beings during that time lies in the principle of imitating the surroundings.

Everything a person does during the years before the change of teeth is done out of imitation. What occurs in the surroundings of a child is enormously important, since the child only imitates. Imitation is one of the strengths of children at that age, and that imitation is directly connected with the same forces that produce the second set of teeth. They are the same forces, and, as we have seen, they are the forces of thinking, of inwardly picturing and understanding the world around us. Thus the forces associated with representational thinking are also the forces connected with physical development. These are the forces active in the child's motive for imitation. Imagine what it means when you grasp that not only intellectually, but when with the entirety of your being, with your soul, when you have a universal, human understanding of it. It means that when I do something in front of a child who is not yet seven years old, not only do I do it for myself, but my doing also enters the child's doing. My deeds do not exist for me alone.

I am not alone with my deeds, with my willing, with my feeling. I am not alone with my thinking; there are intangibles that also have an effect. There is a difference in whether I live alongside a child with a good attitude and allow the child to grow up alongside of me, or whether I do it with a poor attitude. These intangibles have an effect but they are not yet recognized. If we do not honor the connection between the spirit-soul and individual physical human organs, then we do not honor what exists between human beings as a real force, the spirit-soul itself.

When we look at the period between the change of teeth and puberty, the will begins to predominate in the way that I characterized it. With boys, we experience this eruption of the will in the change in the voice. In girls, this is expressed in a different way that we will discuss later. What is active in children at elementary school age shows us that it is connected with the will. Something wants to enter the physical body from the will; something wants to become firmer. There is more than simply a desire to imitate, although, as we will see, that remains important in the curriculum until the age of nine. Something more than simple imitation wants to develop, and that is the desire to honor authority. If I do not live as an authority alongside a seven- to fourteen- or fifteen-year-old child whom I am to bring up and educate, for the child that would be the same as if I cut off a finger or an arm so that he or she could no longer physically behave in the way natural to children. I would take something from the child that wants to develop, namely, the experience of having older people nearby, people who, as genuine authorities, are to educate and raise the child.

We now come to something we will have to make understandable to growing children in a way other than through example or through language. We now come to the role of love in education and upbringing. One of the intangibles we are justified in exercising in educating a growing child is authority over that child, and that our authority be accepted as a naturally effective force. We will not have that authority if we are not permeated in a certain way by what we have to present to the child. If, as teachers, we carry our knowledge within us just as some dry, memorized facts, if we teach only out of a sense of duty, then we have a different effect upon children than when we have an inner warmth, an enthusiasm for what we are to teach them. If we are active in every fiber of our soul, and identify ourselves with that knowledge, then the love for what we carry in our souls is just as much a means of communication as demonstrations and language. An education made fruitful through spiritual science enables us to understand the importance of this kind of intangibility.

4

THE TEACHER AS SCULPTOR OF THE HUMAN SOUL

Basel, April 23, 1920

Up to now I have tried to show how we can approach the human being from the outside. Today I would like to approach our task from the other side, from the side of inner experience. Through this way of considering things—the way of science in the future—the human being becomes transparent from the outside. In a sense, this kind of consideration of the human being, of the activities of the organs and all of human nature, can lead us to discover a person's inner experiences, what he or she experiences as thinking, feeling, and willing. The commonly held perspective confronts us with a dark, impenetrable, incomprehensible being. At the same time, we are concerned with more or less abstract inner experiences of thinking, feeling, and willing that we cannot perceive or feel concretely. We have seen that the human being has three aspects: thinking, feeling, and willing. Let us look at these three aspects from within. We will soon see how the inner and outer paths of consideration are connected.

The content of thoughts is essentially very abstract. As teachers, we cannot approach the developing human being through these thoughts. In a certain sense, there is an impenetrable wall between us. That wall exists in social life and brings us many social problems. It also exists in areas such as teaching and education. Through the scientific materialism that has taken over all our thinking and, to an extent, our feeling, everything we have to say about the soul or spirit has slowly become empty words. We cannot work out of empty words. We can find no relationship to other adults through empty words, nor can we find a relationship to children through them. We need to move forward to reality. We cannot encounter reality if we have only the abstract intellectual reasoning that modern science has implanted in us.

We do, however, come to the spirit through this reasoning. The entire content of reasoning within our intellectually oriented education is spirit, but it is a filtered spirit. It is a spirit that in a way cannot break out of its own confines, which cannot experience itself as real content, and thus remains brutal. This spirit controls our lives. This spirit penetrates nothing; it is a spirit that in art creates only the external form instead of developing the form out of the material itself. It is a spirit that wants to force itself upon the external social relationships connected with the shape of human society instead of developing those relationships directly from living human beings.

We can arrive at a very different position in regard to the spirit if we hold to what spiritual science can give us. The way spiritual science approaches things is much more important than its actual content. If you stay with what is knowledge today, you will find that it simply reflects what already exists. That is how we have arrived at a kind of naturalism that only recreates the external world in art, because our understanding does not penetrate beyond the external world; it has no independent content. We move about in a mere copy of the external world. We do not understand how living content can germinate from the human being, since this living content cannot arise from anything other than the spirit.

Let us contrast spiritual science and conventional science. When they first hear what spiritual science has to say, many modern people understand it as something silly, a fantasy. Why? Simply because people are not accustomed to hearing in the way that spiritual science speaks. People are accustomed to speaking about the world so that it is possible to compare what is said with what we see, with what the eyes perceive or we perceive in other ways. Spiritual science presents things to which we cannot find any correspondence in the external world, things we cannot find when we observe only with our senses. It presents things we can understand only when we work out of our own spirit. Of course, what we create comes from a deeper aspect of the world, but we must actually produce that out of the spirit. This creation out of the spirit is important.

When we study spiritual science, we do not wait until we encounter a tree or an animal that we can then conceptualize. Instead we form the concept in our inner life. In a moment, we will see some examples of how we create concepts inwardly through spiritual science and how they can become alive in the human being. We can therefore say that our intellectual reasoning has slowly lost all meaning, and that spiritual science gives our reasoning something through which it can regain some content.

If you take my book *An Outline of Esoteric Science* and read it like any other book, you may not understand it. Today, even with art, we ask ourselves where in the world we would find something like it. In dramas and novels, that is, in products of our imagination, we demand that their content can be found in exactly, or nearly exactly, the same way as in the world. You cannot do that with the content of *Esoteric Science*. You have to do something else, which is why there is so much opposition to spiritual science: people must do something quite different than in modern conventional science or art. You need to carry out an inner activity for each step described by the writer of such a spiritual scientific book. You will gain nothing from reading such a book if you do not produce something from yourself according to the directions in the book. In this way spiritual science runs quite counter to our modern way of thinking. Today people love to attend lectures that present what they are to learn through slides or other perceptible means. People go to movies because they can see something there. They do not value the fact that there are also some words. People want to remain passive; they just want to be people who watch. You will gain nothing from a spiritual-scientific book or lecture if you allow these modern habits to predominate, as spiritual-scientific lectures or books contain nothing of that sort. Everything depends upon your working inwardly with what such books or lectures offer as a thread.

It is important that reasoning, which has become passive in our intellectual age, should now become active. Spiritual science is an inner activity to the extent that it concerns the world of ideas and is therefore radically different from what modern people are used to. This inner training of self is extremely important, since that is how we can overcome the abstract spirituality connected with modern reasoning. This self-training will renew the entire spiritual and soul constitution of a human being.

Just this morning I received a letter from a teacher at our Waldorf School in Stuttgart, based upon the pedagogical principles we are discussing here. I was quite taken by it. You are perhaps aware that I prepared the faculty of the Waldorf School through a seminar lasting some weeks, and that the teachers continue to reread the transcripts of that course.[1] The teacher wrote in this letter, "When I reread the pedagogical lectures, it is as though I find myself in some foreign territory and suddenly hear the sounds of my homeland." That is a feeling I can well understand. People, at their core, feel like foreigners in our intellectual world. If they rise above themselves to the extent that they bring their inner humanity into activity, as they must do with every spiritual-scientific presentation, they have something like a feeling of coming home to those tones sounding from the spiritual world that actually originated in the human being. It is important that we accustom ourselves to having the spiritual present always. For example, what was important for me with the faculty of the Waldorf School? My goal was that these teachers shed everything that is standard education, all that people used to teach while remembering they should do something in one way or another. According to current education, that is the correct approach. In a way, the core of spiritual science is that you actually forget the spiritual content you have learned and at each moment renew it by creating it again within yourself. You have not really understood spiritual science if you understand it as something you need to remember.

Excuse me if I say something personal here. When I speak thirty, forty, or even fifty times on the same theme, I can never give the same lecture. I can do that just as little—excuse the rather inappropriate comparison—as I can eat again what I ate yesterday. I am in something living, and it is the same with spiritual-scientific content: you are in something living. You need to continually work with it. I prepared the teachers of the Waldorf School so that, in a certain sense, they entered school each morning with a virgin soul, so that they would always be confronted with something new, with new riddles. The ability to forget, which is only the other side of comprehending, is what draws people to spiritual science. It is the result of continual spiritual-scientific learning.

Now you might say that you know a few anthroposophists who could count on their fingers all the things they have learned. But that is only the imperfection of anthroposophists. I was not able to keep some such anthroposophists away, so they will also need to listen to what I am saying. It is a failing to have your anthroposophical knowledge as a memory, to not have it as a source of the inner life of your soul that you must re-create at each moment. That, however, is the attitude you should have when you stand before other human beings who you are to teach and educate. It is important that we work with spiritual science in a way that brings a liveliness to our souls, that is active in the same way that our digestive processes are active each day in our physical body. In this way, everything that is simply memorized disappears into the background, eclipsed by what spiritual science offers; therefore we work with an active, rather than a passive, understanding.

The art of education is enriched in the realm of thought when people allow spiritual science to flow into their way of thinking, into their imagination. Then we can approach the human being in an inner way, through imagination and reason. However, we can also do that through will. Here, I can describe that only briefly, but these ideas will light fires in those people who are to teach and educate if they are comprehended deeply enough. I would like to say something related to a question I was asked.

I attempted to sketch the child's development beginning about age seven until fourteen or fifteen. Someone asked how that development relates to Haeckel's biogenetic law.[2] This law considers the world in an external, scientific way, and says that the embryonic development of the human being repeats the evolution of human beings—that ontogeny recapitulates phylogeny. During the period from conception until birth, human development passes through the various animal forms from the most simple to the most complicated right up to the stage of the human being. I am aware of the exceptions and limitations, but those who understand this law certainly know it is scientifically very important. People have tried to apply this law to the spiritual and soul development of individuals in relationship to all of humanity. In that way, however, we follow a very incorrect path.

Can we find a parallel between human spiritual and soul

development and this biogenetic law? We can do so only if we can say that at the beginning of his or her earthly life, a small child goes through the various stages of humanity and moves through later periods of human development as he or she grows. Thus the development of a child repeats the development of humanity as a whole. We could certainly create such a fantasy, but it would not correspond to reality. In this area we can approach reality only through spiritual science. When we follow the development of the human embryo from the second or third week until it matures, we can see hints of a continuously more perfect form in the developmental stages, the form of a fish, and so on. However, when we observe the early developmental years of a child, we find nothing that indicates a recapitulation of the subsequent stages of human development. We would have to attribute fantasy forces and processes to the child's development to find something like that. It is just a beautiful dream when people like Wolf[3] try to demonstrate that children go through a period corresponding to wild barbarians, then they go through the Persian period, and so forth. Beautiful pictures can result from this, but it is nonsense nevertheless because it does not correspond to any genuine reality. We have to look at human life in its full reality if we want to find something corresponding to the spirit and soul in the biogenetic law. Spiritual science shows that we should not look at the beginning of life, but rather at the end. If we can observe ourselves beyond the age of thirty-five or forty, possibly forty-five, we can then find certain artifacts in the soul life of a human being, in the innermost experiences of a human being. Just as there are vestiges of physical human evolution during the embryonic period, there are strange inner experiences people can have after the age of thirty-five or forty if they are able to accurately observe themselves.

Perhaps this quality of observation is possible only if people develop active thinking through really experiencing spiritual science. We see that later in life, we have inner experiences that do not completely take shape, that are like artifacts. Our physicality can no longer fully develop spirit-soul events later in life. The physical body fails. If we do not let our physical bodies lead us astray, we become enriched in spirit and soul later in life. Of course in modern intellectual culture, only a few people notice what arises as vestiges in our souls. This is because education is founded upon intellectualism, which makes us dependent upon the physical body to an extreme degree. Once we have reached the age of thirty-five, we do not notice events in our souls that cannot really live in our modern physical bodies, but we can experience these events inwardly if we do not sleep through this period of human soul life.

This weighs heavily upon our souls. Most modern people sleep through those experiences in old age, experiences that could guide them into tremendous depths, simply because they are older and are completely awake inwardly. Today a tremendous number of people are simply asleep. If you develop an active understanding, an active feeling and willing, when you are old you will notice these artifacts of the soul's life. An art of education genuinely fructified by spiritual science will enable us to have these experiences of old age. Our society will also know that there are such experiences in old age, so we will move into old age in a different way. We will become curious about what old age can offer us. People will have an entirely different inner experience of life.

Why do such vestigial experiences occur in old age? To understand that, we must focus on real human evolution from the perspective of spiritual science. Materialistic anthropology has rendered real human evolution murky. People believe that humanity began as wild beings. But that is not true. On the contrary, when we go back to the seventh or eighth millennium before Christ, a large portion of the then-civilized humanity possessed a primitive knowledge; of course, it was an instinctive sort of knowledge. But it was knowledge that we need to bow down to in humility if we are to comprehend it today. The last remains of it were retained in the Indian Vedas. However, these do not contain the original knowledge, but something derived from it. Today people enter the early historical remnants of ancient Egypt, Babylon, and India with a tremendous amount of dry intellectuality—a kind of arid, academic perspective. What our modern academic research with all its dryness brings to light is just the corpse of an instinctive, primal human knowledge through which people experienced their connection with the entire universe. People who understand science and then look at that early primal human knowledge, even in its weak historical reflection, know that the world looked different in those ancient periods of human development than modern materialistic anthropology believes. Spiritual science can show what has not been handed down historically. You can read about it in *An Outline of Esoteric Science*. Modern materialistic anthropology believes human beings somehow developed from some wild creatures, so that we now say we have developed far beyond them. However, a true consideration of humanity shows us a period of prehistoric development. Through that consideration, we return to the seventh, eighth, or ninth millennium before Christ, when people had a primal knowledge that was possible only because they could continue to develop their body and soul until a much later age. We can then look back upon the first culture that developed in the southern part of Asia after a major world catastrophe. We can comprehend that primal culture only when we consider the characteristics of humanity at that time. Today physical development runs parallel with that of the soul until the age of seven and continues until puberty, but ceases sometime around age twenty. We are then complete human beings for our modern times. We can no longer believe we can leap over the chasm of development as we leapt over the change of teeth or puberty.

That was completely different in primal times. During the ancient Indian period, people developed physically until their fifties as we do until our twenties. Because their physical development continued in parallel with that of their spirit-soul, they had an instinctive knowledge that their patriarchs experienced simply by becoming old and undergoing the physical transformation that we experience only during puberty.

Then came the period that I called the Primal or ancient Persian period in *An Outline of Esoteric Science*. Here in the fourth, fifth or sixth millennium before Christ, physical development continued beyond the age of forty. Then we have the Egyptian-Babylonian development that goes back to the third or fourth millennium before Christ. At that time, the human being remained capable of physical development until the middle of life, until about the age of thirty-five. Then we come to the Greco-Roman period, when the human being could still develop physically until about the age of thirty. The Greeks as well as the ancient Romans lived differently than we do. Today, people do not want to admit the truth about historical development because they do not want to pay any attention to such things. The Greeks still felt their spirit-soul as a part of their physical body. When they looked out into the world, they knew they were not just looking at things; at the same time, they were aware of a physical process within their body. That was because they remained capable of development much longer than we do today.

You see, everything earlier peoples experienced within their bodies, we experience in old age only in our spirit-souls—if we are not asleep. These are vestiges, artifacts. For the biogenetic law, human embryonic and fetal physical development appears to repeat the evolution of humanity; today we grow into the development of ancient human beings when we consider its remnants in our old age. What we experience as soul artifacts when we are about fifty can give us an idea of the first Indian culture of the seventh or eighth millennium before Christ. Our soul experiences in our forties give us a hint about the ancient Persian period, around the fourth or fifth millennium before Christ. What we experience at the end of our thirties is a hint—no longer physical, only spiritual—of how the ancient Egyptians, Babylonians, and others lived and felt, and why they had a much different social life. Academics describe the Greeks in a way that is quite foreign to how they were. The way modern people base everything on externalities is quite curious. Before the war, we heard that we were to once again celebrate the so-called Olympic Games. We were going to imitate the externalities of games that were entirely based upon the fact that human beings could continue their physical development beyond the age of thirty, something we cannot do. Something of the spirit and soul flowed out of the physical body and into the ancient human being at a much later age.

We can therefore say that in the first cultural period, genuine experiences were possible beyond the age of forty-eight. In the second cultural age, such experiences were possible beyond the age of forty-two; in the third, beyond the age of thirty-five; and in the fourth, beyond twenty-eight to thirty-five years of age. The fifth cultural period is ours, the present time. We have been in that stage of cultural development since the middle of the fifteenth century, and we remain capable of physical development until the age of twenty-seven or twenty-eight at most.

Only this perspective can explain the characteristics of modern people. Modern humanity needs to develop differently than humanity of earlier times. Modern people cannot perceive their spirit-souls by allowing their physical development to occur passively. If we do not want to wither away after we are thirty, we will need to acquire points of view from sources other than those we can obtain through our physical development. At the present time, we suffer under terrible illusions in regard to such things.

I would like to remind you that we have inherited our religious ideas, including those we offer in education. Why are we so afraid of renewing our religious thinking? Because, quite simply, we are reluctant to receive new religious ideas from other spiritual sources. We want to remain with our inheritance because we feel as though we are facing a void. That feeling is justified since the inner spiritual development that results from physical development begins to wither in modern people at about the age of twenty-seven or twenty-eight. If those inherited religious ideas did not continue to play in us, at least unconsciously and instinctively, we would wither. If we did not propagate many of those thoughts from earlier times, we would all wither after the age of twenty-eight. It is very important for us to recognize this law of human development. You will, of course, realize that I mean this figuratively. The more human development progresses, the younger humanity will become. In other words, passive human development continues only until increasingly younger ages; then it ceases to be effective from a spiritual perspective. The development of the Greek physical body continued until the thirties, but today's modern people reach that level only in their spiritual-soul development, inwardly, in tendencies that they need to develop through productive spirituality. The more people cool in regard to traditional religious ideas and have nothing with which to replace them, the more they will experience this cooling. It is absolutely impossible to give human beings something for later in life from a purely intellectual upbringing. It is primarily what occurs with the change of teeth, what occurs in early childhood that can give us sufficient will to bring us further. What is important here, though, is that people today live in a humanity that is actually capable of development through their physical bodies only until the age of twenty-seven or twenty-eight. The impulse for further development in later years must come from spiritual sources. When we look at modern social life, we have to say that humanity is becoming younger, that it reveals an increasing incompleteness of humanity.

Those who can comprehend such things and who have both

knowledge and a sense of responsibility toward human development will be able to fructify the art of education. They will then
look for what they need to accomplish. They will need to bring
from spiritual sources what people need to be human beings, even
when they develop beyond the age of twenty-seven or twenty-
eight. Our deepened understanding of the human developmental
impulse, along with our feeling and concern, will motivate us. We
do not see this clearly enough today. When people are bombarded
with ideas such as that the earth developed out of some kind of
nebular fog along with the other planets and will someday fall back
into the sun, they do not know why human beings exist. When
people have soaked up the attitude about evolution presented by
the natural scientific worldview, they will no longer have any will.
A perspective that looks at the reality of the human being will gen-
erate will: then we will know what we have to do. We will know
that we now need to educate where previously nature carried out
the deed by itself. We can look back to older periods and say the
Greeks were happy because their physicality could develop their
spirit-soul beyond the age of twenty-eight. We will see that the
Egyptians and Babylonians could develop beyond the age of forty
purely because a divine force they could draw upon affected their
physical organs. To draw upon what nature itself, the divine forces
in nature, accomplishes is no longer possible for modern human
beings and will become even less so for humanity in the future. As
human beings, we must take up the responsibility for our own
development. We must more and more find a way to make human
beings truly human.

In that way, science will become will. We can see we have just
moved into that period of human development when new tasks are
arising for education. Until the present, all education was, more
than anything else, instinctive. As I have previously said, there were
good abstract principles. Now, however, comes the time when we
must enliven those abstract principles from within. It lies in our

hands either to enliven those abstract principles into a genuine art of human education or to deliver humanity into the wilderness.

Now that I am at the beginning of what I actually want to discuss about education, you can see that I do not wish to begin with some theoretical discussion, but rather with a feeling. We cannot begin with a pedagogy of rules, but with a feeling. We must feel that the content of the human soul has been given to those who are to teach and educate young people. It is healthy to feel within ourselves the future of humanity. That is the proper starting point, not whether we know one thing or another, but when we feel that the entire task of education is connected with the development of humanity.

You will have correctly comprehended what I have presented today when you can forget all of the individual sentences, all of the theoretical terms I have used, and feel the task of the teacher as a burden upon your soul. If you take with you what is condensed in that feeling, the intent of what I have presented today, when all of what I have said rests in a feeling, we will be able to develop the specifics of the art of education out of that feeling in the following lectures.

Discussion Following Lecture Four

Dr. Steiner (responding to some objection): Today I would like to say only a little about this. It is tremendously tempting to assume, for example, that the drawings made by children are similar to those made by primitive peoples. However, this is based upon the unfounded assumption that the peoples who create such drawings today are the original peoples. Of course, we see that modern children's drawings are similar to those made by primitive peoples, but these people are not primitive; they are decadent. Anthropology errs in saying that those contemporary peoples who live primitively in the wilds are to a certain extent the same as those from which we all descended. We cannot base education upon such errors in science, for if we were to do that, we would overvalue the childlike peculiarities of today's primitive people. Such an overvaluation of those characteristics has been quite thorough in modern times. We can certainly acknowledge the facts of the matter, but the attributed significance of such facts is based upon a misunderstanding of the genuine relationship between the development of individual human beings and that of humanity as a whole. It is also not tremendously important that we find children's rhymes that go back far into the time that I have referred to here as the Fifth Period. Such children's rhymes do not go back any further. Were we to go back further through spiritual science than is possible through anthropology, we would discover that what we find in children's rhymes today did not exist during earlier periods of human development.

Anthropology, which follows human development from the present back to its beginnings and finds a resonance of original human beings in contemporary people, must undertake a new path toward a spiritual-scientific consideration of the development of humanity. Along that path we must, of course, develop a feeling for what remains original, instinctive human culture. I would remind you of the Vedantic literature and of the extremely significant Taoist sayings of Lao Tsu.[1] A person who presents a spiritual-scientific perspective of human development will certainly take everything historical into account before arriving at what I have mentioned here.

It is much easier to go with the flow of general opinion than to fight. Today there is a dangerous pedagogical idea that draws a parallel between what children do and what contemporary primitive peoples, or those of earlier times, have done. What is important is that we find genuine sources of spiritual life. and we must actually seek them first in children.

Then there is something else. Remember that I have said we should develop everything *out of* the child. We hear that today in all its variations and find that people believe they are doing it. But now try to discover what it means not to perceive the nature of a child as some unknown mystery that develops as it should, but rather as something needing to prepare itself through self-education, which is possible only through spiritual science. Try to get an idea through spiritual science for what genuinely lives in children.

I certainly have nothing against the idea that we should not present children with anything from the outside but instead find everything in the child. But first we must learn to see the child. In order to do that, the human being must first become transparent, and what I have presented enables us to truly see human nature from various and differing sides. Through much of what arises from a normal materialistic perspective, many different sides of human nature are obscured. Much of what is now called the spirit or soul is simply an abstraction, an intellectual idea. Of course, much of what is needed to prove what I have just said will be presented only in the later lectures. Nevertheless I am certainly not against people saying that we need to value and develop those things that exist within the child, nor am I against people saying that we should not force into the child what exists within ourselves. On the contrary I consider both of these ideas perfectly obvious. What is important to me is to show how to comprehensively consider both of those ideas.

5.

SOME REMARKS ABOUT CURRICULUM

Basel, April 26, 1920

As you have probably noticed, our previous discussions have differed not only in their content but also in their entire manner of consideration from what we normally find in anthropology or similar areas. Those unwilling to develop the feeling I spoke of at the end of the last lecture will not immediately recognize how such an understanding of the human being can arise in any way other than that which is currently acceptable. It can, however, arise when we comprehend the entire developing human being, that is, the body, the soul, and the spirit, in terms of lively movement. By comprehending the living human being in movement, by placing ourselves in human nature, we can create within ourselves an understanding that is not dead but alive. This understanding is most appropriate if we are to avoid clinging to external materialistic perspectives or falling prey to illusions and fantasy. What I have presented here can be very fruitful, but only when we use it directly, because its primary characteristics first become apparent through direct use.

I would like to mention a few things about our attempts to make this thinking fruitful in the Stuttgart Waldorf School. That school was created because Emil Molt, the director of a factory in Stuttgart,[1] wanted a school based purely upon spiritual-scientific principles for the children of the factory's workers. The school has long since grown beyond its initial boundaries, and it is the first attempt at forming a school whose curriculum and learning goals have been based upon a spiritual-scientific understanding of the human being. Of course we need to recognize that we are still in the first year of the Waldorf School, and that we have students from all possible classes of other schools. For that reason certain compromises are necessary in the beginning.

In the curriculum, our concern is not simply to come to terms pedagogically with a single child or even with a small class where we could work with individual children (an idea that is commonly held). We want each teacher to be so permeated with understanding that even when standing before a large class, he can represent this type of education. Each teacher should be permeated by a living comprehension of the human being so that he understands that the heart does not simply pump the blood through the organism, but that the human being is living, and the movements of fluids and the heart result from that aliveness. When a teacher has absorbed this way of thinking, particular forces within him become active in regard to the development of children. This activity can result in significant insights, even in regard to a child who is part of a large class and with whom we have worked for only a few months. If you have trained your spirit in this way, and thus created a strong contact with it, your spirit can look somewhat clairvoyantly at the individual child. It is not so important that we know that the heart is not the cause of the circulation of the blood. What is important is that we develop within ourselves the possibility of presenting such things in a way contrary to our modern materialistic thinking. Those who develop this possibility within themselves, who configure their spirit in this way, make themselves alive in a different way in regard to developing children, even in large numbers. They gain the capacity of reading the curriculum from the nature of the developing child.

In Stuttgart I had to compromise,[2] since under present social conditions it is not possible to develop a school purely on the basis of this kind of education. I said we needed to take three stages into account. We need complete freedom in how we present the curriculum during the first, second, and third grades, but we want the children at the end of third grade to have learned the same things as children in other schools. The same is true until age twelve, that is, the sixth grade, and again when they leave the school. All we could achieve was to present the curriculum in these stages: in the first three school years, the second three, and in the third stage, the last two school years. These are simply things that we must accept as compromises under today's social conditions. Nevertheless, within these three periods, we have been able to achieve some things. We can, for example, base our work upon the sound principle that we do not begin with the intellectual, as modern instruction generally does. We do not need to begin with this one characteristic of developing human beings—the intellect—instead we can begin with the whole human being.

It is important to first acquire a clear concept of what the whole human being actually is. Today, because people cannot observe how thinking relates to human nature, they believe that we learn to think by logically teaching children how to think. I have to admit that during the first six decades of my life I used to consider people in that way. Those who can observe developing human beings, who can compare the developing human being with what a person becomes, can see certain connections spread out over the various periods of life, which go unobserved if a certain kind of insight has not been developed.

I would like to mention something I often refer to because it shows certain connections in human nature in a textbooklike way. In observing children, you can see how, when those around them relate to them properly, they develop a feeling of respect toward people. If you follow what becomes of these children later in life, you will find that this feeling of respect has so transformed these individuals that, through their words or sometimes simply through the way they look at you, their presence is a deed of goodness. This is simply because when you have learned to respect (or, I could say, to pray) later in life you will have the power to bless. No one can bless later in life who has not learned to respect or to pray in childhood.

We need to look at such things. We need to gain such vision through a living science that can become feeling and will, and not through some dead science such as we have today. Thus we can see how to avoid teaching children mere conventional knowledge, instead taking into account the entire human being.

We have, of course, the task of teaching the children to write, but today writing is a kind of artificial product of culture. It has arisen in the course of human development out of a pictorial writing and has become what we now have today, a purely conventional and abstract writing. If we try to gain a feeling for older writing, for instance Egyptian hieroglyphics, and to understand their basic character, we will see how people originally tended to reproduce the external world in their writing through drawing.

Writing and drawing things in the world are, in a way, also the basis of human speech development. Many theories have been put forward about the development of speech. There is, for instance— I am not making this up, they are called this in the technical papers—there is the so-called Ding-Dong Theory that assumes speech is a kind of model of some inner tonal qualities of our surroundings. Then there is the Bow-Wow Theory,[3] which assumes that speech is based upon sounds produced by other beings in our surroundings. None of these theories, however, begin with a sufficiently comprehensive understanding of human nature. A sufficient comprehension of human nature, particularly one based upon a trained observation of children's speech, shows that human feeling is engaged in a much different way when learning the vowels. They are learned through feeling. If we train our own powers of observation, we will see how all vowels arise from certain human inner experiences that are like simple or more complicated interjections, expressions of feeling. Inwardly, we as human beings live in the vowels. People express external events in consonants. People copy external events through their own organs; nevertheless they reproduce them. Speech itself is a reproduction of external events through consonants, and vowels provide the color. Thus, writing is, in its origins, a pictorial reproduction.

If, as is done today, we teach conventionalized writing to children, it can affect only the intellect. For that reason, we should not actually begin with learning to write, but with an artistic comprehension of those forms that are then expressed through writing or printing.

If you are not very clever, you can proceed by taking Egyptian hieroglyphics or some other pictorial writing, then developing certain forms out of it in order to arrive at today's conventional letter forms. But that is not necessary. We do not need to hold ourselves to such strict realism. We can try to discover for ourselves such lines in modern letter forms that make it possible for us to give the children some exercises in movements of the hands or fingers. If we have the children draw one line or another without regard to the fact that they should become letters, or allow them to gain an understanding throughout their entire being for round or angular forms, horizontal or vertical lines, we will bring the children a dexterity directed toward the world.

Through this approach, we can also achieve something that is extraordinarily important psychologically. At first we do not even teach writing but guide the children into a kind of artistic drawing that we can develop even further into painting, as we do at the Waldorf School. That way the children also develop a living relationship to color and harmony in youth, something they are very receptive to at the age of seven or eight. If we allow children to enjoy this artistically taught instruction in drawing, aside from the fact that it also leads to writing, we will see how they need to move their fingers or perhaps the entire arm in a certain way that begins not simply from thinking, but from a kind of dexterity. Thereby the I begins to allow the intellect to develop as a consequence of the entire human being. The less we train the intellect and the more we work with the entire human being so that the dexterity of the intellect arises out of the movements of the limbs, the better it is.

If you visit the handwork classes at the Waldorf School in Stuttgart, you will perhaps find it somewhat paradoxical when you see that both boys and girls sit together and knit and crochet, and further, that everyone not only does "women's work" but also "men's work." Why is that? The success of this approach can be seen in the fact that boys, when they are not artificially restricted from doing the work, take the same joy in these activities as the girls. Why is that? If we know that we do not develop our intellect by simply going directly to some intellectual education, if we know that someone who moves their fingers in a clumsy way also has a clumsy intellect, has inflexible ideas and thoughts, and those who know how to properly move their fingers also have flexible thoughts and ideas and can enter into the real nature of things, then we will not underestimate the importance of developing external capabilities. The goal is to develop the intellect to a large extent from how we work externally as human beings.

Educationally, it is an enormously important moment when we allow the written forms that are the basis of reading to spring out of what we have created artistically. Thus instruction in the

Waldorf School begins from a purely artistic point of view. We develop writing from art and then reading from writing. In that way, we completely develop the children in relation to those forces that slowly want to develop out of their nature. In truth we bring nothing foreign into the child. As a matter of course, around the age of nine the children are able to write from what they have learned in drawing and then go on to reading. This is particularly important, because when people work against rather than with the forces of human nature, they damage children for the rest of their lives. If, however, we do exactly what the child's nature wants, we can help human beings develop something fruitful for the rest of their lives.

When we turn from external toward more internal things, it is important to see that a child at the age of six, seven, or eight has no tendency whatsoever to differentiate itself from its surroundings as an I-being. In a certain way, we take something away from the healthy nature of the human being when we develop this difference between the I-being and its surroundings too early. You need only observe children as they look at themselves in the mirror. Look at them before the age of nine and then again at ten, and train your eye for their physiological form. Your eye for the physiological form will show that as children pass beyond the age of nine (this is of course approximate, for one child it is one time and for another, another time), something extraordinarily important occurs in human nature. We can characterize this important occurrence by saying that until the change of teeth, human beings develop primarily as imitators. In principle, human beings imitate their surroundings. We would not learn to speak if we were not imitators during that period of our lives. This principle of imitation continues on in the following years until about the age of nine. However, during the change of teeth, a principle begins to develop under the influence of a feeling for authority to validate what respected persons in the child's surroundings recognize as correct. It is important that we really know how to maintain this feeling of authority, which is certainly justifiable during the period from the change of teeth until puberty, because that is what human nature wants.

Some say we should allow children to judge everything, to decide what they need to learn, but such statements ignore the needs of human nature. They ignore what we will carry into later life. Human beings continue to imitate beyond the age of seven up to the age of nine or so, and this principle of imitation affects the feeling for authority. From the age of nine, this principle of authority develops in a purer form. Beginning at the age of twelve, it is again mixed with something new: the capacity to judge.

It is of fundamental significance for all education that we do not force developing human beings to judge at too early an age. Certainly everything we now call illustrative instruction has a certain, though limited, justification. It has great significance in a limited area. However, when we extend illustrative teaching to the point of presenting children only with what can be understood from direct observation, we are ignoring the fact that there are things in the world that cannot be seen but must be presented.

There are things that cannot be seen, for instance, religious things. The same is true of moral things; they also cannot be seen. At best, we can show the effects of these things in the world, but not those things themselves. Aside from that, there is something else that is important. We need to teach children how to properly accept something because an authority presents it or to believe something because an authority believes it. If the children are incapable of doing this, we take something away from them for the remainder of their lives. Just look at what happens then. If someone at the age of thirty or thirty-five looks back on something they were taught in school, they will recognize that they did not understand it at that time. But because they loved their teacher, they accepted it. Such a person had the feeling that she did not learn but that she *experienced*. She had a feeling that she needed to honor, to respect the teacher, and since the teacher thought something, she should think it also. Thus, at the age of thirty or thirty-five, a person may recall something she did not understand but accepted out of love. Now, however, that person is more mature and looks at what arises out of the depths of her soul as an older person and realizes the following: what was accepted many years before out of love resurfaces later in life and now becomes clear. We need only consider what that means. It means that through such a resurfacing of something that is now understood for the first time at maturity, a feeling for life—which we need if we are to be useful human beings in social life—increases. We would take a great deal away from people if we took away the acceptance of truths through love, through a justifiable feeling for authority. Children must experience this justifiable feeling of authority, and we need to use all the powers of our souls in practicing education to work toward maintaining that justifiable authority for the child between the change of teeth and puberty.

The fact that we must divide elementary school into three periods gives us the basis of discovering the curriculum and the learning goals. During the first years of elementary school, imitation is affected by the principle of authority. From the ages of nine until twelve, the principle of authority becomes more and more important and imitation recedes. After the age of twelve, the power of judgment awakens. At the age of nine, children begin to separate their I from their surroundings in their inner experiences, and it is the I that awakens the child's power to judge at about the age of twelve.

In this realm there is a strong connection between the way we think and feel about life and the way we think about the proper way to teach. You have, perhaps, heard of the philosopher Mach, whose views arise out of a natural-scientific perspective. He was a very honest and upright man, but throughout his life he represented the modern materialistic attitude. Because he was so honest, he also lived the inner structure of materialistic thinking. Thus he tells with a certain kind of naive honesty how once, when he was very tired, he jumped onto a bus. Now, just as he entered the bus, at the same time someone who looked like a schoolmaster jumped on the bus from the opposite side. This person made quite a special impression upon him. He first realized what it was after he had sat down. He realized that there was a mirror opposite the entrance to the bus and that what he had seen was himself. That is how little he knew his external form. The same thing happened to him another time. There was a mirror placed behind a display window, and he looked at himself but did not recognize himself. There is a connection between the fact that this man had so little capacity to recognize himself and the fact that he was a fanatical representative of certain pedagogical principles. In particular, Mach was a fanatical enemy of working with children's youthful fantasy. He did not want any fairy tales told to children, or to teach children anything other than scientific trash about external sense-perceptible reality. That is how he brought up his own children, something he told me with a naively honest openness.

People can think what they want about the spiritual content of external, sense-perceptible reality, but it is poison for developing human beings when, from the ages of six or seven until the age of nine, their capacity for fantasy is not developed through fairy tales. If a teacher is not some radical, then he or she will present everything concerning the surroundings of a human being to a child, everything that is to be taught about animals, plants, or other things in nature to the children in the form of fairy tales. Children do not yet differentiate between themselves and their surroundings; that occurs only later, at the age of nine. If only people would learn what an enormous difference it makes whether children are read fairy tales or if you create such fairy tales yourself. No matter how many fairy tales you read or tell your children, they do not have the same effect as when you create them yourself and tell them to your children. The process of creation within you has an effect upon children; it really is conveyed to them. These are the intangible things in working with children.

It is an enormous advantage for the child's development when you attempt to teach children certain ideas through external pictures. For example, if I want to teach the child at the earliest possible age to have a feeling for the immortality of the soul, I could attempt to do that by working with all the means at my disposal. I could attempt to do that by showing the child how the butterfly emerges from the cocoon and by indicating that in the same way the immortal soul flies off from the body.

Now certainly that is a picture, but you will only succeed with that picture when you do not present it as an abstract intellectual idea but believe it yourself. And you *can* believe it. If you genuinely penetrate into the secrets of nature, then what flies out of the cocoon will become for you the symbol for immortality that the creator placed into nature. You need to believe these things yourself. What you believe and experience yourself has a very different effect upon children from what you only accept intellectually. For that reason, during the children's first years of school, we at the Waldorf School attempt to imaginatively present everything connected to the surroundings of the human being. As I said, a teacher who is not lost in dreamland will not cause the children to become lost in fantasy no matter how many stories about bugs or plants, about elephants or hippopotami they are told.

It is important to begin artistically, with a genuine enthusiasm for artistic writing. Allow writing to develop out of drawing, and for these first years of elementary schools, allow it to have an effect upon the imagination. Everything you teach in the way of scientific descriptions is damaging before the age of nine. Realistic descriptions of beetles or elephants or whatever, in the way we are used to giving them in the natural sciences, are damaging for children before this age. We should not work toward a realistic contemplation, but toward imagination.

We need to genuinely observe students when we stand before a class. It does not seem to me to be so bad if classes are very large as long as they are healthy and well ventilated. What we might call individualization occurs of itself if the teacher's work arises out of a living comprehension of human nature and the nature of the world. In that case, the teacher is so interesting for the students that they become individualized by themselves. They will become individualized and do it actively. You do not need to work with each individual student, which is a kind of passive individualization. It is important that you always attempt to work with the entire class, and that a living contact with the teacher is present. When you have shaped your own soul to comprehend life, life will speak to those who wish to receive it.

If you develop a genuine talent for observation, you can perceive something when standing even before a large class. You can see that when you artistically present things that will become abstract and intellectualized only later, the physiognomy of the children changes. You will see how small changes in physiognomy occur, and that between the ages of seven and nine the children understand themselves. You can see how their faces express something healthily and not nervously active. It is of enormous import for the remainder of the children's lives that this takes place. If the physiognomy develops healthily and actively, later in life people can develop a love of the world, a feeling for the world, an inner power of healing for hypochondria and superfluous criticism and similar things. It is terrible if you as teachers do not achieve that, for children after the age of nine have externally a quite different physiognomy than before.

I also think it is best for the teacher to not change classes throughout the entire elementary school period. I believe it is best for a teacher to begin with a class in the first grade of elementary school and continue moving up with the class through the grades until the end of elementary school, at least as far as this is possible. While I am aware of all the objections to this approach, I believe it can create an intimate connection with the students that outweighs all the disadvantages. It will counterbalance all the problems that can occur at the beginning because the teacher is unacquainted with the individuality of the class or the students. The teacher and students will achieve a balance over the course of time. They will grow together more and more with the class and will learn in that connection. It is not easy to see the subtle changes in the physiognomy of the children.

For me it is not important to describe some theoretical basis for following the spiritual and soul forces of human beings in such a way that you can see their connection with the physical body. What is important is understanding that the human being is a unity and actually being able to see this in individual cases. By developing these skills, you can train yourself to observe how people become different. Perhaps you will even develop a talent for observing how a person will listen later in life. You can read in the physiognomy whether people listen as a whole, that is, whether take in what they hear with thinking, feeling, and will, or whether they only allow what they hear to affect their wills, as a choleric might. It is good for teachers to develop such a talent for observation for life in general. Everything we learn in life can help us when we want to teach children. When you see, as I can see at the Waldorf School, how the teacher works in a way appropriate to her own individuality, you will notice how each class becomes a whole together with the teacher. Out of that whole arises the development of the child. This process can be very different with each individual teacher, since these processes can always be individualized. One teacher who instructs nine-year-old boys and girls could do something very well in a particular way and another who teaches quite differently could teach them just as well. In that way there is complete individualization.

I also believe it is possible to determine the curriculum and learning goals for each grade in the elementary school out of the nature of the human being. For that reason it is of great importance that the teacher be the genuine master of the school, if I may use the term "master." I do not mean that there should be any teaching directives. Instead the teacher should be a part not only of the methods but also of the plans of the school. Whether she is teaching the first grade or the eighth, the teacher should be totally integrated with the whole of the school, and should teach the first grade in the same manner that the eighth grade will be taught.

In my lecture the day after tomorrow, I want to characterize the curriculum in more detail and also justify the learning goals for each year. Today, of course, since we are stuck in a materialistic culture that also has an effect upon our curriculum and learning goals, we can view such things only as an ideal for the future and put them into practice only to a limited degree. If there is a loophole in the law somewhere, as there is in the elementary school law in Württemberg, it is possible to make some compromises. Nevertheless such things need to be taken up since I believe they are connected with what must occur for us to move beyond the misery of the past five or six years.

6

TEACHING EURYTHMY, MUSIC, DRAWING, AND LANGUAGE

Basel, April 28, 1920

To illustrate some things I will discuss later, I will begin today with a remedy I attempted at our Waldorf School in Stuttgart. After I had observed the teaching in the eighth grade, I mentioned in a faculty meeting how various teachers were unable to cope with some of the children. I also mentioned that what we want to accomplish in a particular period could not be accomplished by a certain number of the children due to that problem. I had the teachers prepare a list of children who were lagging behind, and then I met with each of the children from the various grades who appeared to be weak during the previous school year. Since it was possible for me to be in Stuttgart only during the Christmas holiday, these meetings were made possible by the extraordinary willingness of the parents and children at the school. It was important for me and the respective class teachers to determine what the problem with each child could have been, from either a physio-

99

logical or psychological perspective. When testing the capabilities of students in this way, you need to start from somewhat deeper principles than those commonly used today that are derived from so-called experimental psychology. (But I do not want to say anything against this so long as it remains within its own boundaries.)

I attempted to show how it is possible to test insufficient capacities on things that actually lie very far from the capacity in question. For example, we can take the situation where a child in the third grade, for instance, that is, about eight or eight-and-a-half years old, is not sufficiently attentive. When the child is attentive, we can teach him or her something that he will most likely soon forget. It is, however, not possible to properly develop the desired level of attentiveness in that child.

I examined one such child. As I said, the children there are very willing, because of the faculty's general attitude, which was prepared in the way I characterized for you recently. I examined such a child and presented him with the following test. I said to the child, grasp the lower part of your left arm with your right hand. I also drew the outline of an ear and asked him if it was a left ear or a right ear. Then I drew some geometric figure that the child did not actually need to understand alongside another figure and attempted to determine whether the child had some feeling that the one figure was formed symmetrically to the other. I also attempted to determine how long the child needed, measured through a kind of feeling, not a watch.

In this way we could see whether a child was quick or slow in regard to things with a direct connection to life. After a few months, I returned to the school. In the intervening time, such things had been taken into account and right in the middle of class similar questions were asked of this same child. This had been done two, three, or four times. When I returned, it was apparent that they had had a certain effect upon him. When you begin with pictures, that always has an effect upon the child, but particularly when you use such pictures that are connected with the child's own body and not those that the child simply views, which lie outside him. Pictures such as "grasp your left arm with your right hand" are particularly effective.

Illustrative teaching, where the child is directly placed in the picture, has a lasting effect. Those who are unacquainted with spiritual science will not be able to properly differentiate between the impression made upon a child by such a picture from the impression made by a more abstract, more externally viewed picture. If we do not begin from the perspective of spiritual science, we underestimate the influence it has upon the entire development of the child, particularly during the time when the child is sleeping. Much too little attention is paid to what occurs during the period from falling asleep until awakening. It is certainly true that within our materialistic view of the world and in our practical understanding we are more or less forced to see the spirit-soul as something that directly results from the physical body, even though we may deny this. We are therefore never aware that during the period of wakefulness, from awakening until falling asleep, we work with a connection of the spirit-soul with the physical human being and, in contrast, during the period from falling asleep until awakening, quite a different being is lying there in bed. That being lying there in bed has actually been robbed of its higher spirit-soul aspect, and that spirit-soul exists outside the physical body during sleep. Even though the spirit-soul receives its consciousness through physicality—that is, the physical body is necessary for us to be aware of the content of our soul—the physical body is not necessary in order for us to experience that content. There is continual activity in the content of the soul during the period from falling asleep until awakening, and what occurs there can be studied only with the help of spiritual-scientific research. Through such research, it is apparent that we take into our soul only what we receive pictorially, that is, only what awakens corresponding feelings. Everything we receive as mere abstract concepts—things we learn as unpictured, unmovable concepts—does not work within us during the period of sleep. It does not directly enter our souls.

A child learns things presented pictorially in a healthy way only when they are in some way connected with the child's own physical body. The basis of education is extraordinarily dependent upon such subtle differences in life. We need to take into account the activity of the spirit-soul during that state in which human beings live from falling asleep until awakening. If we do not learn to recognize that, we will achieve very little during school or through education in general for the child's later life.

Only when we look at these two aspects of human nature will we become aware of what it is within a child that appears to bring about a unified activity. We need to be completely clear that when we attempt to teach a child something from a purely intellectual perspective, we can, at least under some circumstances, completely fail with some children. If, on the other hand, we attempt to support something that is missing in the child, through pictorial instruction, for example, a quick comprehension, then we can give the child something that is, perhaps, just what is needed in a specific case.

Even when we are forced by social conditions to work with a large number of students in the class, we can to a certain extent relate individually and with goodwill. For example, we can find the weaker children and give some attention to attempting to help them through details that sometimes appear unrelated. I do not want to suggest that what I have described here is the ideal; nevertheless the ideal does lie in that direction. Through such a study of a child's life, you begin to comprehend how activities within human nature that appear quite unified are the result of a duality that we must respect.

The day before yesterday I showed how instruction in writing should be developed from instruction in drawing, or perhaps, from simple instruction in painting. That instruction will also serve for many other things I will mention. In the Waldorf School, I have generally made the attempt—and I believe there are certain indications that it was relatively successful after a short period of time—to begin with artistic activities even with the youngest children. Our youngest children in the Waldorf School are actually only occupied with school subjects for two hours a day. A relatively large period of time is spent with the younger children in teaching foreign languages. Although I am aware of the prejudices against this, there is a tremendously deep effect in regard to the children's liveliness and attentiveness, that is, in regard to the awakening of their souls, when you attempt to teach foreign languages to young children without any grammatical pedantry, simply through speaking. Our children begin to learn French and English as soon as they enter school. In doing so, we use more time than is usual. The instruction in the afternoons consists almost only of music. We include in the normal school instruction what I have referred to as a drawing-basis for writing. Thus the younger children are primarily taught drawing in the way that I will describe later. Exception for a few hours in which the pastors and spiritual leaders provide religious instruction and where we need to work according to their schedule, afternoons are used almost exclusively for physical exercises and singing and music. When you begin in this way with the youngest children, you can see how you can include really the entire human being with this kind of artistic foundation of instruction.

The children have primarily an inner experience through the musical instruction. We have divided the physical exercises in such a way that we alternate between simply physiological gymnastics and what we call eurythmy.[1] What we call eurythmy is, from a pedagogical perspective, something we could call "ensouled gymnastics." We could also look at eurythmy from an artistic perspective, but I will discuss that at another time. Eurythmy is added to the normal physiological gymnastics. Physiological gymnastics, by which I mean gymnastics as they are normally done today, start more or less from a study of the human body (even though people deny this). In general, even in regard to an "ensoulment of gymnastics," we actually are only concerned with the physiological or, at best, the psychological aspects, as modern science gives no reason for thinking of anything more. Eurythmy differs from that in that each movement the child makes is ensouled. Each movement is not simply a physical movement; it is at the same time an expression of the soul in just the way that the spoken word is an expression of the soul.

We have found that among the entire 280 children that we have in eight classes in the Waldorf School, only three do not wish to participate in this instruction. They did not want to do it at all, whereas the others enjoy it a great deal. When we looked into this, we discovered that these three did not at all like any physical activity. They were simply too lazy. They preferred more passive activities. They did not want to pour themselves into this ensouled movement.

In the end, eurythmy is such, when you understand it, that you can read it in just the same way as you can read words and sentences. If I may use a Goethean expression, eurythmy developed through a sense-perceptible and supersensible observation of the tendencies in the movement of the larynx, gums, and lips, and then applying the Goethean principle of metamorphosis[2] to transfer the movement of those organs to the entire human being. Goethe's view was that an entire plant is only a more complicated leaf. What I mean here is that everything that a human being does in movement according to her will is a reflection not of the actual movements, but of the tendencies of those movements found in the organs of speech, so that the entire human being becomes a lively, moving larynx.

Eurythmy has an enormous effect upon the nature of the child.

We need only recall that speaking is simply a localization of the entire activity of a human being. In speaking, the activities of thinking and will come together. In encountering one another, they also become an activity of feeling. The intellectual activity, which in our civilized language is very abstract, is left out in eurythmy so that everything flows out of the human will. Thus the will is what is actually utilized in eurythmy. Eurythmy is the opposite of dreaming. Dreaming brings human beings into experiencing the world of thought. People simply lie there and the movements that they imagine do not actually exist. They may travel through a large area of land, but in reality they do not move. All this is only present in the person's imagination. In eurythmy, it is just the opposite. In dreaming a human being is half asleep, whereas in eurythmy a person is more fully awake than he or she is during normal wakeful life. In eurythmy, a person does just what is left out in dreams and suppresses what is the main aspect of dreaming. Thus each thought is immediately carried out as a movement. For many children, this activity is not always what they want to do. I am convinced that while simple physiological gymnastics achieves its intended effects, it does nothing to strengthen those activities of the will that begin in the soul, or at best it strengthens them indirectly in that people more easily overcome a certain physical clumsiness. However, simple physiological gymnastics does not actually do anything to strengthen the will. This is a conviction that I have from the short time in which we have divided the required time for gymnastics between normal gymnastics and eurythmy. Of course, this is a question that must be considered further. Nevertheless I believe it has major social significance.

I ask myself today how it is that, in spite of the suffering we have gone through in the past years, we are confronted with a humanity that has so little understanding of how the will has been crippled. Those of you who live here in Switzerland and have never seen, for example, such areas as we find in Germany today do not have any real understanding of what this means. You will only gain such an understanding in five or six years, or perhaps later. What is now occurring in some areas will, if some redress is not found, spread through Europe. In those areas that have not yet been affected there is little idea of how crippled the will is in the Central European population. This is something terrible. You can expend much effort over weeks or months in pointing out to people one thing or another, and then when you speak with someone later, they tell you that may all be correct what you have said, but it doesn't matter. That is a statement I have often heard in the course of a year. I have put much effort into finding the foundation of such things, but I can find no other reason than that they are the result of excessive praise of physiological gymnastics. That does not strengthen the will. The will is strengthened when, as a child, you carry out movements where each movement is at the same time connected with the soul, so that the soul pours itself into each individual movement.

If you attempt to approach things artistically, or perhaps we could say, artistically-humanly, then you will see what the youngest children in particular gain from such an artistic form of instruction. Through ensouled gymnastics, their interest for the external world grows. The growth of their interest for the external world is a necessary result. In various discussions, Herman Grimm,[3] the art historian, told me about his frustrations with the gymnasts who came to the university and to whom he was to lecture about art history. When he presented them with a painting by Raphael,[4] they were unable to determine which figures were in front and which were toward the back. They hadn't the least idea about what was in the foreground and what was in the background. Grimm often said to me that he was absolutely unsure of what to do with such students when he was to lecture to them about art history. I believe that children who in their early years of school do their exercises with awareness in their soul would not at all have this problem.

They have an astonishing interest in observing the external world. In addition to this cultivation of will, we also need to cultivate inner reflection in a corresponding way through the proper teaching of music and singing. Both must be kept in balance. We have tried this harmony by having the same teacher teach singing, eurythmy, and gymnastics. If you try to do this, you will find that the relationship to the external world, something that arises from the will, is strengthened by eurythmy and gymnastics. It is permeated with a kind of initiative. You will also find that inner reflection with feeling is strengthened by music in all forms. This is extremely important. If you attempt to study the developing child in this way, then you will notice how particularly by developing things that appear to be unified actually arise out of two sources of human experience.

I have studied the primitive drawings of children for decades. You will not understand children's drawings if you attempt to simply follow the primitive forms in which children make them. In order to properly understand such drawings, which is actually a representation of what is occurring in the child while drawing, you need to observe children who for some reason or another at the age of six or seven have a talent for drawing as well as children who for whatever reason are unable to draw before the age of nine or ten. It is not good that there are such children, but there is certainly sufficient opportunity to observe them. There is a major difference in the drawings produced by those children around the age of ten who earlier could not draw at all when compared with those drawings made by children at the age of six, seven, or eight. The difference is that those children who at an early age draw something, this is certainly something you all know, those children draw in a very primitive way. They draw, for instance, a head like this [Steiner draws], a head, two eyes, and a mouth. They also often draw the teeth and the legs immediately below. Or they may draw a head, then the torso, make two lines here [for the arms], and sometimes they are aware that on the end of them they need a hand or something.

You can certainly pursue such drawings, and there is also much such material collected in pedagogical references. What is important here, however, is that we learn to understand such drawings from the perspective of the entire nature of a human being. Today that is extremely difficult because we have no comprehensive view of art. This in turn is because we do not properly comprehend the process of how people create art. Our view of art has been influenced by the way artistic creation has developed in modern times. In the most recent years there has often developed a very insufficient opposition to what has developed. I am expressly using the term *insufficient*. Fundamentally, our entire artistic creation is connected in some way with a model, that is, with an external perspective.

I have spent a great deal of my life in art studios and have seen how everything that modern artists produce, that is, sculptors and painters, depends upon a model. This leads people to think, for example, that the Greeks also depended upon models for their artistic creation, yet that is not the case. Those who properly understand something like the Laocoön group, or some other such figure—those of course are from the later Greek period—those who really go into such things will slowly come to recognize the independence, particularly of Greek artists, from the model. Certainly Greek artists could see things well and retain them in a picture. However, that alone is insufficient. The Greek artist, particularly as a sculptor, created from the feeling of a limb, from their own feeling and perception of a limb and its movements. Thus in their artistic creations they inwardly felt, for example, a bent arm and a balled-up fist, and that inner feeling was not simply what they saw with their eyes in an external model. It was not the external model that was reproduced in a material, but that inner feeling, the feeling of the human form. It is in fact this inner feeling of the human being that has been lost to European civilization since the time of the Greeks. We need to study the transition from the feeling of the human being, from an organic self-recognition that existed with the Greeks and that in the end is contained in every Greek poem, in every Greek drama. We need to recognize the difference between that feeling, between the organic self-recognition, or, better, self-observation or self-feeling of a human being, and what occurs through a simple imitation of what is seen, through basing work upon a model. It is clear that the Greek artists were able to achieve what they wanted. It is easy to say that the Greeks gained an overview of forms through the Olympic Games and such things, and certainly that was of some help. However, the most important aspect of artistic creation was that inner feeling, the feeling organ. Thus the Greeks were in their artistic creations very independent of the model, something that for them was a kind of preliminary design, which they held to externally.

When I look at the drawings of a child, as primitive and sketchy as they are, I can find in each of them a confluence of the child's perspective and the child's primitive feeling of himself in his organs. In every individual line of a child's drawing, we can see how the child attempted to put down what originated in the eye and attempted also to put down those things that originate in inner feeling. If you take a large number of children's drawings and attempt to see how children draw arms and legs, you will see that that originates from an inner feeling. When you look at how children draw profiles, you will see how that originates from viewing. The drawings thus originate from two separate sources. The situation is even more interesting when you look at drawings done by children who have been unable to draw until a certain age. They draw more or less out of the intellect. Small children do not draw from their intellect; they draw from experience, from primitive views enlivened with a primitive feeling. I believe it is possible to always differentiate when a child draws a mouth: then the outline of the mouth has been seen. But when it draws teeth, that is in some way taken out of an inner feeling. If, however, you look at a child who has begun to draw only at the age of nine or ten and study the child's drawings, you will see how the child actually often makes more beautiful expressionist drawings than the expressionists themselves. The child draws often with colored pencils and draws what it thinks, what it has thought up. It is often quite curious how children often draw something we do not recognize and will then say that it is a devil or an angel. The drawing does not at all look like an angel, but the child says this is an angel. In such cases, the child is drawing its own intellect; the child is drawing what it has thought up.

If a feeling for the inner organs is not cultivated in the years when it is important, that is, between the ages of six and nine, the intellect will take over. This intellect is essentially the enemy of intellectual human life as well as of social life. I of course am not in favor of making people dumb. It is important, however, that we recognize the parasitic nature of the intellect and that we recognize the intellect as being complete only when it arises out of the entire human being and not in a one-sided way. That, however, is possible to achieve only when drawing and music instruction are supported in all areas of instruction, most importantly in speech and arithmetic.

As for teaching languages, you first need to gain a sense of how to do this. I first became aware of this sense of teaching languages when I had the opportunity of pursuing the result of having children who spoke dialect sit in the same classroom as other children who did not speak the dialect. It is very interesting to observe children who speak a dialect and how they carry themselves. A dialect, every dialect, has a certain characteristic. It arises out of what I would call an inner feeling of the human being just in the same way as the inner organic feeling arises, something that is much less important in today's intellectualism. Dialect is an inner experience that pushes the entire human being into speech. In modern conversational speech, the so-called educated speech, which has become abstract, there is no longer a proper connection between inner experience and what is expressed in a sound or series of sounds. Certain subtle differences in the relationship between the person and the person's surroundings are often wonderfully expressed in dialect. That is something you can no longer detect in educated speech. For example, when as a child I heard the word *sky-flash (Himmlitzer)*, I knew immediately that it was something that must be similar to the sound. Try to feel the word *Himmlitzer*. In certain dialects, that is the word for *lightning*. There is something in the sounds or in the series of sounds. Here the language is drawing a picture; it paints in a kind of inner music. The close connection between language and inner experiences of feeling is enormously stronger in dialect than it is in educated language.

There is something else to consider. It is curious that when we compare languages, we discover that the inner logic of a language is greater in primitive languages than in more educated speech forms. You would actually expect the opposite. This is, of course, not true with the languages of black Africans. But those are *really* primitive languages and I will come back to those in a moment. In certain primitive languages there is a remarkable inner logic, which is much more abstract yet simpler than when the language becomes more civilized. Thus there is in dialect a greater inner logic than in educated language, and we can achieve a great deal. If, for example, in a village school we have to work with dialect, then we must begin with dialect, as we need to attempt to make conscious what already exists unconsciously in the language, namely, the grammar. Grammar should be taught in a very lively way. It should be taught in such a lively way that we assume that it already exists when the child speaks. When the child speaks, the grammar is already there. You should allow the children to speak sentences in the way they are used to speaking so that they feel the inner connection and inner flexibility of the language. You can then begin to draw the child's attention and make them aware of what they do unconsciously. You certainly do not need to do that through a pedantic analysis. You can develop the entirety of grammar by simply making the children more aware of the life of the grammar that is already there when the child has learned to speak.

We can certainly assume that all grammar already exists in the human organism. If you take that assumption seriously, you will realize that by making grammar conscious in a living way, you work on the creation of an I-consciousness in the child. You must orient everything toward that knowledge that exists in the body around the age of nine, when a consciousness of the I normally awakens. You need to bring forth into consciousness everything that exists unconsciously in the child's organism. In that way the child will reach the Rubicon of development at the age of nine in a favorable way. In that way you bring into consciousness what is unconscious. You then work with those forces in the child that want to develop, not the forces that you bring from outside the child. There is a way of teaching language by using the way the child already speaks and supporting the instruction through a living interaction between those children who speak a more cultivated language and those who speak a dialect. In this way you can allow them to measure themselves against each other, not in some abstract way, but using feeling to guide a word, a sentence, in dialect into another. If you do that for an hour and a half, you will really make the children break out into a sweat. The teachers who teach this way in the Waldorf School certainly have enough when they do this for an hour and a half or so each morning! If you give instruction in language by working with the knowledge in the body so that you create an actual self-consciousness, you are working in harmony with the foundation you have laid in drawing and musical instruction. Thus you have two processes that support each other.

I was quite startled as I found in some more recent pedagogical literature a statement that teaching drawing was negatively influenced by language class because instruction in language or speaking in general forces people into abstractions. People forget how to see and how to view what exists in the external world as forms and colors. That is what is asserted there. That is not the case if you give instruction in language not in an abstract way, but instead develop it out of an inner experience. Then they support one another and what develops as a consciousness of the self around the age of nine becomes visible, piece by piece, as it goes on to imbue an external view of things with an artistic feeling for form.

I have had the teachers in the Waldorf School do the following exercises because they should be working entirely out of an artistic perspective. Our teachers may not be satisfied when the children can draw a circle or a square or a triangle. Instead, our children need to learn how to *feel* a circle, triangle, or square. They need to draw a circle so that they have a feeling of roundness. They should learn to draw a triangle so that they have a feeling for the three corners and that when they have first drawn one corner they should feel that there will be three. In the same way, when they draw a square, they should have a feeling of the right angle, a feeling that is carried throughout the whole drawing process from the very beginning. Our children need to learn what an arc is, what vertical or horizontal is, what a straight line is, not simply in seeing it, but an inner feeling of how the arm or the hand follows it. This is done as a basis for teaching writing. None of our children should learn to write a *P* without first having the experience of the vertical and an arc, not simply that a child has an abstract understanding of that, of the vertical and the arc, but a feeling for a felt experience of such things.

By slowly developing everything intellectual out of the artistic, that is, out of the entire human being, you will also develop the entire human being, people with real initiative, with a real force of life in their bodies. They will not be like people in our own population who no longer know where they are after they have done their final examinations. This is a real tragedy. If your professional task is to understand human beings, then it is possible that you can experience the following. You are, for example, to test someone around the age of twenty-five or thirty whether he is to receive a given position. You approach him with the expectation they should develop some initiative, particularly if he is to go into a practical profession. The person tells you, however, that you expect one thing or another but that he wants to go to India or to America in order to learn more about the profession. What that means is that he actually wants to move into the profession passively. He does not want to develop anything out of his own initiative, but instead wishes to have the opportunity that the world will make something of him. I know that saying this is something horrible for many people, but at the same time I am pointing out something we can see in people who have completed their education in the last decades. It has not developed a genuine initiative, initiative that reaches down into people's souls when it is necessary later in life. It is of course easy to say that we should develop initiative. The question is, though, how we do that, how we can arrange the material we are to present in education so that it acts not against initiative in the will, but strengthens it.

Discussion Following Lecture Six

I would now like to answer a few questions. To begin with, I would like to go into the question of psychoanalysis. Psychoanalysis is a child of our materialistic times. In our time, people do not try to seek the harmony between the sleeping spirit, which I might refer to as the artist of the body, and the physical organization of our bodies. Both of these aspects stand next to one another. Psychological theories attempt to form bridges between them. Just think of all such bridges we have seen in modern times that were to be formed between the spirit-soul and the physical body, beginning with the views of Descartes,[1] psychophysical parallelism, and so forth. All these theories have essentially been born out of an incapacity to view the human being as a whole. People do not see how the physical is formed out of the spiritual and how the spiritual is revealed simultaneously in the physical body. We need only to understand how the one has been separated from the other through abstractions. Thus certain things have been totally misunderstood in modern times, even though they are understandable when we recognize the harmony between the physical and the psychological.

Take, for example, a young person who has had a traumatic experience. Every traumatic experience that occurs before the age of twenty has an effect upon the physical body. Even in later years such an effect is present, though to a much lesser extent. Today the only thing that is seen in that regard plays out only at the most extreme, superficial level. People see, for example, how a person reddens when he or she is ashamed, or turns pale when afraid. They do not see how a traumatic experience that perhaps over a period of several weeks pushes human feeling in a particular direction also causes the physical body to develop in a different direction than it would have otherwise taken. The body begins with a normal structure, but this structure changes as a result of traumatic experience.

Since human life follows a rhythm, after a particular number of years a special kind of repetition of the original organic trauma will occur. If you meet a person who is thirty-eight years old and has some anomalies in his or her soul, you understand that this anomaly indicates an earlier experience that must have occurred as many years *before* the age of thirty-five as the recurrence does *after* that age. Thus the psychic anomaly that we observe in the thirty-eight-year-old can be connected with an experience that person had at about the age of thirty-two. We can also understand the recurrence of this experience at the age of thirty-eight when we recognize the relationship between the traumatic experience at the age of thirty-two and certain physical organs. In other cases, the present experience may be related to an experience that occurred just as many years before the age of twenty-eight as the number of years that have passed since that age. We need to acquire a capacity of observation in order to recognize the connections between experiences in the spirit-soul and their relationship to the organs.

But what is done in modern times? If you are a physician, regardless of how materialistically you think, you still cannot deny that there is some life of the soul. Materialism is characterized by the fact that it understands nothing of the material, and in our time of materialism we experience the tragedy of how materialism does not even understand material processes. It is just for that reason that people do not relate things experienced in the soul to material things. On the contrary, they erroneously say that an isolated experience that has been hidden for many years now suddenly has risen to the surface and we must become conscious of it. What is important is to study the person's organic state of health rather than poking around in that person through psychoanalysis.

The same is true with regard to the use of psychoanalysis in education. People do not understand the interaction between the spirit-soul and the physical body. Only for this reason do they speak about the use of psychoanalysis in education. We cannot simply work one-sidedly with the spirit-soul.

I would now like to say something about the difficulties that arise during puberty. These arise only when children have not been properly brought up. If children have the kind of introspection and inner experience that I described today, then that will have an effect upon the entire physical body and soul of the child. The child will have different perceptions and a different relationship to the external world than it would have had had it developed it too intellectually or with too little experience in art when the child was about seven or eight years old. The errors made in teaching children when they are seven or eight years old reappear in their problematic feelings during puberty. If we were to speak about the things that we often hear mothers and fathers tell about their children, we would be able to see how materialism has taken control of our feelings. People come to me and tell me about their five- or six-year-old child who has undesirable sexual behaviors. This shows only that people can no longer differentiate. If a knife has been made into a razor blade, then it is no longer a pocketknife. In the same way, activities that occur with children and which at a superficial level appear to expose some sexual desires are in fact not actual sexual activities, but simply demands that the child be brought up according to his or her own nature. When that is done, then abnormal feelings will not occur during puberty. It is no more a sexual act if a child scratches herself in the region of the sexual organs because there is a small sore (which may be easy to miss) than it would be if she were to scratch herself on the nose or cheek.

If we understand this, we will not fall into the craziness of Freud.[2] Instead of recognizing that it makes no difference whether a child scratches herself on the cheek or somewhere else, he claims that it is a sexual act when a child enjoys sucking on a pacifier. Freud's perspective puts everything into one hat. This is something that Goethe tried to do with one of his most humorous poems, "The World Is a Sardine Salad,"[3] in which he attempted to counter the argument that the world consists simply of so-and-so-many different atoms and the views of the world according to which will and unconscious existence are simply constructs. Gustav Theodor Fechner,[4] the humorist, did something really funny in his book, *The Moon Is Made of Iodine*, which appeared in the early nineteenth century. He proves through formal logic that the moon is made up simply of iodine. We could use that little book as an example of the way people think of the world today.

Steiner replies to an objection that he has referred only to Freud and has not mentioned other directions.

To fully answer your question, I would need to hold a whole series of lectures. Since that is not possible, I would like to say only the following. How strongly the fanaticism for particular views is in our time is especially clear with supporters of psychoanalysis. In answering a question, I used an example indicating the Freudian position with regard to sexuality. It is, of course, correct that other psychoanalysts have a view different from that one-sidedly sexual interpretation. In recent months, some psychiatrists have strongly distanced themselves from the original Freudian direction, and even from Jung's[5] direction. However, those who can judge psychoanalysis in connection with the development of civilization in modern times will never be able to see something new, not even a seed of something new, in psychoanalysis. They will always see only the final consequences of materialism.

It is characteristic of materialism that instead of examining the relationship of the spirit-soul with the physical, in a living way it attempts to characterize the physical in only the most superficial ways, in the ways that are valid for physics and chemistry. On the other hand, it remains an abstract characterization of the spirit-soul, which has been carried to an extreme in the way that psychoanalysis simply follows the path of the status of the soul throughout the life of the human being. I certainly do not deny the positive things that some people have in mind when they speak of psychoanalysis today when those things are correct. It is certainly correct that certain experiences in the soul have a lasting effect and can be recognized and observed as causing a particular change. What is important here, though, is that during the period lying in between, an interaction occurs that psychoanalysis considers to be something isolated in the soul. The effects upon the physical organism that become apparent as a strong one-sidedness are not recognized.

Such theories, of which psychoanalysis is one, have something unusual about them at the present. I have studied these things intensely. What is important to recognize here is that there is a tendency today to take theories that are correct for a particular and limited situation and extend them into general laws. Psychoanalysis exemplifies that. Summarizing theories into a law is justifiable only when they can be used in all practical situations. This is not true of psychoanalytical theory. Since the psychoanalyst does not understand the true relationship between the physical and the psyche, he or she tends to relate the psychic facts only to earlier psychic states. This is something that is quite strongly apparent with Jung. Jung is quite far from a comprehensive consideration of events in the world. We should, however, recognize that Jung has understood certain complexes and has traced them back in the evolution of the soul. The so-called Oedipus complex is, in the way that some psychoanalysts have described it, something that is very interesting and captivating. The problem lies in the way that the described series of symptoms does not comprehensively include all other symptoms connected with it.

What I mean here can be demonstrated through a simple picture. If you place a rose and a crystal on a table, you can say that both are objects. Equating a rose and a crystal through the concept of "object" is, however, only justified in an extremely superficial way. A rose is not simply an object alone, and you cannot consider it in the same way as you would a crystal, which is, in a certain way, something complete. (Of course, we should not forget that a crystal also needs to be considered in relationship to its normal surroundings.) Thus we need to seek the full context of symptoms in which we place a complex. We cannot simply take the most obvious things into account. The blossom of a tree, for example, cannot be simply considered as an object in itself. The tree must also be taken into account. Looking still further, we would need to take into account the qualities of the soil and of the air and so forth as well.

The primary error of psychoanalysis is that it considers symptoms in isolation that can only be explained in connection with other symptoms. I previously referred to the sexual example because psychoanalytic literature declares the fish symbol to be the symbol for the male sexual organ, and this is proven in a completely unscientific way. Such declarations are simply grotesque. Nor should the so-called Oedipus complex and its symptoms be considered in isolation. Instead we need to bring it into relationship with the entire development of humanity.

7

THE PROBLEM
OF TEACHER TRAINING

Basel, April 29, 1920

What is most important for me in these lectures is to show to what extent spiritual science can make education more fruitful. Of course it is not possible to develop a complete system of pedagogy in fourteen lectures. In these first considerations, I have already indicated that I do not believe a renewal of education is necessary, since present educational principles contain many good things. I believe that primarily a refreshing of education is necessary. Spiritual science is certainly appropriate for bringing new life into educational practice based upon many of the wonderful educational theories that already exist, because spiritual science attempts to comprehend the living spirit. Such comprehension of the living spirit, which is a source of enlivening for both the will and the feeling, is particularly necessary in pedagogy. Furthermore, spiritual science is a source of a genuine understanding of the human being that is particularly appropriate for working with children.

I would like to remark that it is clear that alongside of any form of education, whether it is oriented more toward the intellect or toward the soul, the human being must also be educated in feelings, primarily in a moral and religious sense. Particularly in the development of ethical and moral attitudes and of a religious sense, we need to work with the entire human being. Whenever we wish to have an effect upon the attitudes or will of the entire person, we must take into account the transformation and changes that human beings undergo both as children and in later life. To such changes in later life it is necessary that we give the proper impulse, particularly during the time of education.

But it is impossible to teach anything in connection with morals, attitudes or religion if, during the course of education, we do not first create some way of accessing the human soul and spirit. It would be a major error to believe that we can simply set up rules that people should do this or that in regard to their attitudes or religion or morality. The situation is actually quite different, and we can describe it in the following way.

If in my teaching, particularly with children up to the age of nine, I can create a connection with the child's soul, the child will allow me to guide her in a moral or religious connection. If I cannot create such a relationship, if I teach in such a way that the child closes her feelings off from me, the child will be unreachable by even the best moral or religious guidance. It is particularly unhelpful to give in to illusions, even if we are doing so on the grounds that we are overcoming some of the cultural damage of our times. We cannot, for example, allow ourselves to be influenced by doctrines that understand the immortality of the human soul only in one sense.

In this area we chiefly try to make sure that people have a good understanding and a healthy feeling in regard to going through the gates of death, in regard to the further life of the soul after death. Such knowledge might seem to be merely theoretical, but it is not. Every action that we undertake in life, everything we do or say, particularly how we do or say it, depends upon a person's view of this major life question. Although the various confessions of the immortality of human soul are absolutely correct, they nevertheless arise out of egotism in a certain number of people. They have developed out of human egotism. While it is necessary to speak to people (and to children in particular) about life after death—a truth that is certainly well-anchored in spiritual science—when we speak about this by itself, we reflect only the egotism of human nature that wants to continue to live after the body has been given over to the earth. But in doing so, we shut people out from the tasks of their earthly life. In particular, we as teachers shut ourselves out from the task of developing human beings when we think and act under the influence of such one-sided perspectives.

We need to recognize that earthly life is the continuation of a supersensible life. We need to look at what lives in us as spirit-soul as something that has moved from a supersensible world and connected itself with our physical bodies. It is very important to look at growing children in that way. If you look without prejudice, every child is a riddle to be solved, particularly for educators. If you look in this way at a growing child and say to yourself that what is presented here in earthly life is a continuation of the spiritual life, and it is our responsibility to guide what that divine being wanted in being incarnated in a human being, then we will be overcome by a feeling of holiness without which it is not possible to educate. We will have a feeling of solving a riddle when we are confronted with a developing human being. To imbue life here in the physical world with the character of a continuation of a spiritual life is something very important when we recognize it.

This is an important example of how differently an educator will act depending on his attitude. In external life, what is of primary importance is how a person acts. However, in being confronted by developing human beings, by children, we are also confronted with the innermost aspect of human nature. Our attitudes will inevitably affect theirs, and what is important here is the influences which lie at the basis of our attitude. An attitude of reverence will encourage a sense of responsibility toward the task of education. And without that sense of responsibility, we can achieve nothing in teaching. Everything must be permeated by it. I particularly hope that you will be permeated by this feeling, even though it appears to be so distant from the topic we are here to discuss.

Human beings derive their activities from two sources, as I said yesterday. One source is an indication more of what a human being brings into physical life from superphysical life. The other source is more an indication of what the human being should create out of life here. When we realize this, we will also be able to see the difference between what a human being brings into life and what is to be developed through this life. When I said how the intellect is born with the change of teeth and how the will moves into a human being with puberty, I characterized these two sources from two standpoints, although there are many others. When we focus upon the intellect, we are looking more at what a person brings into physical existence through birth. When we turn our attention to the will, we should be aware that we are primarily dealing with what a person should take in from the physical world in order to embed it into his higher nature. In every disharmony and harmony with the world that occurs through physical life, the human will is developed; that, in a certain sense, *becomes* human will. What is present as the intellect in human nature we must attempt to coax out.

In simply stating that, we can see many misunderstandings that arise in stating educational truths. People always want to say things in one-sided ways when these things actually have two sides in life. They either say that we must draw everything out of the human being or that we must put everything into it. Both are incorrect, of course. It is true that to a certain extent we need to draw everything that is naturally imaginative out of human nature. On the other hand, for everything concerned with the will, the experiences that we present to a human being are what is formative. People draw upon life for their will. For this reason it is important how we are connected to the children's developing will, so that they can imitate us, seeing that what we say we also do. At around the age of seven, these patterns become authority for them. We need to place the child in such an environment so that she herself can draw upon as many experiences as possible to develop the will.

Here you can see how much of what people call the question of education is actually a question about the qualities of the teacher. Before I continue in this consideration, which I began yesterday, I would like to characterize the element that should permeate all of instruction, at least from one perspective.

Once again, it is possible to be very one-sided. Because of your own nature, you could fill your instruction with seriousness, with a face that can never laugh, that can only reprimand. It is also possible, if you have the tendency, to bring very little seriousness into your teaching. Both of these lead to extraordinarily damaging results later in life. It is as if someone were to think about whether inhaling is better than exhaling. Of course what is important is that human beings must both inhale and exhale; when a person who should exhale wants to inhale, that goes against nature. Just as there is a strict rhythm in the human being according to which there are on the average eighteen breaths taken in a minute, the entirety of human life is based upon rhythm. One part of that rhythm is the interplay between humor and seriousness.

Humor is based upon people getting away from themselves in a certain way. With humor, we move onto the path toward dreaming. Although we remain completely conscious, moving toward humor is the beginning of the path to dreaming. This loss of self is expressed through smiling or laughing. In these acts, the spirit-soul—or what we in spiritual science call the I and the astral body—moves out in a certain way from the physical and the etheric, although people still remain in control. Through humor, people expand in their soul and spirit aspects.

Let us now look at extreme examples of seriousness, such as crying and becoming sad. In these cases people are more compressed. The spirit-soul is more closely connected with the physical body than it is when we are in a neutral mood. A humorous attitude is an expansion of the soul and spirit, whereas a serious mood brings the spirit-soul aspect of human nature into closer contact with the physical body. We could also say that through laughing, a human being becomes more altruistic, and through seriousness, more egotistic.

An objection could be made to this assertion. If I say that seriousness makes people egotistical, then we can certainly preach that human beings should fight egotism. But what would happen if people fought egotism out of their own egotism, so that they perceived themselves as being unegotistical, as being unselfish? So that when they thought about the situation, they realized that they had created within themselves a passion for unselfishness? When someone satisfies her egotism by taking pleasure in loving many people, that is a much better gift than being unselfish in order to earn self-praise. We need to consider such things in a way that corresponds to human nature rather than interpreting them in a way that leads to an increase of passion within the soul. What is important here is that the rhythm in the human being between humor and seriousness supports the soul-spirit life in the same way that inhaling and exhaling support physical life. Just as exhaling is a kind of turning toward the external world and becoming more foreign to oneself, while inhaling gives physical pleasure to a person's egotism, humor is something whereby the human being expands and seriousness is something whereby the human being collects himself egotistically. Children need to move between these two moods through a teacher's guidance.

Now it is of course extraordinarily difficult if, when you enter the classroom with a kind of self-imposed responsibility, you say to yourself that you should alternate between being humorous and serious. To give yourself such a task is impossible. It's silly. It is something that cannot be. No one could expect me to include humorous things in my instruction immediately after a difficult personal experience. However, such an abstract feeling of responsibility is not necessary if you determine the content of what you should be enthusiastic about in the instruction in spiritual science. If you prepare for the class in a spiritual-scientific way, you will live in the individual portions of what you are to teach in an objective and impersonal way. If I come into a classroom at three in the afternoon to present something to the children and if I have schooled myself in the material in the same way I have learned to school myself in spiritual science, the material will be something through which I no longer need to take the external world into account. My own attitudes will disappear. The material itself will provide me with humor and seriousness at the right times, and things will just go by themselves.

This is an example of how spiritual science can help in practical education, right down to affecting the attitude of the teacher. It is necessary to see a doctor if I cannot properly breathe in order to restore the breathing process if possible. So the health-giving influence of a spiritual-scientific education is necessary for those people who are to have a healthy influence upon children. It is quite possible, of course, that on the way to school you may be justified in hanging your head in thinking about some terrible things that have happened to you. However, when you enter the classroom, you will become aware of what the task is for today, and you yourself no longer speak. It is not joy and sorrow that speaks. The things we teach are what speak; they move our fingers when we draw with chalk or when we write or do something else.

This shows that what is important at present is not to create new principles of education. Instead what is needed is a new spiritual structure that enables us to carry out our tasks without subjective influences. The teachers at the Waldorf School attempt to train themselves in this or at least to draw it out of human nature. During the short time we have worked there, we have in fact achieved something I could describe in the following way. For the sake of discretion, I will describe it as abstractly as possible.

Some have disagreed with my selection of teachers. They have told me that one teacher or another may not be very good, he may be too pedantic. I have not allowed myself to be influenced by that. But if a person has correct spiritual moral and feeling capacities, it is not necessary to consider whether that person is pedantic or not. What is important is to show the person how his or her pedantic tendencies can be properly brought into the service of humanity. If we had to remove all pedantic tendencies in people, we would certainly see how little is left over. If you take up spiritual science in a living way, it makes it easier to explain a specific, concrete area of life in an objective way, because the subjective characteristics of pedantry cease to be effective. In fact those people who were described as pedantic have become very exciting teachers after they found their way into teaching through a spiritual-scientific attitude. It is not at all important to act according to one or another preconceived idea. Instead we should act according to life. That is something we need in the present. Socialism wants to reform the entire world according to a theory. With regard to the development of humanity, the task of the present is to act according to life.

Everything I have said today is, in a way, the flip side of what I said yesterday about teaching languages, eurythmy, gymnastics, and so forth. What I discussed yesterday can be properly achieved by the teacher only when the teacher behaves in the way I have described today.

This leads me into a particularly interesting question that I was asked and which is closely connected with what I have just now described. It was indicated to me that a twelve-and-a-half-year-old girl had a B in behavior. While discussing an essay, she mentioned that in a private school, she always had good grades, but always a B in behavior. She told me that she then had a teacher she liked very much and never had a B, but that later his son taught the class and these bad grades in behavior started up again and continued in our school until the present time.

Much of what we have said today could have an extraordinarily high impact upon this question. You see, there are two things that are necessary in teaching. One is that we understand how to draw as much as possible out of the child, something we do at first through imagination. The other is that we work with the children in such a way that the child can like us.

There are all kinds of things in which we can, with some effort, try to train ourselves so that they become instinct. This is a complicated psychological problem into which we really cannot enter today. It is, however, true that many things that may require much effort to learn will come to others so simply, almost instinctively. One such thing is that a group of children just loves the person. That is very beautiful when it happens. What is important in regard to the development of culture and civilization, though, is that we achieve something similar through a certain kind of self-training. We can achieve that if we try to relate to the world in the way that we must if we are to take up spiritual science. As I mentioned before, we cannot take up spiritual science as though we were sitting in the theatre and watching a film. We can only take it up when we are inwardly active. As I said before, you should read my book *An Outline of Esoteric Science,* but if you read it without any inner experience and take what I say there simply as a guide for your own thoughts, then the entirety of spiritual science will be just like straw. For that reason, spiritual science is for many people simply straw. If, however, you read it so that it is like an orchestral score that you first only understand when you have drawn all the details out of yourself, then, through drawing that out of yourself, you will develop those forces that otherwise remain hidden in human nature.

It is just those forces that develop relationships, particularly in children, that in a sense draw children's attention to us. If we have gone through the process of drawing out those spiritual forces within us, then we can create a direct connection from one soul to another between ourselves and the child. That connection has tremendous significance in attitudinal and moral guidance as well as in training the child's will. It would be hardly possible for you to keep a class that is made up of 40 percent uncontrollable children simply through moral reprimands that come out of you like abstract rules. Often, through the tone of your voice or the energy you put into your voice, you can achieve that for a short period. But you can achieve nothing lasting in that way.

Perhaps, however, you could attempt to have some experiences with the following. When preparing for your classes, in addition to your normal preparation, try to add a kind of meditative preparation. Add something that has not the least to do with the material you are to present, but has more to do with raising your own soul, that has something to do with imbuing some material or some feeling that opens the world to you. When in the evening you have gone through such a meditative inner view, and you enliven that view so that on the next morning you can recall it and in a sense reexperience it, then you will notice an effect when you go into the classroom. This may sound as though I am telling you some superstition, but these are things that cannot be comprehended through any theory. You need to see them. When you observe them you will find them confirmed. Most people today are not particularly interested in observing such things. But we will have to become accustomed to such observations if we are to come out of the misery of the present time. From them corresponding convictions will arise, particularly for a type of education that is meant to include all of humanity. With the student I described before, it is quite clear that when she said she loved the teacher, her training in will was under the direct influence of that personal relationship. Although we can philosophize about this as much as we want, all training in will is always under the sway of personal relationships until children are past the age of puberty.

Now I come to another extremely interesting question. In every elementary school, particularly in boys' schools, you will find at least one boy who, although not in any way weak-minded, appears to be extraordinarily dumb in every subject, but who has a considerable talent for drawing. He has a certain instinct for observing and a genuine feeling for art. The remaining dumbness is nearly always connected to a kind of moral weakness and a brooding egotism. Such a boy does not seem to have the energy to come out of himself. What insight can a spiritual-scientific consideration of such a situation give? How should a teacher treat such a student in order to develop his intellectual capacities as well as the moral strength to carry out his own decisions?

When confronted with so concrete, so personal a question, I have the feeling of standing before unscalable walls. If you attempt to penetrate facts in the world through spiritual science, you can no longer consider such things superficially. At first you will have an uneasy feeling when working from the spiritual-scientific perspective in regard to such basic questions, even though you may have a great deal to say about them based upon all the many theories. You know, however, that regardless of how much you philosophize, you cannot find anything that will lead to an answer because life nearly always shows individual facts in individual situations and with special nuances, and you must first understand those nuances. With spiritual science you will almost always be led to the experience. Out of that experience you will work to find an answer.

I would now like to show you how you can attempt to find a

way of overcoming to an extent the insurmountable hindrances that life may present. I knew a boy who I could also continue to observe as a young man who had a remarkable weakness in the will. It was so acute that he could stand in the street, for instance, and decide to take a given streetcar to go somewhere. But when the streetcar came, he was unable to sufficiently gather his will together and board it. He thought about going to his destination with the streetcar, but he was unable to board it, so he stood there after the streetcar had gone by. I knew just such a boy who as a young man was an extraordinarily intelligent and progressive person, and that was a real riddle for me at first. I solved the riddle in a rather remarkable way. I was aware that the boy's father, whom I also knew, held the view that it was unnecessary to develop the will.[1] His thoughts were thus concentrated upon, in a sense, talking away the will as a characteristic of the soul. Now I had a path. The father's perspective was not actually a part of his nature; it had not actually affected his own organs. But what was a thought with the father had become habitual with the son. Possibly what the son had received from the father through heredity was strengthened by hearing similar thoughts expressed. Maybe the father did not always say explicitly that the will was not a part of the soul, but this was the perspective implied. People grow into life through very complicated situations.

It lies in human nature to develop the three capacities of the soul, namely, thinking, feeling, and willing. But some feeling also enters into our thoughts. We never actually have pure thinking unless we strictly train ourselves to do it, or when we devote ourselves to the ideals of morality or religion. In normal life, however, in thinking about the external world or when thinking together with other people, we are always using thoughts that contain some degree of feeling. We can therefore say that our thoughts are related to our feelings. Our feelings are reflected in our thoughts because they are stimulated by those thoughts, by the kind of thinking we do. On the other hand, our will also interacts with our feeling. There is quite a difference between will and *will*. The will can be what I would call a more neutral impulse or it can contain the warmth of feeling. Some people have a tendency to strengthen feeling at the cost of willing so that feeling is overemphasized and the will comes up short. With such people during childhood, what should actually enter the will is held in feeling. Thus they are satisfied with the picture of an action and never actually go on to act. That is the sort of person I am talking about here. We need to see how the feelings of such children react to one thing or another. Then we should not be satisfied only with what we see, but we should try to direct them toward the things that bring them into movement.

With children who exhibit this kind of moral weakness, an ensouled gymnastics of the sort I have described as eurythmy has a healthy effect. This is assuming that eurythmy, where human beings draw not only with their hands but with their entire bodies in space, is taught to them by the age of nine.

It is important to look at the interactions between human capacities. If you have learned to observe life, you will learn to guide the influences that act upon the child in such a way that the forces of the soul and those of the entire human being are brought into appropriate interaction. Spiritual-scientific training, when properly carried out, guides a person toward observing life. In general, people forget the most important facts of life, or they do not find the proper rhythm between humor and seriousness. You have not found the proper rhythm if you simply laugh at a young person who allows the streetcar to pass by. Such a person is certainly an object of humor, but you need to be able to move from humor into seriousness. We cannot remain merely with one or the other. This view of life is particularly necessary for teachers, and this is what is developed in us through a proper spiritual-scientific training.

8

TEACHING ZOOLOGY AND BOTANY TO CHILDREN NINE THROUGH TWELVE

Basel, May 3, 1920

I have attempted to indicate from various perspectives how we can base curriculum and teaching goals upon human development. I have particularly tried to show that we can characterize the period that begins around the age of six or seven with the change of teeth, and continues until puberty, about age fourteen or fifteen, as one stage of life. I also attempted to show that there is a shorter stage within the earlier stage that lasts until approximately the age of nine. There is another important change around the age of twelve. We should view these three times, that is, about the age of nine, then about twelve, and then again around fourteen or fifteen, which is approximately when the students leave school, as important when we create the whole curriculum and teaching goals. You can easily see the importance of comprehending the development of the human being when you realize that what is important in education is that we completely develop those forces that lie buried in human nature. If we look at things in the proper way, we have to admit that we need to use all our teaching material and education to reveal those forces. It is not nearly so important to use the forces within children to teach them one detail or another. What is important is that we use the material the children are to learn in such a way that the effects of what they learn develop the natural forces within them. That is something we fail to do if we do not take into account how different the child's physical and soul nature is before the age of nine, and then again before the age of twelve, and so forth. We must be aware that the power to differentiate through reason, which enables human beings to reason independently, in essence occurs only at puberty and that we should slowly prepare for it beginning at the age of twelve. We can therefore say that until the age of nine children want to develop under authority, but their desire to imitate is still present as well. At nine, the desire to imitate disappears, but the desire for authority remains. At about the age of twelve, while still under the guidance of authority, another important desire, namely, to reason independently, begins to develop. If we use independent reasoning too much before the age of twelve, we will actually ruin the child's soul and bodily forces. In a certain sense, we deaden human experiencing with reason.

To anyone not completely devoid of feeling, it is not insignificant that we say yes or no to something through making a judgment. Depending upon whether we need to say yes or no, we have feelings of liking or disliking, joy or sorrow. As much as modern people tend to have egotistical feelings of liking or disliking those things that they judge, they have hardly any feelings, whether of joy or sorrow, about the world and life as a whole. That is precisely why people miss so much today. Aside from that, their incapacity to experience the world influences social desires as a whole. That is why our teaching should not only emphasize the development of proper concepts, but it should also develop a proper feeling for the world, a proper feeling for a person's place in the world.

Today people have one overriding judgment in regard to social issues. They say to themselves that we must make the world into an earthly paradise for all human beings. In the end, what do the extremists, the radical socialists of Eastern Europe, want other than to develop a kind of earthly paradise out of some theories, even though the paradise that results is a hell? But that is something else again. Where does this come from? We need only replace that judgment with another, and we will immediately see the problem in wanting to create an earthly paradise through enforced socialization.

I don't really want to discuss Nietzsche here, but I do want to mention the following in order to explain something else.[1] Nietzsche's first work was entitled *The Birth of Tragedy from the Spirit of Music.* Among the many thoughtful ideas contained in that work (even though you could argue against them), Nietzsche suggests that the Greek people were not the eternally happy, laughing folk many people say they were, but instead the life of the Greeks was rooted in tragedy, in a kind of sadness. The Greeks felt that our life here upon earth between birth and death could not always be one of great happiness, and that the task of human beings lay beyond this earthly life. Nietzsche thought the Greeks had a particularly strong feeling of this and needed a strong solace for the disharmonies of earthly life, which they found in art. Nietzsche's view of the rise of art was that art, particularly Greek art, was a solace for earthly disharmonies. Nietzsche sees music in particular as something that leads people beyond earthly disharmonies. There is certainly a contrast between what we experience in our dry, calculating thinking and what we experience through music, but these contrasts relate to one another in a quite peculiar way. Consider that we can compute tones and the relationships of tones in terms of numbers; the result is musical physics, or acoustics. However, those who give themselves over to the musical world of tones leave what we can compute completely behind. They leave the intellectual aspects of music aside. What is intellectual sleeps in music. Nietzsche had a particular feeling for what he called the tragedy of music. The tragedy of music is that people can feel in music what they should otherwise feel throughout the world. Now Nietzsche was a man who could feel throughout his body what the materialism of the nineteenth century had brought to humanity. He was the kind of a teacher who dreamed of educational institutions based upon ideas such as I just described, which could have been the source of a genuine solace for life. Someone like Nietzsche revealed through his own life what was needed by the nineteenth century. The problem is, he collapsed under the experiences of those disharmonies. If we read between the lines, we will see that fate in a way determined that this man could deeply experience things that others of his century passed through in a more or less sleepy state of soul. We can also see that he always points to those things that were missing in his own education, specifically the education he had to go through in school. In Nietzsche you have the feeling that the forces within him remained deeply buried, that they were never developed. Surely such an insightful person as he felt the tragedy of that much more strongly than others. You could easily say that here and there he had some awareness of the three main stages of childhood, particularly the stage between the ages of six or seven and fourteen or fifteen, but he never brought that understanding into the service of education. That is something that must happen now.

At the age of nine, the child experiences a truly complete transformation of her being that indicates an important transformation of her soul life as well as her physical experience. At that time, the human being begins to feel separated from her surroundings and learns to differentiate between the world and herself. If we can observe accurately, we have to admit that until that transformation, the world and the I are more or less conjoined in human consciousness. Beginning at the age of nine (of course I mean this only approximately), human beings can differentiate between themselves and the world. We must take that into consideration in what and how we teach children starting at the age of nine. Until then, it is best not to confuse them with descriptions and characterizations of things that are separate from the human being, or that we should consider separate from the human being. When we tell a child a story or a fairy tale, we describe the animals and perhaps the plants in the way we would speak about people. In a certain sense, we personify plants and animals. We can justifiably personify them because the child cannot yet differentiate between herself and the world. That is why we should show the child the world in a way similar to the way he or she experiences it. You should be clear that what I am suggesting does not diminish childhood before the age of nine, but enriches it.

My last statement may seem quite paradoxical to you. But much of what people say about the child's life is said in such a way that the child's life does not actually become richer but rather poorer. Think for a moment of what modern people often say when a child injures himself on the corner of a table and hits the table in rage. Today people say that children's souls have something called animism. In a certain sense, the child makes the table alive by pushing his or her soul into the table. This is an impossible theory. Why? Because children do not directly perceive themselves as something living, something that can put itself into the table and personify it. Rather, children do not think of themselves as any more alive than the table. Children look at the table and experience no more of themselves than they do of the table. It is not that the child personifies the table but, if I can express it this way, the child "tables" his or her own personality. Children do not make their personality anything more than the table. When you tell a child a fairy tale or story, you speak only of what the child can comprehend of the external world. That is what must occur until the age of nine. After that, you can count upon children's ability to differentiate themselves from the world. At that time, we can begin to speak about plants and animals from the perspective of nature.

I have put a lot of effort into studying the effects upon children of teaching about nature too early. Teaching about nature too early really does make children dry; so dry, in fact, that a well-trained observer can see in the changes of someone's skin that that person was taught about the concepts of nature at too early an age.

When they are nine we may begin to teach children the concepts of nature, but only through living thoughts. Wherever possible, we should avoid teaching them about minerals, about dead things. What is living, what lives outside the human being, exists in two areas, that of animals and that of plants. However, if we attempt to present the popular descriptions of animals, their scientific characteristics and the scientific descriptions of plants, we will not really be able to teach children about them. You can see in nearly every natural history book that the content is nothing more than a somewhat simplified academic natural science—that is horrible. Of course, people have also attempted to create an illustrative teaching of nature. There are numerous books about that method too, but they suffer from the opposite mistake. They contain a great deal of triviality. In that case, the teacher attempts to discuss nothing with the children, nothing more than what they already know. As people say, the teacher tries to create a picture of nature solely out of the nature of the children themselves. We easily fall into triviality that way. We can only throw our hands up in frustration about so many of those method books because they are so terribly trivial. We may feel that if schools use such things, only triviality will be implanted in children. This triviality will come to expression later as many other things I have already mentioned, as a kind of aridness in later life, or at any rate it will make it impossible for people to look back upon their childhood with joy.

That is, however, precisely what human beings need. Throughout life, we need to be able to look back upon our childhood as something like a paradise. It is not just that we had only happy experiences then; it is really not so important that as children we had only happy experiences. Many people may have gone hungry during their childhood or have been beaten by their teachers out of a lack of understanding or were treated unkindly. Of course, nothing other than an intent to fight against all such things in the best possible way should ever form the basis of education. Nevertheless such things can occur, and even so thinking back upon childhood can still be a source of enlivening when, in one way or another, we gained a relationship to the world during childhood. As children, we need to develop that relationship by being taught about nature in the proper way. It is of no help whatsoever when we describe the various classes of animals or types of plants and so forth to children and then, in order not to be too dry, we go on a walk with the children to show them the plants outdoors. That is not at all useful. Of course, through certain instinctive tendencies, one teacher will be able to accomplish more and another less. A teacher can, through his or her own love of nature, enliven a great deal for children. However, what spiritual science can give to people's feeling is something really quite different, something that gives people a feeling for the connections living between the human being and the remainder of the world.

In the first third of the nineteenth century, many people still felt that the entire animal world was an extended human being. In this model, we have different groups of animals. One group is one-sidedly developed in one direction, another in another direction. We can create an overview of the various groups and kinds of animals for ourselves. The human being contains all those forces, all the inner forms that are distributed among the animals. That was, for example, the view of nature that someone like Oken took.[2] At that time people looked for the lower animals in nature. Today's materialistic natural science says that these lower animals existed in very early times and that they slowly developed and become more complete. The result was today's human being, a completely developed physical being. We do not need to go into all the details today, since our concern is not with conventional science, but with education. However, can't we see that the human head, which is a bony structure outside with the softer parts inside, looks similar to that of certain lower animals? Look at a snail or a mussel and see how similar they are to the human head. If you look at our more or less developed birds, you would have to admit that they have adjusted to the air, they have adjusted their entire life to something that corresponds to the inner form of the lungs and such things in human beings. If you remove from your thoughts all those aspects of the human being contained in the limbs and imagine the entire human inner organization as adjusted to living in air, the result will be the form and function of a bird. You could also compare the organic form of a lion or a cat with that of a bovine.

Everywhere you will see that in one group of animals, one part of its form is more developed and in another group, a different part. Each group of animals is particularly well-developed in one direction or another. We can say a snail is almost entirely head. It has nothing other than the head aspect, only it is a simple and primitive head. The human head is more complicated. Of a bird we can say that it is, in a certain sense, entirely a lung developed in a particular way because all other aspects are rudimentary. Of a lion we can say that it is, in a certain sense, primarily the blood circulation and the heart. We could say cattle are entirely stomachs. Thus in external nature we can characterize the various groups of animals by looking toward individual human organs. What I have just said can be said very simply, in a primitive way. If we look at the world of animals and look at the great diversity there, then compare that with the human organism and see how in the human being everything is well-rounded—how no part of the human being is one-sidedly developed, but each part complements the other—then we can see that in animals the various organs are adapted to the external world, whereas in human beings the organs do not adapt to the external world, but rather one organ complements another.

The human being is a closed totality.

Now imagine that we used everything available to us, the nature exhibits in the school, each walk with the children, everything the children have experienced, to show in a living way how the human being is, in a certain sense, a summary of the animal world. Imagine showing children that everything in the human being is formed harmoniously, is well-rounded, and that the animals represent one-sided developments and, for that reason, are not fully blessed. We can also show that the human being represents an adaptation of one system of organs to the other and for that reason has a possibility of complete being. If we are completely convinced of this relationship of the human being to the world of animals, if it fully permeates us spiritually, we can describe that relationship in a lively way so that the description is quite objective, but at the same time children can feel their relationship to the world.

Think how valuable it is for modern people to be able to say, in our materialistic times, that they are the crown of earthly creation. People do not really understand it—they look at themselves, and they look at individual animals. However, they do not look at each individual animal and try to understand how one system of organs is one-sidedly developed in one animal and another in another animal. They also do not consider how that all comes together in the human being. If we do that, our knowledge will directly become a feeling, a perception of our position relative to the world. We will then stop experiencing ourselves only egotistically, and our feelings will go out into the universe.

You need only attempt to teach in that sense once, and you will see what value such teaching has for the feelings of the child. Such knowledge is transformed completely into feeling, and people slowly become more modest under the influence of such knowledge. In that way, the material to be taught becomes a genuine means of education. What is the use of saying we should not teach in a dry way, we should not teach the children only facts, if we have no possibility of transforming the material to be taught so that it becomes a direct means of education? Sometimes when people stress that teaching children too many facts hinders their proper development, we want to ask, "Why don't you throw out all the material you teach if it is of no use?" We cannot do that, of course. We must make the material we teach into educational material. Teaching about nature, particularly in connection with the animal world, can become educational material when we shape it in the way I described, and when we do not teach it to children before the age of nine.

With the plant world, we cannot take the individual plants or kinds of plants, present them one-sidedly, summarize everything we find there, and expect to see it again in the human being. The approach that is so fruitful with animals and gives us such a good basis for an artistic and living presentation of the nature of animals fails with plants. We cannot consider them in the same way; it does not work. With plants, we need to use a very different approach. We need to consider the entire nature of plants in relationship to the earth as something that enlivens the entire earth.

Materialism has brought us to the point where we consider the earth only as a ball made of stones and minerals in which plants are simply placed. We cannot use the same principle with, for instance, the human head and hair. We need to consider the growth of hair as something connected with the human head. In the same way, we must consider plants as belonging to the organism of the earth. We create an abstract picture if we only think of the earth as a stone, which can at most call gravity its own.

We speak of the real earth when we think of the earth as an organism with plants that belong to it just as the hair on our heads belongs to us. When we consider it that way, our picture of the earth grows together with our picture of plants, and we get the proper feeling for how to think of the earth in connection with the plant world. We can do that when we look at the earth in the course of the year. If we are to really teach children about plants, we should not compare one class or group of plants with another. Instead we need to use all the fresh plants we have, the nature exhibits in the school, walks, everything the children remember, and everything we can bring into the classroom as fresh plants. Then we can show the children how spring magically draws the plants out of the earth. We can show them how plants are magically drawn out, then go on to May, when the earth becomes somewhat different. We then continue on into summer, and the earth looks different again.

We try to consider flowers and plants in the same way children understand the development of the earth throughout the course of the year. We tell the children how, in the fall, the plant seeds return to the earth and the cycle begins anew. We consider the earth an organism and follow the sprouting and dying back of the plants. We call everything by its proper name (which of course is only convention) only after we have taught the child by saying, "Look, here is a plant (under a tree or perhaps somewhere else). We have this little plant because this kind of plant grows so well in May. It has five little petals. Remember, these plants with five little yellow petals are part of the life of the whole earth in May. It is a buttercup." You can go on in that way and show them how the world of plants is connected with the yearly cycle of the earth. You can then go on further to more hidden things, how, for example, some plants bloom at Christmastime, and some plants can live through winter and others much longer. You go from the life of one plant that decorates the earth for one year and leaves, to others, such as the growth of a tree and so forth. You would never consider simply comparing one plant with another; you always relate the earth to its plant growth and how the growth of plants arises out of the living earth.

You now have two wonderful points in the life of nature. Everywhere in the animal realm you find things that point to the human being. People can feel how they are a synthesis of all the one-sided aspects of the animal realm. We do not take up any species of animals without indicating which aspect of the human being that animal species has developed one-sidedly. The animal kingdom becomes, therefore, a picture of the human being spread out before us—the human being unfolded like a fan. As I said, modern people laugh about such things, but during the first third of the nineteenth century that sometimes took on grotesque forms. People such as Oken have said such grotesque things as "the tongue is a squid," and I certainly do not want to defend them. Oken had the right principle in mind. He looked at the human tongue and then sought something among the animals which he then compared with that human organ. He found the greatest similarity to the human tongue in the squid; thus the tongue is a squid. He went on to say that the stomach is a cow. All that is, as I said, an extreme presentation. We certainly do not need to go that far. At that time, people were really unable to find the proper things. Today, however, we can certainly present the entire animal world as a spread-out human being and the human being as a synthesis of the entire animal world. We thus connect everything the children observe in the animals with the human being. We therefore have a possibility of placing all the aspects of a human being in front of the child's eyes by directing the child's eyes outward.

In the plant world we have just the opposite. There we completely forget the human being and consider the world of plants as entirely growing out of the earth itself, out of the planet upon which we wander. In the one case we bring the animal world into a close relationship to the human being, and in the other case we bring the plant world into the same close relationship to something that exists outside the human being. In other words, on the one hand we bring forth a feeling understanding of the world of animals and the human being by observing the animal world itself. On the other hand, we teach children to objectively consider the earth as an organism upon which we run about and from which we live, and where we see in the growth of plants, in the life cycle of plants, particularly in how plants live from year to year, something that is separate from ourselves. Through these two ways of looking at things, we can bring a tremendous amount of balance between the intellect and feeling into the human soul. We will leave mere intellectualism, which is so boring and arid, behind.

Once people comprehend annual plants, green plants that grow out of the earth with their roots in the earth, leaves, and stems above it, and the green leaves that then go on to form the flower and seed; once people perceive a living connection with the earth and have enlivened that through their experiences of the yearly cycle; once they have experienced how the blossom comes forth when sunlight has connected itself in love with what pours forth out of the earth; once that is felt throughout people's entire being as a felt knowledge; once people have felt the growth from the root through the leaf to the flower and finally to the seed from spring until fall; once people have felt all that, then they will realize something else. Here is the earth, here is a plant, an annual. This plant that lives only one year is rooted in the earth. Now let us look at a tree. Here it is wood. Here are the branches. What appears on the tree during the course of one year appears similar to an annual plant and sits on the tree in a way similar to an annual plant sitting in the earth. In a certain sense the earth and the part of the tree that is wood are the same. Through that we can create a picture that will have an enormously strong effect upon us. In the same way a tree grows into wood, the earth is built upon what lies under the surface. Where no trees, but only annual plants grow, the forces that are otherwise in the trunk of the tree is in the earth itself. We can achieve a living feeling about how to seek the flowing of the sap in the tree trunk under the surface of the earth. Just as the sap that flows within a tree brings forth the blossoming of the year, the sap flowing beneath us, which we can see is identical to the sap flowing in the tree, brings forth annual plants. What I want to say is that we can intimately connect what we see in trees with our view of the earth. We therefore gain an understanding of what is living.

Through such a living characterization of the earth, plants, animals, and human beings, you can directly enliven something in the children that they would otherwise feel as only dead, specifically, in the period from about the age of nine until twelve. During the time when children are particularly interested in gradually differentiating themselves from the world and unconsciously want to learn about the relationship between the human being and the world of animals, on the one hand and, on the other hand, the earth and earthly life separate from the human being, something will grow within children that gives them the proper relationship to the historical life of humanity on Earth. In this way the appropriate feelings develop that allow children to learn about history properly. Before the age of ten or eleven, we have told children about history only in the form of stories or biographies. At about the age of ten or eleven, we include history within the teaching of natural history, so that everywhere a feeling develops in the child through the teaching of natural history that is, in a certain sense, also held in all the concepts and ideas and feelings that can enliven the teaching of history. Only at the age of twelve can we begin to go on to actual reasoning. We will speak more of that tomorrow.

For centuries, no one has been educated in a way appropriate to human nature, which makes it quite impossible to accurately look at human life and compare it with the life of the earth.

People express themselves through their view of the world. Quite understandably, people say, for example, that spring is the morning of the year, summer the day, fall the evening, and winter the night. But in reality it is quite different. When we are sleeping, everything that differentiates us from plants slips out of our human form. When we are sleeping, we are not at all justified in looking as we do. Actually, we look the way we do only because we are shaped in accord with our soul and spirit. While sleeping, we are actually more at the level of plants. At that time, as individual human beings, we are no different from the earth with its plant growth. But to which season does our sleep correspond? When we are sleeping, that corresponds to summer, that is, to that period of the year in which the plants are here. To which season does our wakefulness correspond? That is like winter, when plant life ceases and, in a sense, recedes deep within the earth. In the same way, plant life recedes into the human being and is replaced by something else during the period of awakening until falling asleep again. If we do not follow some vague analogy but follow reality, we would have to say that we need to compare human sleep with summer, and the period of human wakefulness with the earth's winter. Thus the reality of the situation is actually just the opposite of some vague analogy.

At this point I need to say something rather unusual. I have attempted to determine if anyone working in conventional science has even the slightest idea of what I have spoken of as a result of spiritual-scientific research, namely, that the earth is actually awake in winter and asleep in summer. The only small hint I have found which, if properly developed, would lead to what I have just described, I found in the Basel school program developed in the 1840s or '50s. In that school program there is a discussion about human sleep that is treated in a manner contradictory to normal considerations. I think it is important to make mention of that school program in Basel. At the moment, I have forgotten the name of the person who created it, but I hope I will remember it by tomorrow.[3]

9

DIALECT AND
STANDARD LANGUAGE

Basel, May 4, 1920

The question I was posed after yesterday's lecture is directly connected with what I explained in the previous days. It can also be
considered today in connection with what we have been talking
about. Yesterday I attempted to sketch out a description of how
the content of the teaching material may actually not be the most
important thing. I said we cannot make directly out of the material we obtain through science or from something else a popular-
ized form adjusted for children, as often is done with biology or
zoology, so that a simplified content is taught the children. I
drew your attention to how the task of teaching can only become
a task of education when we are in a position of being able to
transform the material we have to present, regardless of what
form it has, into an educational experience. Yesterday, I gave
some indication of how to do that for biology and zoology. In
education, we need to work more and more toward presenting
everything, particularly with children from the ages of six or
seven until puberty, in such a way that the forces that are trying

to develop in a child can actually be brought to development.

If we are going to be able to do that, we must also be capable of properly using everything the child brings into school. I also mentioned that a large number of children bring into school something that we can well use in teaching, namely, their dialect. The children speak in dialect, and they speak in such a way that the dialects have developed in them under the influence of the instinct for imitation. If we have a talent for observing such things, we can recognize that those children who speak in dialect have a much more intimate relationship to language than those children who do not speak in dialect. The question I was asked yesterday was connected with how we can use the capacity of the children to speak in dialect in school, in teaching them to speak the so-called standard language.

We certainly cannot overlook the fact that the intimate relationship that children who speak in dialect have to their languages exists because the dialect as such, in its words and sentences, has been formed out of a much more intense feeling and willing than standard language, which is based more upon thinking or upon a thinking derived primarily from feeling. In any event, emotion is much less present in standard language when a child learns standard language originally than it is in dialect. The same is also true in regard to the will impulse.

Now this points us at the very beginning to something extremely important for teaching and education, namely, that human beings, more than we normally assume, develop themselves from two sources that are really related to one another like the North and South Poles. If we work in one direction or the other in education or in forming our teaching, if we work to primarily base everything upon visualization so that the child reasons visually and thus slowly develops through a comprehension of the pictures presented, we are going to one extreme. If, on the other hand, we educate the child through using the child's capacity of memory or count upon the child's acceptance due to obedience to our authority, we are going to the other extreme.

It is particularly clear in language that these two extremes always belong together in human nature. Language itself has a clearly perceptible musical element, an element which is closely connected with that innermost aspect of the human being. Language also has at the same time a sculptural or drawing element. As very small children, we attempt to imitate, though unconsciously, in our language what we perceive through the senses. It is especially clear in language how the musical and sculptural elements work in two diverging directions. If we educate children more according to the musical element, which in school is expressed primarily through a feeling for authority, we will destroy what exists in the child as a sculptural desire. The musical element of language develops under the influence of authority such that the child continuously has an instinct or a desire to speak, even in the details of the tones, in the same way that a person who is felt to be an authority speaks. A conformity to the authority's musical element is, whether we want to believe that it is right or wrong, simply there because of the nature of the child. If you have a talent for observing such things, you will quickly notice how the musical element of the child's language conforms to that of the person educating the child.

A one-sided development of the musical element in language destroys language's sculptural element. When people only follow the musical element, they are forced more and more to make language an inner experience, to follow their feelings in a certain way by recreating the tone, the intonation, and particularly the nuances of the vowels to conform to those of the people whom they perceive as authorities. This is most certainly true when a child enters elementary school. It is less true for a child in that age between birth and elementary school, when he or she first learns language. During that time, the child is an imitator and develops language out of the entirety of human nature and with a continuous adjustment of the remainder of the human organism to the environment. At that point much enters into speaking which guides language into a more sculptural form. However, because human beings are imitators and imitate right into the innermost activities of their nature, the sculptural element also forms during this time in an inner way. Here we can see one major difference in language development. From birth until the change of teeth, children develop their language sculpturally. If a child has the good fortune to be able to adjust to a dialect during that period of life, one that is more inwardly connected to the human being than standard language, then the child is, in regard to willing and authority aspects of language development, more intimately connected to language than it is with standard language.

Upon entering elementary school, the musical element then replaces the sculptural element, as I mentioned before, and the inner feelings have an effect. However, since the musical element as such counteracts the sculptural element, it is necessary for us to appropriately use in teaching elementary school what the children bring with them, what they have developed in language through their own forces until the age of six or seven.

In language, broadly speaking, the unconscious has had a great effect on the child. We should also learn from the fact that primitive peoples have often developed a much richer grammar than those present in the languages of more civilized peoples. This is seldom taken into account outside of spiritual science, but it is something we should consider as a result of a genuine observation of human beings, namely, that the human being develops a logic from within so that language is actually logically formed. Thus we do not need to teach grammar in a way other than by bringing what already exists as a completely developed language structure into consciousness. When teaching and learning grammar, we need only to follow the general tendency of awakening the child and of bringing that into consciousness. We need only to develop those forces that can be developed until the age of nine, in the sense that I described before. We need to use the instruction in language in order to continue to awaken the child. We can best do that if we use every opportunity that occurs to work from dialect. If we have a child who before the age of seven has already learned a more educated informal language, the so-called standard language, it will be extremely difficult to reach the aspect of the child's unconscious that has a natural relationship to the logical formation of language, since that has already withered. Thus if we have children who speak dialect and others who do not in the same class, we should always connect our instruction in grammar with what those children who do speak in dialect already provide us.

We first want to try to find the structure of a sentence and then a word from the perspective of dialect. We can do that if we proceed by having a child say a sentence, for example, one that is as simple as possible. The main thing the sentence will always contain is something that is an inner enlivening of an activity. The more often we begin with an inner enlivening of an activity, the more we will be able to achieve an awakening of consciousness in the child while teaching language.

There is a very extensive and clever literature about so-called subjectless sentences, for instance, "It is raining," "It is lightning," "It is thundering,"[1] and so forth. The most important point about this is hardly mentioned in all of that research, however. What is most important is that these sentences correspond to the child's actual understanding. The sentences correspond to that feeling in children that exists in people who are not educated, and where the soul feels itself to be at one with the external world. A differentiation between the I and the external world has not yet been developed. If I say, for example, "It is raining," this is based upon an unconscious feeling that what is occurring as an activity outside of myself continues in that space within my skin, and that my I does not confront the external world. When saying something like "It is raining" or "It is lightning," we do not feel ourselves separate from the world. In a certain sense, these subjectless sentences are the original sentences of human nature. They are simply the first step of language development which arrests an activity. Originally, we perceived all of the world as an activity, something we do not consider enough. In a certain sense, in our youngest childhood, we see everything substantial as a substantiated verb[2] and accept it simply as it is. Later, what we become aware of, what is active, is what is active and then occupies our own activity. Now you might say that contradicts the fact that children first say "Papa" or something similar. That is not at all a contradiction, since in speaking the series of sounds, the child brings into life that activity which the corresponding person presents to the child.

Learning to speak is at first the enlivening of an activity whose substantiation occurs only afterwards. This is something that, when we look at dialect, we can certainly take into account. You can attempt to feel that by having a child say something and then trying to feel that within yourself. The words in dialect are such that they are extremely close to what lives in the gesture that accompanies the word in dialect. To a much greater extent dialect words require the person to participate, to live into the word. By feeling the word in dialect you can determine what is an abstraction, and what the subject and the predicate are. The predicate is derived from the activity, whereas the subject is actually more of an intellectual abstraction of the activity. When we have children speak sentences in dialect and we then consider the pictures they provide us with, and we can see those as representing what human beings actually feel when we go on to develop the rules of grammar, we are using instruction in grammar and sentence structure to help the child to awaken.

We can now allow these two things to interact in a wonderful way. We can translate what has been presented in dialect into standard language and then show, through a direct feeling and with a lively interaction with the children, how a certain "aroma" of language is given to the so-called educated informal language, to standard language. From there we can go on to the inner characteristics of standard language. This creates a certain development of thinking. In standard language we need to give much more attention to the development of the thoughts that are its basis than we do with dialect.

Dialect shows us directly that human beings did not develop speech from thinking. Instead they learned to think from language, so it was language that first developed out of the human unconscious. As human beings thought about language, thoughts first arose from language. If we can properly feel this, then we can connect a living feeling with what I would call the genius of language. In many regards language is much more clever than individual human beings. In earliest childhood we can in fact find our way through the complicated organism of language. Only later do we discover those remarkable connections that only a sharp logic can reveal and which exist in language out of our unconscious nature. The spirit has an effect upon language. However, we will not understand that spiritual aspect if we only consider how the spirit, in an abstract form, has an effect upon human beings, in the way that people in our materialistic age like to do.

Perhaps I can again touch something which is often said to be the basis of psychoanalysis but which needs to be understood in a quite different sense than psychoanalysts often do. Let us take something that often occurs in life. A lady is invited to a home where guests have been invited, but the lady of the house is absent that evening because of illness. This lady now attends the party. On the same evening, the lady of the house needs to leave. The party breaks up because the man of the house needs to take his wife to the train. The group of people now go along the street, and a coach comes around the corner. At first the carriage is going very quickly and the group of people move to the left and right of the street to make way. However, the one lady who had been invited that evening runs in front of the horses. She runs and runs, and in spite of all the coachman's shouting, he is unable to get her to move to one side. She keeps on running in front of the coach, and as they come to a bridge, she recognizes the situation and jumps into the water. She needs to be rescued. The group of people who were at the party don't know what to do with her except bring her back to the house where they had been invited that evening.

The psychoanalyst would say that this lady was mentally isolated, that she had been startled as a child by a horse that had chased her or something similar, and that this experience was carried in the depths of her mind. Now, on this evening, this experience surfaces again. This is a very clever theory. But those who have learned to observe reality and who have learned to place themselves into reality through spiritual science will not see this as valid.

The truth is quite different. The lady is infatuated with the man of the house, and is quite happy to have been invited to the party on just that day when the lady of the house has to leave. Of course, this lady would not admit this, since she is a very correct person. She could be, in fact, a very correct lady in her consciousness, but what she does not admit has an effect in her subconscious. For that reason, she arranges everything so that all of the guests invited that evening will bring her back to the house when the lady of the house has left. That is what she wanted from the very beginning, but was not at all conscious of it.

Here you can see how thinking, cleverness, and intelligence work without having an effect through the human consciousness. Those who can observe life know that there are people who can arrange things from a distance to achieve what they want without having any conscious idea that they are doing so. Nevertheless everything is all very systematically arranged toward a particular goal. We need to be aware that reason is not only something that we develop, it is also something that acts within us in our nature, something which is active within us long before we become aware of it.

What we want to teach children about language has an effect upon them long before they become aware of it. We should therefore avoid trying to teach them the rules for speaking or writing, but instead enable them to awaken and become aware of what subconsciously acts within. Whether we have one intention or another in our instruction is tremendously important. We should always pay attention to the intention behind teaching.

Speaking a dialect has an intimate connection with the subconscious, so we can develop real grammar and rules for sentence structure from the dialect language by basing our work upon the reason that lives within human nature. If, however, we need to work with children who already speak the standard language, we should whenever possible not work in such a way to develop a kind of grammar through the intellect, and not direct our work by teaching about the dative and accusative and how we write, how periods and commas are placed at particular locations and so forth. We instead need to work in a different way. When we need to teach children who do not speak in dialect, then we must create our instruction and grammar in an artistic way and appeal to a feeling for style.

Children bring an instinct for language with them into elementary school, and we need to develop this feeling wherever possible until the child reaches the age of nine. We can only do this by developing a feeling for style in an artistic way. That is something we can achieve—although in this age where authority is being undermined everywhere this may be laughed at—by using the natural desires of children to follow authority, and thus to form those sentences that we present to the children in the most artistic way. We need to artistically form the sentences so that we draw from the child a feeling for their artistic form. That is something we can do when we make the children aware of the difference between an assertion or a question, or perhaps a statement of feeling, and have the child speak it in such a way that a statement with feeling is spoken with the intonation of an assertion. We can then make the children aware of how an assertion is spoken in a neutral, objective way; whereas a statement of feeling is spoken with certain nuances of feeling. We can work with this artistic element of language, then out of that element develop grammar and syntax.

If we use dialect in order to develop the natural human instinct for language while using standard language in order to awaken an inner feeling for style, we can achieve what is necessary in teaching language. I will speak about this in more detail later, however; for now I simply want to indicate the principles.

This principle shows that we must keep the developing child in mind at all times. We need to ask what is developing at this particular age. If we do not have the feeling that with the change of teeth children are, in a certain sense, born a second time, then we will not have the proper enthusiasm for our teaching. Of course, the physical birth is much more obvious than what occurs at around the age of seven. At birth the physical body of a human being is separated from that body of the mother. With the change of teeth, the human etheric body becomes separate from the physical body, with which the etheric body was intimately connected. The etheric body worked within the physical body to develop the second set of teeth, but now it becomes free. What children bring to school in terms of capacities are actually the free and newborn capacities of the etheric body. This is the first spiritual aspect that a child presents.

When we have a child younger than seven before us, we have it before us only as a physical body. All the child's spiritual and soul aspects are active within that physical body, and we can reach the child only through the fact that the child itself has a desire to imitate. At the age of seven, the etheric body, that is, all those aspects of human nature which have an etheric component in their substance, now become free and have a life for themselves.

I have already mentioned that the human being is more than 75 percent composed of water. Why do people in physiology and anatomy always speak as though the human being consisted of a solid body? What occurs within a human being works in just the same way in fluids. It also occurs in the gaseous state. What develops in a child in regard to spiritual and soul capacities after the change of teeth occurs neither in a solid nor in liquid nor in gaseous state. It occurs instead in what we carry within our body as the etheric, what we carry within us in the form of heat, light, chemical, and life ethers.

It is nonsense to say that thoughts are only processes within the nervous system, imagining the nerves as semisolid or at least soft forms. No, thoughts occur through direct development, by not being transformed into memories. Thoughts occur in such a way that they do not even have contact with the physical body after the age of seven.

When people think, they think only in their etheric element, which fills their physical bodies. You might, however, object by saying that thoughts become memories and thus remain within the human being. The etheric element is very volatile; all thoughts would dissolve if they were to live only in it. Memory is a much more complicated process than people normally think. Often they have the idea—which is based upon materialism—that when people think, the thoughts they have seek out a place to live somewhere in the human soul, and that we bring them forth again when we recall them. But that is not how it is. If you can observe the process of thinking, you will find that when you see something through your senses in the outer world, you connect thoughts with it. But when you recall something and form a thought, then what you have is something that otherwise comes from the external world but now arises within your own inner world. Just as you comprehend thoughts connected with the external world, you also comprehend thoughts which arise within you. Memory does not occur because thoughts sink down into the soul, but because what physically acts upon the eye and the ear is continued within the physical body. Thinking is a parallel process. This process leaves behind a rhythmical element which can be brought forth inwardly at a later time, so it can be perceived in the same way that external perceptions are.

Probably all of you have observed how young children help themselves so that they can better bring up their memories. They do everything possible in order to strengthen thinking through the senses if they are to remember something. Recall how many children study, how they seek to include within their physical body what they are to learn as a thought, how a physical inclusion occurs in parallel with thinking. When children simply think, they often do not remember. They only remember when they again hear what they have memorized, or are in some other way physically reminded of what they have memorized.

In order for us to remember, there must be some process that works in parallel to thinking. For thinking, it is totally unimportant whether it is developed through the external world or through a memory that arises within. Thinking is something that is fleeting. Thoughts are not retained. It is something else which is retained that then each time gives rise to a new thought. There is no difference between whether I remember something and then create a thought and when I see something in the external world that gives rise to a thought. In the one case, there is a process connected with the external world and in the other case there is a process connected with an inner experience. In any event, when I recall something, my organs go into a rhythmic movement and repeat what they carried out under the impression of the experience. When I have the experience for the first time, that is, while

I observe it in the external world, my thoughts develop only in connection with the external world. When I remember something, my thoughts are ignited from within by my organs, which begin to vibrate in the same way as when I first had the experience.

Such things cannot be directly proven in the same way that external processes can be proven. These things must be slowly comprehended so that they become a certainty through a genuine observation of life. When we look at this particular kind of thinking that actually occurs within the volatile element of the etheric and when we determine how the physical organs must be capable of vibrating in the same sense as the etheric vibrates, we will properly comprehend the enormous transformation that human life undergoes through the change of teeth. Up to this point the entire etheric body is active. The heat, chemical, light, and life ethers are active in the organs, forming them in such a way that they can vibrate in material along with the etheric. The etheric body is the architect and sculptor of the physical body. Once the physical body is developed to this degree, under the influence of the etheric body—which actually thinks—the intellect is emancipated from the physical body so that the physical body can vibrate like a violin string when another string is struck. Thus when the physical body has developed to the point that the change of teeth has begun, we can then count upon developing the etheric body as such. We form the physical body at the same time as we form the etheric body. But we need to have a feeling for this birth of the etheric body at the time of the change of teeth.

Going on, we again need to sense that something still higher in human nature is born at puberty, something that previously had been working on a further formation of the human organism. Whether we call what is born at the age of fourteen or fifteen in a human being the astral body and whether we are pleased with that description or not is unimportant. What is important is to realize that just as the intellectual element is born through the etheric body around the age of seven, the entire nonphysical soul aspect is born around the age of fourteen or fifteen. Prior to that, feeling and willing are closely connected with the physical organism. Just as thinking is connected with the physical organism until the age of seven, feeling and willing are closely connected with the physical organism, that is, until puberty.

We must therefore be aware that before the age of puberty, which is also when the students graduate from elementary school, we do not under any circumstances bring into thinking—which is slowly developing with the etheric body—anything that could lead to an independence of the will or feeling too early. When the child is educated with love under the guidance of authority—when the child learns feeling and willing under the guidance of others, under the guidance of adult instructors—then at the proper moment, namely at puberty, the child's own independent feeling and willing will be born. We can only properly develop our feeling and willing in that we allow them to develop under the authority of other people. If we achieve an independent development of will too early, if we achieve what I might call certain secret functions of the will too early, that will damage us for the remainder of our lives. We achieve a subtle functioning of the will too early if we are tempted to subject our moral and religious impulses to our own judgment at too early a time.

Until puberty, children should learn morality and religion through the influence of moral and religious authorities. Only at puberty does the spiritual and soul nature of the human being begin to become free of the body so that we can allow it to make its own judgments. When you say such things today, you have the prejudices of our times against you. As I mentioned this question of a natural feeling for authority in a more or less public lecture in Germany at a time when everything seemed to be under the influence of a revolution (though it did not turn out to be), everyone objected to this because they all wanted to keep the authorities away from children. What they really wanted was that teachers cease to exist and that the children would teach and raise themselves in a democratic way.

I had to answer that this is something that children do not want at all. Children want to be guided, they want to love and learn from authority. What develops within children as a love of authority is connected with their own nature.

When human beings reach sexual maturity, there, of course, develops a love for the other sex. This then becomes individualized into the love of a man for a woman. However, what is thus individualized is at the same time an individual expression for a general love for humanity, for a love for humanity in general. The general love of humanity as well as a love for particular persons develops in the same way as love for the other sex does at sexual maturity. This love that one person has for others develops as an independent force only with sexual maturity, since love must be freed of authority. This kind of love is genuine devotion. Until sexual maturity, love is a need. It is something that the child's own being demands egotistically. We must recognize that children in elementary school egotistically demand to be able to love. They need to have that person of authority near them on whom they hang, to whom they are devoted because they find pleasure in devotion, into which they are forced by their own nature. That is the primary element in love, whether it be love of humanity or love of nature, love of the stars, or love of supersensible beings and God. It is what lives in the human beings as love, and it is essentially the content of the astral body.

Only when you have thoroughly accepted these things will you be able to develop a proper understanding of how language, at least to the extent that the child brings language to school in the form of a dialect, has developed under the influence of the physical body itself. In contrast, from the age of seven onward, we no longer have a possibility of bringing style into the imaginative element of language if we do not develop a feeling for style itself through our own individual personal relationship, our love for the child. Out of this loving relationship, a feeling for style in more educated, standard language, can grow.

A child that learned a dialect just as it learned to walk already has a feeling for the dialect. It is something we can develop out of the child itself. But it is also useful to make children aware of dialect even if they have not had the good fortune of learning it. Compared to standard language, a dialect is more artistic. Standard language is more related to reason and adheres more to convention. In doing this, we are using something we need to use in education—the artistic element. In a certain sense, we use something existing in the child's blood that forms the dialect.

I still need to speak about the actual teaching of grammar, about what is, in my opinion, the proper method of teaching arithmetic and so forth. In teaching arithmetic it is important to be able to look closely at what occurs in a young person between the ages of seven and fourteen or fifteen. If we develop a person contrary to what occurs naturally, we will damage that person for his or her entire life.

It is very easy to teach a person in a way that is against human nature because human nature is split. We thus need to be aware that we damage people when we do something that is correct but take it to an extreme: one side always needs to be rounded off by the other. In language, we need to round off the sculptural element with the musical element. We will see what the situation is with arithmetic. What damages people so much is often the result of their instruction in arithmetic. The way that we learn to do arithmetic generally goes against human nature. Everything that occurs in many people today as a tendency toward materialism is essentially the result of improper instruction in arithmetic around the age of nine. Another thing that is so destructive for the later development of the soul in many people is that they begin to reason too early, and we present the material there to learn in a way for which they are not yet mature enough. They take in a large number of predetermined judgments that then continue to affect them. People often speak about the fact that in human beings one concept or idea associates itself with others. There is nothing more unfortunate than this talk about the association of ideas. When ideas associate with one another in us, when they clump and we run after them, then in our thinking, we are under their control and no longer have power over ourselves. Through education, we must protect people from allowing these associations to gain the upper hand over the will. I will speak more of that tomorrow.

10

SYNTHESIS AND ANALYSIS IN HUMAN NATURE AND EDUCATION

Basel, May 5, 1920

You have seen how spiritual science works toward using educational material as a means for raising children. The scientific forms of the instructional material are presented to the child in such a way that those forces within the child that prepare him or her for development are drawn out. If we are to work fruitfully with the instructional material we have, we need to pay attention to the course of activity of the child's soul.

If we look at the activity of a human soul, we see two things. The first is a tendency toward analysis and the second is a tendency toward synthesis. Everyone knows from logic or psychology what the essential nature of analysis and synthesis is. But it is important to comprehend these things not simply in their abstract form, as they are normally understood, but in a living way.

We can recall what analysis is if we say to ourselves the following: if we have ten numbers or ten things, then we can imagine these ten things by imagining three, five, and two, and adding to it the idea that ten can be divided, or analyzed as three, five, and two.

When working with synthesis, our concern is just the opposite: we simply add three, five, and two. As I said, in an objective, abstract, and isolated sense, everyone knows what analysis and synthesis are. But when we want to comprehend the life of the human soul, we find that the soul is continuously impelled to form syntheses. For example, we look at an individual animal out of a group of animals and we form a general concept, that of the species. In that case, we summarize, that is, we synthesize. Analysis is something that lies much deeper, almost in the unconscious. This is a desire to make multiplicity out of unity. Since this has been little taken into account, people have understood little of what human freedom represents in the soul. If the activity of the human soul were solely synthetic—that is, if human beings were connected with the external world in such a way that they could *only* synthesize, they could only form concepts of species and so forth—we could hardly speak of human freedom. Everything would be determined by external nature.

In contrast, the soul aspect of all of our deeds is based upon analysis, which enables us to develop freedom in the life of pure thinking. If I am to find the sum of two and five and three, I have no freedom. There is a rule that dictates how much two and five and three are. On the other hand, if I have ten, then I can represent this number ten as nine plus one, or five plus five or three plus five plus two, and so forth. When analyzing, I carry out a completely free inner activity. When synthesizing, I am required by the external world to unfold the life in my soul in a particular way.

In practical life, we analyze when, for example, we take a particular position and say we want to consider one thing or another from this perspective. In this case, we dissect everything we know about the thing into two parts. We analyze and separate everything and then put ourselves in a certain position. For instance, I could consider getting up early purely from the standpoint of, say, a greater inclination to do my work in the early morning. I could also consider getting up early from other perspectives. I might even go so far in my analysis that I have two or three perspectives. In this analytical activity in my soul, I am in a certain way free. Since we develop this analytical soul activity continuously and more or less unconsciously, we are free human beings. No one can overcome the difficulties in the question of human freedom who does not understand this analytical tendency in human beings.

And yet it is just this analytical activity that is normally taken too little into account in teaching and education. We are more likely to take the view that the external world demands synthesis. Consequently synthesizing is what is primarily taken into account rather than analyzing. This is very significant. If, for example, you want to pursue the idea of beginning with dialect when teaching language, it is clear how necessary it is to analyze. The child already has a dialect language. When we have the child speak some sentences, we then need to analyze what already exists in those sentences in order to derive the rules of speech formation from them. We can also develop the analytical activity in instruction much further.

I would like to draw your attention to something that you have probably already encountered in one form or another. What I am referring to is how, for example, when explaining letters we are not primarily involved in a synthetic but rather in an analytic activity. If I have a child say the word *fish* and then simply write the word on the blackboard, I attempt to teach the child the word without dividing it into separate letters. I might even attempt to have the child copy the word, assuming he or she has been drawing in the way I discussed previously. Of course the child has at this time no idea that there is an *f-i-s-h* within it. The child should simply imitate what I put on the board. Before I go on to the letters, I would often try to have the child copy complete words.

Now I go on to the analysis. I would try to draw the child's attention to how the word begins with *f.* Thus, I analyze the *f* in the context of the word. I then do the same with the *i* and so forth. Thus we work with human nature as it is when, instead of beginning with letters and synthesizing them into words, we begin with whole words and analyze them into letters.

This is something we also need to take into account, particularly from the perspective of the development of the human soul in preparation for later life. As you all know, we suffer today under the materialistic view of the world. This perspective demands not only that we only accept material things as being valid. It also insists that we trace everything in the world back to the activities of atoms. It is unimportant whether we think of those atoms in the way people thought of them in the 1880s, that is, as small elastic particles made up of some unknown material, or whether we think of them as people do today—as electrical forces or electrical centers of force. What is important in materialism is material itself, and when the tools of materialism are transferred to our view of the spirit and soul, we think of them as being composed of tiny particles and depending upon the activities of those particles. Today we have come so far that we are no longer aware that we are working with hypotheses. Most people believe it is a proven scientific fact that atoms form the basis of phenomena in the external world.

Why have people in our age developed such an inclination for atomism? Because they have developed insufficient analytical activities in children. If we were to develop in children those analytical activities that begin with unified word pictures and then analyze them into letters, the child would be able to activate its capacity to analyze at the age when it first wants to do so; it would not have to do so later by inventing atomic structures and so forth. Materialism is encouraged by a failure to satisfy our desire for analysis. If we satisfied the impulse to analyze in the way that I have described here, we would certainly keep people from sympathizing with the materialistic worldview.

For this reason in the Waldorf School we always teach beginning not with letters, but with complete sentences. We analyze the sentence into words and the words into letters and then the letters into vowels. In this way we come to a proper inner understanding as the child grasps the meaning of what a sentence or word is. We awaken the child's consciousness by analyzing sentences and words.

When you accept a child as he is and see how he speaks a dialect, then it is not at all necessary to begin with the opposite method. Children understand the unity of sentences much more than we think. Children whose tendency to analyze is accepted develop a greater awareness than is generally the case in today's population. We have sinned a great deal in education in regard to the awareness in people's souls. We could actually say that we sleep not only in the time between falling asleep and awakening, nor are we simply awake during the period from awakening until falling asleep. To some extent during daily life we alternate continually between being awake and being asleep. The activity of inhaling and exhaling is at the same time an illumination and a darkening, though we may not notice it. We do not notice it because it occurs quite quickly and because the darkening and illumination are very weak. The rapidity of the process and the subtlety of the changes make this imperceptible. Nevertheless it is true that with every inhalation we go to sleep in a certain sense, and when we exhale, in a certain sense we awaken. In this sense wakefulness and sleeping continually alternate within us.

This is also true of the mind. As a rule, with every analytical activity we awaken, and with every synthesizing activity we fall asleep. Of course this does not mean the ordinary states we are in during the night or day. Even so there is a relationship between analyzing and awakening and synthesizing and falling asleep. We therefore develop a tendency in the child to confront the world with a wakeful soul when we use the child's desire to analyze, when we develop the individual details from unified things.

This is something we must particularly take into account in teaching arithmetic. We often do not sufficiently consider the relationship of arithmetic to the child's soul life. First of all we must differentiate between arithmetic and simple counting. Many people think counting represents a kind of addition, but that is not so. Counting is simply naming differing quantities. Of course, counting needs to precede arithmetic, at least counting up to a certain number. We certainly need to teach children how to count. But we must also use arithmetic to properly value those analytical forces that want to be developed in the child's soul. In the beginning, we need to attempt, for instance, to begin with the number ten and then divide it in various ways. We need to show the children how ten can be separated into five and five, or into three and three and three and one. We can achieve an enormous amount in supporting what human nature actually strives for out of its inner forces when we do not teach addition by saying that the addends are on the left and the sum is on the right, but by saying that we have the sum on the left and the addends on the right. We should begin with analyzing the sum and then work backwards toward addition.

If you wish, you can take this presentation as a daring statement. Nevertheless those who have achieved an unprejudiced view of the forces within human nature will recognize that when we place the sum on the left and the addends on the right, and then teach the child how to separate the sum in any number of ways, we support the child's desire to analyze. Only afterward do we work with those desires that actually do not play a role within the soul, but instead are important with interactions of people within the external world. What a child analyzes out of a unity exists essentially only for herself. What is synthesized exists always for external human nature.

Now you might say that what I had said previously regarding the concept of species, for example, is the result of syntheses. And that is true. However, we cannot understand the process of synthesizing as simply the creation of abstract concepts. Certainly people believe that when we form general concepts such as *wolf* or *lamb*, these are general concepts that develop only in our reasoning. This, however, is not the case. The things that exist outside of all substance, and which we comprehend in the idea of a wolf or lamb, are also real. If they were not real, if only material substance were real, then if we were to cage a wolf and feed it only lamb, after a period of time it would have to become like a lamb. Clearly this is something that will not happen because a wolf is something more than simply the matter out of which it is made. The additional aspect of which a wolf consists becomes clear to us through the concept that we form through synthesis. It is certainly also something that corresponds to an external reality. On the other hand, what we in the end separate out of something into various parts corresponds to something subjective in many cases, but particularly in those cases where our concern is to find a point of view. It is certainly a subjective activity when I separate the sum on the left into the addends so that I have the addends on the right. In that case, I have what needs to be on the right. If I have the sum on the left and then separate it into parts, then I can do the separation from various points of view and thus the addends can take on numerous forms. It is very important to develop this freedom of will in children.

Similarly, in multiplication we should not attempt to begin with the factors and proceed to the product. Instead we should begin with the product and form the factors in many various ways. Only afterwards should we turn to the synthesizing activity. This way through arithmetic people may be able to develop the rhythmic activity within the life of the soul that consists of analyzing and synthesizing. In the way we teach arithmetic today, we often emphasize one side too strongly. For the soul, such overemphasis has the same effect as if we were to heap breath upon breath upon the body and not allow it to exhale in the proper way. It is important to take the individuality of the human being into account in the proper way. This is what I mean when I speak of the fructification that education can experience through spiritual science.

We need to become aware of what actually wants to develop out of the child's individuality. First we need to know what can be drawn out of the child. At the outset children have a desire to be satisfied analytically; then they want to bring that analysis together through synthesis. We must take these things into account by looking at human nature. Otherwise even the best pedagogical principles—although they may be satisfying to use and we believe they are fulfilling all that is required—will never be genuinely useful because we do not actually try to look at the results of education in life.

People are curiously shortsighted in their judgment. If you had lived during the 1870s, as I did, you would have heard in Prussia (and also from some people in Austria) that Prussia won the war with Austria in 1866 because the Austrian schools at an earlier time were worse than those in Prussia. It was actually the Prussian teachers who won. Since October 1918 I have not heard similar talk in Germany, although there would perhaps be reason to speak that way. But of course the talk in Germany would have to be the other way around.

We can learn from such things. They show how people have too strong a tendency to form judgments not according to the facts, but according to their sympathies and antipathies, according to what they feel. This is because there are many things in human nature that are not developed, but actually demand to be developed as human forces. We will, however, always find our way if we take the rhythmic needs within the whole human being into account. We do that when we do not simply teach addition, subtraction, multiplication, and division. When teaching addition, we should not simply expect answers to the question of what is the sum of so and so much. Instead we should expect answers to the question of how a sum can be separated in various ways. In contrast, the question with regard to subtraction is, from what number do we need to remove five in order to have the result be eight? In general, we need to pose all these kinds of questions in the opposite way to which they are posed in synthetic thinking when interacting with external world.

Here we can place the teaching of arithmetic in parallel with teaching language, where we begin with the whole and then go on to the individual letters. In our Waldorf School it is very pleasing to see the efforts the children make when they take a complete word and try to find out how it sounds, how we pronounce it, what is in the middle, and so forth, and in that way go on to the individual letters. When we atomize or analyze in this way, children will certainly not have any inclination toward materialism or atomism such as everyone does today, because modern people have been taught only synthetic thinking in school and thus their need to be analytical, their need to separate, can only develop in their worldviews.

We must, however, take something else into account. Human nature, as I mentioned yesterday, basically begins with activity and only then goes on to rest. Just as a baby begins by kicking and waving its arms and then becomes quiet, the entirety of human nature begins with activity and must learn how to come to rest. This process actually needs to be developed quite systematically. Thus what is important is that we, in a sense, educate people based upon their own movement.

It is very easy to make an error in that regard today. I have already tried to show how important it is at the beginning of elementary school to work with the musical and singing elements. We need to work with the child's musical needs as much as possible. Today, however, it would be very easy for an erroneous prejudice against these ideas to arise. If we look at the modern world—and most of you will have already noticed this—there are nearly as many methods of teaching singing as there are singing teachers. Of course each one always believes his or her own method is the best. If we simply apply these methods of teaching singing and music to adults, who are already beyond the age of development, we can allow them to pick and choose the method they want. Essentially all such methods begin with an erroneous position. They assume that we need to quiet the human organs in order to develop the activity that is desired. Thus, in a sense, the activity of the lungs, for example, must be quieted in order to develop that activity in the lungs which in this case, in singing, should predominate. However, just the opposite occurs within human nature. Nearly all methods of teaching singing that I have every seen actually begin with our modern materialism. They begin with the assumption that the human being is somehow mechanical and needs to be quieted in order to be able to develop the necessary activity. This assumption is something that can never be important when we genuinely see the nature of the human being.

The proper method of teaching singing or developing a musical ear assumes that children normally hear properly, and then a desire develops within the child to imitate so that the imitation adjusts to that hearing. Thus the best method is for the teacher to sing to the children with a certain kind of love and to adjust to what is missing in them musically. In that way, the natural need of the students to imitate and have their mistakes corrected is awakened though what they hear from the teacher. However, in singing, children need to learn what instinctively results from quieting the organs.

In the same way, speaking serves to regulate the human breathing rhythm. In school we need to work so that the children learn how to bring their speech into a peaceful regularity. We need to require that the children speak syllable for syllable, that they speak slowly and that they properly form the syllables so that nothing of the word is left out. The children need to grow accustomed to proper speech and verse, to well-formed speech, and develop a feeling rather than a conscious understanding of the rise and fall of the tones in verses. We need to speak to the children in the proper way so that they learn to hear.

During childhood the larynx and neighboring organs adjust to the hearing. As I said, the methods common today may be appropriate for adults, as what results from those methods will be included or not included in one way or another by life itself. In school, however, we need to eliminate all such artificial methods. Here what is most needed is the natural relationship of the teacher to the student. The loving devotion of the child to the teacher should replace artificial methods. I would, in fact, say that intangible effects should be the basis of our work. Nothing would be more detrimental than if all the old aunts and uncles with their tea-party ideas of music and methods were to find their way into school. In school what should prevail is the spirit of the subject. But that can only occur when you, the teacher, are enveloped by the subject, not when you want to teach the subject to the children through external methods.

If in the school education becomes more of an art such as we have been discussing, then I believe people will be less inclined to learn things according to some specific method than they are today. If children at the age of six or seven are taught music and singing in a natural way, later on they will hardly take any interest in the outrageous methods that play such a large role in modern society.

In my opinion, modern education should also require the teacher to look objectively at everything in the artificiality of our age, and eliminate it through instruction during elementary school. There are many things—such as the methods I just mentioned—that are very difficult to overcome. The people who use such methods are fanatical and can see only how their methods may reform the world. In general, it is useless to try to discuss such things reasonably and objectively with these people. Such things can only be brought into their proper context by the next generation. Here is where we can make an impact. In regard to society it is always the next generation that accomplishes a great deal. The art of teaching and education consists not only of the methods used, but also of the perspective that results from the teacher's interest in the general development of humanity. Teachers need to have a comprehensive interest in the development of humanity, and they need to have an interest in everything that occurs during the present time. The last thing a teacher should do is to limit his or her interests. The interests we develop for the cultural impulses of our age have an enlivening effect upon our entire attitude and bearing as teachers. You will excuse me when I say that much of what is properly felt to be pedantic in schools would certainly go away if the faculty were interested in the major events of life and if they would participate in public activities. Of course, people don't like to see this, particularly in reactionary areas, but it is important for education not to simply have a superficial interest.

A question was asked of me today that is connected with what I have just said. I was asked what the direction of language is, what we should do so that all of the words that have lost their meaning no longer form a hindrance to the development of thinking, so that a new spiritual life can arise. An English mathematician who attempted to form a mathematical description of all the ways of thinking recently said, in a lecture he gave on education, that style is the intellectual ethical aspect. I think this could be a genuine literary ideal. In order to speak or write ethically each person would need a particular vocabulary for himself, just as each people does now. In language as it is now, the art of drama only develops the words, but seldom develops general human concepts. How can we transform language so that in the future the individual thought or feeling, as well as the generality of the individual concept, becomes audible or visible? Or should language simply disappear and be replaced by something else in the future?

Now that is certainly quite a collection of questions! Nevertheless I want to go into them a little today; tomorrow and the next day I will speak about them in more detail. It is necessary to look into how more external relationships to language exist in our civilized languages, since they are in a certain way more advanced than external relationships that exist in other languages. There is, for example, something very external in translation by taking some text in one language and looking up the words in a dictionary. When working this way you will in general not achieve what exists in the language beyond anything purely external. Language is not simply permeated by reason; it is directly experienced, directly felt. For that reason, people would become terribly externalized if everyone were to speak some general language like Esperanto. I am not prejudiced; I have heard wonderful-sounding poems in Esperanto. But much of what lives in a language in regard to the feelings, the life of the language, would be lost through such a universal language. This is also something that is always lost when we simply translate one language word for word into another using a dictionary. We therefore need to say that in one sense the man who spoke about that here was quite correct, although it is not good to make such things into formulas. It is not good to try to formulate thoughts mathematically or to do other things that are only of interest in the moment. What we can say, though, is that it is important for us to try to imbue our language with spirit. Our language, like all civilized languages, has moved strongly into clichés. For that reason, it is particularly good to work with dialect.

Dialects, where they are spoken, are more alive than so-called standard language. A dialect contains much more personal qualities: it contains secret, intimate qualities. People who speak in dialect speak more accurately than those who speak standard language. In dialect, it is more difficult to lie than it is in standard language. That assertion may appear paradoxical to you, but it is nevertheless true in a certain sense. Of course I am not saying there are no bald-faced liars who speak dialect. But it is true that such people must be much worse than they would need to be if they were to lie only in educated, standard language. There you do not need to be as bad in order to lie, because the language itself enables lying more than when you speak in dialect. You need to be a really bad person if you are to lie in dialect because people love the words in dialect more than they do those of standard language. People are ashamed to use words in dialect as clichés, whereas the words in standard language can easily be used as clichés. This is something that we need to teach people in general—that there are genuine experiences in the words. Then we need to bring life into the language as well.

Today hardly anyone is interested in trying to bring life into language. I have tried to do that in my books in homeopathic doses. In order to make certain things understandable, I have used in my books a concept that has the same relationship to force as water flowing in a stream does to the ice on top of the stream. I used the word *kraften* (to work actively, forcefully).[1] Usually we only have the word *Kraft*, meaning "power" or "force." We do not speak of *kraften*. We can also use similar words. If we are to bring life into language, then we also need a syntax that is alive, not dead. Today people correct you immediately if you put the subject somewhere in the sentence other than where people are accustomed to having it. Such things are still just possible in German, and you still have a certain amount of freedom. In the Western European languages—well, that is just terrible, everything is wrong there. You hear all the time that you can't say that, that is not English, or that is not French. But, to say "that is not German" is not possible. In German you can put the subject anywhere in the sentence. You can also give an inner life to the sentence in some way. I do not want to speak in popular terms, but I do want to emphasize the process of dying in the language. A language begins to die when you are always hearing that you cannot say something in one way or another, that you are speaking incorrectly. It may not seem as strange but it is just the same as if a hundred people were to go to a door and I were to look at them and decide purely according to my own views who was a good person and who was a bad person. Life does not allow us to stereotype things. When we do that, it appears grotesque. Life requires that everything remain in movement. For that reason, syntax and grammar must arise out of the life of feeling, not out of dead reasoning. That perspective will enable us to continue with a living development of language.

Goethe introduced much dialect into language. It is always good to enliven written language with dialect because it enables words to be felt in a warmer, more lively way. We should also consider that a kind of ethical life is brought into language. (This, of course, does not mean that we should be humorless in our speech. Friedrich Theodore Vischer[2] wrote a wonderful book about the difference between frivolity and cynicism. It also contains a number of remarks about language usage and about how to live into language.) When teaching language, we have a certain responsibility to use it also as a training for ethics in life. Nevertheless there needs to be some feeling; it should not be done simply according to convention. We move further and further away from what is alive in language if we say, as is done in the Western European languages, that one or another turn of phrase is incorrect and that only one particular way of saying things is allowed.

11

RHYTHM IN EDUCATION

Basel, May 6, 1920

If we look again at the three most important phases of elementary school, then we see that they are: first, from entering elementary school at about the age of six or seven until the age of nine; then second, from the age of nine until about the age of twelve; and finally from twelve until puberty. The capacity to reason independently only begins to occur when people have reached sexual maturity, even though a kind of preparation for this capacity begins around the age of twelve. For this reason, the third phase of elementary school begins about the age of twelve.

Every time a new phase occurs in the course of human life, something is born out of human nature. I have previously noted how the same forces—which become apparent as the capacity to remember, the capacity to have memories, and so forth—that appear at about the age of seven have previously worked upon the human organism up until that age. The most obvious expression of that working is the appearance of the second set of teeth. In a certain sense, forces are active in the organism that later become important during elementary school as the capacity to form thoughts. They are active but hidden. Later they are freed and become independent. The forces that become independent we call the forces of the etheric body.

Once again at puberty other forces become independent which guide us into the external world in numerous ways. Hidden within that system of forces is also the capacity for independent reasoning. We can therefore say that the actual medium of the human capacity for reason, the forces within the human being that give rise to reasoning, are basically born only at the time of puberty, and have slowly been prepared for that birth beginning at the age of twelve.

When we know this and can properly honor it, then we also become aware of the responsibility we take upon ourselves if we accustom people to forming independent judgments too soon. The most damaging prejudices in this regard prevail at the present time. People want to accustom children to forming independent judgments as early as possible.

I previously said that we should relate to children until puberty in such a way that they recognize us as an authority, that they accept something because someone standing next to them who is visibly an authority requests it and wants it. If we accustom children to accepting the truth simply because we as authorities present it to them, we will prepare them properly for having free and independent reasoning later in life. If we do not want to serve as an authority figure for the child and instead try to disappear so that everything has to develop out of the child's own nature, we are demanding a capacity for reason too early, before what we call the astral body becomes free and independent at puberty. We would be working with the astral body by allowing it to act upon the physical nature of the child. In that way we will impress upon the child's physical body what we should actually only provide for his soul. We are preparing something that will continue to have a damaging effect throughout the child's life.

There is quite a difference between maturing to free judgment at the age of fourteen or fifteen—when the astral body, which is the carrier of reasoning, has become free after a solid preparation—than if we have been trained in so-called independent judgment at too early an age. In the latter case, it is not our astral aspect, that is, our soul, which is brought into independent reasoning, but our physical body instead. The physical body is drawn in with all its natural characteristics, with its temperament, its blood characteristics, and everything that gives rise to sympathy and antipathy within it, with everything that provides it with no objectivity. In other words, if a child between the ages of seven and fourteen is supposed to reason independently, the child reasons out of that part of human nature which we later can no longer rid ourselves of if we are not careful to see that it is cared for in a natural way, namely, through authority, during the elementary school period. If we allow children to reason too early, it will be the physical body that reasons throughout life. We then remain unsteady in our reasoning, as it depends upon our temperament and all kinds of other things in the physical body. If we are prepared in a way appropriate to the physical body and in a way that the nature of the physical body requires—that is, if we are brought up during the proper time under the influence of authority—then the part of us that should reason becomes free in the proper way and later in life we will be able to achieve objective judgment. Therefore the best way to prepare someone to become a free and independent human being is to avoid guiding the child toward freedom at too early an age.

This can cause a great deal of harm if it is not used properly in education. In our time it is very difficult to become sufficiently aware of this. If you talk about this subject with people today who are totally unprepared and who have no good will in this regard, you will find yourself simply preaching to deaf ears. Today we live much more than we believe in a period of materialism, and it is this age of materialism that needs to be precisely recognized by teachers. They need to be very aware of how much materialism is boiling up within modern culture and modern attitudes.

I would now like to describe this matter from a very different perspective. Something remarkable happened in European civilization around 1850, although it was barely noticed: a direct and basic feeling for rhythm was to a very large extent lost. Hence we now have people a few generations later who have entirely lost this feeling for rhythm. Such people are completely unaware of what this lack of rhythm means in raising children. In order to understand this, we need to consider the following.

In life people alternate between sleeping and being awake. People think they understand the state called wakefulness because they are aware of themselves. During this time, through sense impressions they gain an awareness of the external world. But they do not know the state between falling asleep and awakening. In modern life, people have no awareness of themselves then. They have few, if any, direct conscious perceptions of the external world. This is therefore a state in which life moves into something like a state of unconsciousness.

We can easily gain a picture of the inner connections between these two states only when we recognize two polar opposites in human life that have great significance for education. I am referring here to drawing and music, two opposites I have already mentioned and which I would like to consider from a special point of view again today.

Let us first look at drawing, in which I also include painting and sculpting. While doing so, let us recall everything in regard to drawing that we consider to be important to the child from the beginning of elementary school. Drawing shows us that, out of his or her own nature, the human being creates a form we find reflected in the external world. I have already mentioned that it is not so important to hold ourselves strictly to the model.

Instead we need to find a feeling for form within our own nature. In the end, we will recognize that we exist in an element that surrounds us during our state of wakefulness in the external world, in everything that we do forming spatially. We draw lines. We paint colors. We sculpt shapes. Lines present themselves to us, although they do not exist in nature as such. Nevertheless they present themselves to us through nature, and the same is true of colors and forms.

Let us look at the other element, which we can call musical, that also permeates speech. Here we must admit that in what is musical we have an expression of the human soul. Like sculpting and drawing, everything that is expressed through music has a very rudimentary analogy to external nature. It is not possible to simply imitate with music that which occurs naturally in the external world, just as it is not possible, in a time where a feeling for sculpting or drawing is so weak, to simply imitate the external world. We must ask ourselves then if music has no content. Music does have its own content. The content of music is primarily its melodic element. Melodies need to come to us. When many people today place little value upon the melodic element, it is nothing more than a characteristic of our materialistic age. Melodies simply do not come to people often enough.

We can well compare the melodic element with the sculptural element. It is certainly true that the sculptural element is related to space. In the same way the melodic element is related to time. Those who have a lively feeling for this relationship will realize that the melodic element contains a kind of sculpting. In a certain way, the melodic element corresponds to what sculpting is in the external world.

Let us now look at something else. You are all acquainted with that flighty element in the life of our souls that becomes apparent in dreams. If we concern ourselves objectively with that element of dreaming, we slowly achieve a different view of dreams than the ordinary one. The common view of dreams focuses upon the content of the dream, which is what commonly interests most people. But as soon as we concern ourselves objectively with this wonderful and mysterious world of dreams, the situation becomes different. Someone might talk about the following dream.

I climbed up a mountain, but just before I came to the peak there was an obstacle that I was unable to overcome. I was therefore unable to reach the peak. As I attempted to overcome that obstacle, I was met by evil, unfriendly animals, beings with demonic forms.

Another person might describe the following:

I was walking along a path and came to a cave. I went into the cave and it grew suddenly dark so I could go no further. I then encountered all kinds of obstacles, but I could go no further and could not reach my goal.

A third or a fourth person could tell still other stories. The pictures are quite different. One person dreams about climbing a mountain, another about going into a cave, and a third about still something else. It is not the pictures that are important. The pictures are simply woven into the dream. What is important is that the person experiences a kind of tension into which they fall when they are unable to solve something that can first be solved upon awakening. It is this moving into a state of tension, the occurrence of the tension, of becoming tense that is expressed in the various pictures.

What is important is that human beings in dreams experience increasing and decreasing tension, resolution, expectations, and disappointments, in short, that they experience inner states of the soul that are then expressed in widely differing pictures. The pictures are similar in their qualities of increase and decrease. It is the state of the soul that is important, since these experiences are connected to the general state of the soul. It is totally irrelevant whether a person experiences one picture or another during the night. It is not unimportant, however, whether one experiences a tension and then its resolution or first an expectation and then a disappointment, since the person's state of mind on the next day depends upon it. It is also possible to experience a dream that reflects the person's state of soul that has resulted from a stroke of fate or from many other things. In my opinion, it is the ups and downs that are important. That which appears, that forms the picture at the edge of awakening, is only a cloak into which the dream weaves itself.

When we look more closely at the world of dreams, and when we ask ourselves what a human being experiences until awakening, we will admit that until we awaken, these ups and downs of feeling clothe themselves in pictures just at the moment of awakening. Of course, we can perceive this in characteristic dreams such as this one:

> A student stands at the door of a lecture room. He dreams about how another student comes up to him and says such nasty things that it is obvious that this is a challenge to duel. The student dreams that the seconds are chosen, that they go out into the forest, and that everything is prepared. First shot. The student hears this sound and awakens to find that he has knocked over a chair standing next to his bed: that was the shot. That was the only external event.

Thus the entire picture of the dream flashed through his head at that moment. However, what was clothed in those pictures is a lasting state of his soul.

Now you need to seriously compare what lies at the basis of these dreams—the welling up and subsiding of feelings, the tension and its resolution or perhaps the tendency toward something which then leads to some calamity and so forth. Compare that seriously with what lies at the basis of the musical element and you will find in those dream pictures only something that is irregular (not rhythmic). In music, you find something that is very similar to this welling up and subsiding and so forth. If you then continue to follow this path, you will find that sculpture and drawing imitate the form in which we find ourselves during ordinary life from awakening until falling asleep. Melodies, which are connected to music, give us the experiences of an apparently unconscious state, and they occur as reminiscences of such in our daily lives. People know so little about the actual origins of musical themes because they experience what lives in musical themes only during the period from falling asleep till awakening. This exists for human beings today as a still-unconscious element, though revealed through forming pictures in dreams. However, we need to take up this unconscious element that prevails in dreams and which also prevails as melody in music in our teaching, so that we rise above materialism.

If you understand the spirit of what I have just presented, you will recognize how everywhere there has been an attempt to work with this unconscious element. I have done that first by showing how the artistic element is necessary right from the very beginning of elementary school. I have insisted that we should use the dialect that the children speak to reveal the content of grammar, that is, we should take the children's language as such and accept it as something complete and then use it as the basis for presenting grammar. Think for a moment about what you do in such a case. In what period of life is speech actually formed? Attempt to think back as far as you can in the course of your life, and you will see that you can remember nothing from the period in which you could not speak. Human beings learn language in a period when they are still sleeping through life. If you then compare the dreamy world of the child's soul with dreams and with how melodies are interwoven in music, you will see that they are similar. Like dreaming, learning to speak occurs through the unconscious, and is something like an awakening at dawn. Melodies simply exist and we do not know where they come from. In reality, they arise out of this sleep element of the human being. We experience a sculpting with time from the time we fall asleep until we awaken. At their present stage of development human beings are not capable of experiencing this sculpting with time. You can read about how we experience that in my book *How to Know Higher Worlds*. That is something that does not belong to education as such. From that description, you will see how necessary it is to take into account that unconscious element which has its effect during the time the child sleeps. It is certainly taken into account in our teaching of music, particularly in teaching musical themes, so that we must attempt to exactly analyze the musical element to the extent that it is present in children in just the same way as we analyze language as presented in sentences. In other words, we attempt to guide children at an early age to recognize themes in music, to actually feel the melodic element like a sentence. Here it begins and here it stops; here there is a connection and here begins something new. In this regard, we can have a wonderful effect upon the child's development by bringing an understanding of the not-yet-real content of music. In this way, the child is guided back to something that exists in human nature but is almost never seen.

Nearly everyone knows what a melody is and what a sentence is. But a sentence that consists of a subject, a predicate, and an object and which is in reality unconsciously a melody is something that only a few people know. Just as we experience the rising and subsiding of feelings as a rhythm in sleeping, which we then become conscious of and surround with a picture, we also, in the depths of our nature, experience a sentence as music. By conforming to the outer world, we surround what we perceive as music with something that is a picture. The child writes the essay—subject, predicate, object. A triplet is felt at the deepest core of the human being. That triplet is used through projecting the first tone in a certain way upon the child, the second upon writing, and the third upon the essay. Just as these three are felt and then surrounded with pictures (which, however, correspond to reality and are not felt as they are in dreams), the sentence lives in our higher consciousness; whereas in our deepest unconsciousness, something musical, a melody, lives. When we are aware that, at the moment we move from the sense-perceptible to the supersensible, we must rid ourselves of the sense-perceptible content, and in its place experience what eludes us in music—the theme whose real form we can experience in sleep—only then can we consider the human being as a whole. Only then do we become genuinely aware of what it means to teach language to children in such a living way that the child perceives a trace of melody in a sentence. This means we do not simply speak in a dry way, but instead in a way that gives the full tone, that presents the inner melody and subsides through the rhythmic element.

Around 1850 European people lost that deeper feeling for rhythm. Before that, there was still a certain relationship to what I just described. If you look at some treatises that appeared around that time about music or about the musical themes from Beethoven and others, then you will see how at about that time those who were referred to as authorities in music often cut up and destroyed in the most unimaginable ways what lived in music. You will see how that period represents the low point of experiencing rhythm.

As educators, we need to be aware of that, because we need to guide sentences themselves back to rhythm in the school. If we keep that in mind, over a longer period of time we will begin to recognize the artistic element of teaching. We would not allow the artistic element to disappear so quickly if we were required to bring it more into the content.

All this is connected with a question that was presented to me yesterday and which I can more thoroughly discuss in this connection. The question was, "Why is it not possible to teach proper handwriting to those children who have such a difficult time writing properly?" Those who might study Goethe's handwriting or that of other famous people will get the odd impression that famous people often have very strange handwriting. In education, we certainly cannot allow a child to have sloppy handwriting on the grounds that the child will probably someday be a famous person and we should not disturb him. We must not allow that to influence us. But what is actually present when a child writes in such a sloppy manner? If you make some comparisons, you will notice that sloppy handwriting generally arises from the fact that such children have a rather unmusical ear, or if not that, then a reason that is closely related to it. Children write in a sloppy way because they have not learned to hear precisely: they have not learned to hear a word in its full form.

There may be different reasons why children do not hear words correctly. The child may be growing up in a family or environment where people speak unclearly. In such a case, the child does not learn to hear properly and will thus not be able to write properly, or at least not very easily. In another case, a child may tend to have little perception for what he or she hears. In that case, we need to draw the child's attention to listening properly. In other situations it is the teacher who is responsible for the child's poor handwriting. Teachers should pay attention to speaking clearly and also to using very descriptive language. They do not have to speak like actors, making sure to enunciate the ending syllable. But they must accustom themselves to *living* into each syllable, so that the syllables are clearly spoken and children will be more likely to repeat the syllables in a clear way. When you speak in a clear and complete way, you will be able to achieve a great deal with regard to proper handwriting for some children. All this is connected with the unconscious, with the dream and sleep element, since the sleep element is simply the unconscious element. It is not something we should teach to children in an artificial way.

What is the basis of listening? That is normally not discussed in psychology. In the evening we fall asleep and in the morning we awake; that is all we know. We can think about it afterward by saying to ourselves that we are not conscious during that period. Conventional, nonspiritual science is unaware of what occurs to us from the time we fall asleep until we awaken. However, the inner state of our soul is no different when we are listening than when we are sleeping. The only difference is that there is a continual movement from being within ourselves to being outside ourselves. It is extremely important that we become aware of this undulation in the life of our souls. When I listen, my attention is turned toward the outer world. However, while listening, there are moments where I actually awaken within myself. If I did not have those moments, listening would be of absolutely no use. While we are listening or looking at something, there is a continual awakening and falling asleep, even though we are awake. It is a continual undulation—waking, falling asleep, waking, falling asleep. In the final analysis, our entire relationship to the external world is based upon this capacity to move into the other world, which could be expressed paradoxically as "being able to fall asleep." What else could it mean to listen to a conversation than to fall asleep into the content of the conversation? Understanding is awakening out of the conversation, nothing more. What that means, however, is that we should not attempt to reach what should actually be developed out of the unconsciousness, out of the sleeping or dreaming of the human being in a conscious way.

For that reason, we should not attempt to teach children proper handwriting in an artificial way. Instead we should teach them by properly speaking our words and then having the child repeat the words. Thus we will slowly develop the child's hearing and therefore writing. We need to assume that if a child writes in a sloppy way, she does not hear properly. Our task is to support proper hearing in the child and not to do something that is directed more toward full consciousness than hearing is.

As I mentioned yesterday, we should also take such things into account when teaching music. We must not allow artificial methods to enter into the school where, for instance, the consciousness is mistreated by such means as artificial breathing. The children should learn to breathe through grasping the melody. The children should learn to follow the melody through hearing and then adjust themselves to it. That should be an unconscious process. It must occur as a matter of course. As I mentioned, we should have the music teachers hold off on such things until the children are older, when they will be less influenced by them. Children should be taught about the melodic element in an unconscious way through a discussion of the themes. The artificial methods I mentioned have just as bad an effect as it would have to teach children drawing by showing them how to hold their arms instead of giving them a feeling for line. It would be like saying to a child, "You will be able to draw an acanthus leaf if you only learn to hold your arm in such and such a way and to move it in such and such a way." Through this and similar methods, we do nothing more than to simply consider the human organism from a materialistic standpoint, as a machine that needs to be adjusted so it does one thing properly. If we begin from a spiritual standpoint, we will always make the detour through the soul and allow the organism to adjust itself to what is properly felt in the soul.

We can therefore say that if we support the child in the drawing element, we give the child a relationship to its environment, and if we support the child in the musical element, then we give the child a relationship to something that is not in our normal environment, but in the environment we exist in from the time of falling asleep until awakening. These two polarities are then combined when we teach grammar, for instance. Here we need to interweave a feeling for the structure of a sentence with an understanding of how to form sentences.

We need to know such things if we are to properly understand how beginning at approximately the age of twelve, we slowly prepare the intellectual aspect of understanding, namely, free will. Before the age of twelve, we need to protect the child from independent judgments. We attempt to base judgment upon authority so that authority has a certain unconscious effect upon the child. Through such methods we can have an effect unbeknownst to the child. Through this kind of relationship to the child, we already have an element that is very similar to the musical dreamlike element.

Around the age of twelve, we can begin to move from the botanical or zoological perspective toward the mineral or physical perspective. We can also move from the historical to the geographical perspective. It is not that such things should only begin at the age of twelve, but rather before then they should be handled in such a way that we use judgment less and feeling more. In a certain sense, before the age of twelve we should teach children history by presenting complete and rounded pictures and by creating a feeling of tension that is then resolved. Thus, before the age of twelve, we will primarily take into account how we can reach the child's feeling and imagination through what we teach about history. Only at about the age of twelve is the child mature enough to hear about causality in history and to learn about geography.

If you now look at what we should teach children, you will feel the question of how we are to bring the religious element into all this so that the child gains a fully rounded picture of the world as well as a sense of the supersensible. People today are in a very difficult position in that regard. In the Waldorf School, pure externalities have kept us from following the proper pedagogical perspective in this area. Today we are unable to use all of what spiritual science can provide for education in our teaching other than to apply the consequences of it in how we teach. One of the important aspects of spiritual science is that it contains certain artistic impulses that are absorbed by human beings so that they not only simply *know* things, but they can *do* things. To put it in a more extreme way, people therefore become more adept; they can better take up life and thus can also exercise the art of education in a better way.

At the present time, however, we must refrain from bringing more of what we can learn from spiritual science into education than education can absorb. We were not able to form a school based upon a particular worldview at the Waldorf School. Instead from the very beginning I stipulated that Protestant teachers would teach the Protestant religion. Religion is taught separately, and we have nothing to do with it. The Protestant teacher comes and teaches the Protestant religion, just as the Catholic religion is taught by the Catholic priest or whomever the Catholic Church designates, the rabbi teaches the Jews, and so forth. At the present time we have been unable to bring more of spiritual science in other than to provide understanding for our teaching. The Waldorf School is not a parochial school.

Nevertheless the strangest things have occurred. A number of people have said that because they are not religious, they will not send their children to the Protestant, Catholic, or Jewish religion teachers. They have said that if we do not provide a religion teacher who teaches religion based solely upon a general understanding, they will not send their children to religion class at all. Thus those parents who wanted an anthroposophically oriented religion class to a certain extent forced us to provide one. This class is given, but not because we have a desire to propagate anthroposophy as a worldview. It is quite different to teach anthroposophy as a world-view than it is to use what spiritual science can provide in order to make education more fruitful.

We do not attempt to provide the content. What we do attempt to provide is a capacity to do. A number of strange things then occurred. For example, a rather large number of children left the other religion classes in order to join ours. That is something we cannot prohibit. It was very uncomfortable for me, at least from the perspective of retaining a good relationship to the external world. It was also quite dangerous, but that is the way it is. From the same group of parents we hear that the teaching of other religions will soon cease anyway. That is not at all our intent, as the Waldorf School is not intended as a parochial school. Today nowhere in the civilized world is it possible to genuinely teach out of the whole. That will be possible only when through the threefold social organism cultural life becomes independent. So long as that is not the case, we will not be able to provide the same religious instruction for everybody. Thus what we have attempted to do is to make education more fruitful through spiritual science.

12

TEACHING HISTORY AND GEOGRAPHY

Basel, May 7, 1920

When you have taught the children in the way I have indicated, at around the age of twelve you will see they are mature enough to comprehend history on the one hand and to learn about geography, physics, and chemistry on the other. At that age they are also mature enough to prepare for genuinely practical life. Today I would like to give you an outline of this.

Children are not mature enough to understand history before the age of twelve. You can certainly prepare them for learning about history by telling stories or by giving them short biographical sketches, or even by telling them stories with a moral. They become mature enough to learn history through learning about botany and zoology as I have described it. You can achieve a great deal in regard to history if, in botany, you have presented the earth as a unity and shown how the various plants grow upon the earth's surface during the different seasons of the year, and if they understand the human being as a synthesis of various groups of animals—that is, if you have presented each of the animal groups as something one-sided which then harmoniously unites with the others in the human being. When children move through such ideas, you prepare them for learning history.

When we begin to teach children history, it is important that we use it to develop and support certain forces of human nature and, in a certain sense, to fulfill the longings of human nature during this period of life. If we present history in the ordinary fashion, however, we encounter considerable resistance. Today's usual presentation of history is actually only the narration of certain events or the summarizing of those events or cultural forms from a particular causal perspective. It essentially emphasizes the superficiality of what occurred. If you remain objective about it, you will feel that this form of history fails to properly describe what really lies at the basis of human development.

We often hear that history should keep from talking about wars or other external events, and that it should instead present the causal relationships of cultural events. It is very questionable whether we are justified in assuming such causal relationships as, for example, that what occurred in the second half of the nineteenth century resulted from what occurred in the first half, and so forth. We could certainly express the basis of human historical development in a quite different way. In teaching history, it is important not to let ourselves go and try to teach in such a way that we ourselves understand only very little. Of course, we assume that we all learned history at the university, that we understand history as a whole, but that is not what I am talking about. What I mean is that when we begin to teach a particular history class, we normally just start somewhere and assume that what follows the given period will be properly taken up at a later time. That is why history is generally taught as just a series of events in time.

Teaching this way does not actually take into account the forces that emanate from human nature. And yet that is what we must do. We should, for example, be clear that the most important thing is what we, as human beings living in the present, experience as history. If we take the children back to Greek history in an abstract way, even if they are at a college-preparatory level, it leads only to an abstract placement in an earlier time. The children will not concretely understand why modern people need to know anything about the Greek era. They will immediately understand what is important, however, if you begin by describing how we experience the effects of the Greek period in the present. Therefore we first need to give the children a picture of these effects, which we can do in various ways. We could have prepared that previously, but in teaching history, we must begin by describing how what existed at a particular historical time still exists in the present.

An objective survey of our culture will easily show you the following. If I were to describe in detail what I now wish to outline, it would take too much time, but each of you can do that for yourself. Here I want only to indicate the general guidelines. Everything we have as comprehensive and universal ideas, that is, everything we live by in terms of ideas, we essentially have inherited from the Greek period. Certain feelings about art that occupy our souls are only a result of the Greek period. Take any of the most common examples, things we work with every day, for example, the concept of cause and effect, or even the concept of the human being itself. The Greeks developed every universal concept we have. They even developed the concept of history. Thus if we look at our entire life of ideas, we will find we have inherited it from the Greeks.

We can describe our entire universe of ideas and concepts for students at a quite elementary level without even mentioning that they arose in Greece. We can speak completely from the perspective of the present and leave it at that for the time being. We could then attempt to do something dramatic or lyrical with the children, so that we indicate, for instance, how a drama is divided into acts, how the drama is built up, leading to a climax, which is then resolved. In that way we can develop an elementary concept of catharsis. We do not need to develop any complicated philosophical ideas in children, but we can provide them with the concept of catharsis by showing how a certain feeling of tension is developed in the drama, how we are led into a feeling of sympathy or fear, and then how we can learn to have a balance in our feelings of fear or sympathy. Then we can tell them how the Greeks developed all these as the most important aspects of drama. This is all possible when we have properly prepared the children for what they are to learn around the age of twelve. We can then show the children some Greek work of art, say, a figure of Aphrodite, and explain how beauty is revealed in it. We could even go so far as to explain the artistic difference between what is at rest and what is in movement. We can also give them some ideas about public life if we discuss the basic political ideas during the Greek period in connection with modern public life.

After we have discussed all of these things, we can try to present the basic character of Greek history to the children. We should try to make it clear to the children how the Greek city-states worked, and that people with a certain character lived in Greece. Our main task, therefore, is to show that these things we are discussing are still alive today and that they arose with the Greeks, for example by showing how sculpture developed during the Greek period or how cities developed and so forth. Begin with what still exists today, then go on to show the children how such things first developed and took control of human development during the Greek period. That will give the children a very concrete idea of everything the Greek period gave to the development of humanity.

Through such a presentation, the children should get the idea that historical life is not something that endlessly repeats itself. Instead a specific period achieves something quite specific for humanity, something that then remains. The children should also learn how later periods achieved other things, which also remain.

In that way they can gain a firm footing in the present and can then say to themselves that their own period of history has something quite specific to achieve for eternity. Such a presentation of history has a genuine effect upon the soul and excites the will. How you give such a presentation is extremely important. Through the presentation you have the opportunity to give the children a large number of ideas and impressions and to show that it was the Greeks who introduced such things into human life.

You can also speak to the children about things that happened a long time ago and are still living but do not contain any Christian aspects. When we speak about the ancient Greek culture in such a way that it is perceived as living, we are working with material that contains nothing of Christianity. However, it is precisely in awakening ideas in the children that have remained alive over a long period of time, and are neutral in relationship to Christianity, that we have the possibility of clearly presenting the effects of the event of Golgotha and the rise of Christianity. After we have presented Greek history by characterizing the entirety of Greek culture, we can go into the details. If we have covered Greek history this way, we will have properly prepared the children for an awakening of a feeling for Christianity.

Many of you may say, with a certain amount of justification, that my suggestion to avoid discussing the details of history at first and instead discuss the great movements and tendencies in ancient Greece is not the proper method because we would not begin with specific events and then put them together to form a picture of Greek history in its entirety. Here we come to an important question of method that we cannot answer out of our own desires and prejudices but instead should answer from a complete understanding of life. I would ask you in turn if the whole of life is always formed from individual events. If you were to make that demand of normal perception, you would have to teach people how to form a human head out of its individual parts, the brain, and so forth. In normal life, we look at the whole directly. We can gain a living relationship to life only when we look directly at the whole. We should never study the individual parts of the whole in some random fashion. Instead we need to characterize as a whole those things that occur as a whole. The Greeks themselves lived in a given decade and experienced as individual human beings the impressions that arose during that decade. The part of ancient Greece that is alive today is a summary. It forms a whole that the children will look past if we do not begin by characterizing what was alive within the entirety of Greek culture.

This also resolves another more practical question. I have experienced time and again what it means in a specific situation when the teacher does not complete the required material in a given grade. It can lead to complete nonsense in two ways. In the first case, you are not finished, which is simply silly. In the second case, you do finish, but you pile things together so much in the last weeks that all the work is for nothing. However, if you first present the material as a whole, you will have covered the period of history that you want to teach the class. In that way you don't do nearly so much harm when you skip over some of the details in your discussion. If you have an overview of the subject, it is very simple later to look up the details in an encyclopedia. Not to have learned the overview is, under some circumstances, a lasting loss. You can get a proper overview of a subject only under the guidance of a really lively person, whereas you can learn the details yourself from a book. We will discuss how to divide the material throughout the curriculum and among the grades later.

In examining teachers, what is important is to get an impression of their worldviews and then leave it up to the individual teachers to determine what they need to know in order to teach on a daily basis. Teachers' examinations that test for details are complete nonsense. What is important is to gain a summary impression of whether someone is suited for being a teacher or not. Of course, we should not carry such things to an extreme. However, what I just said is true in general.

We can consider everything I have just described as living today as a kind of transition into Greece. We could then go on to those things living today that were not yet living in ancient Greece. You could certainly give a lively presentation about such concepts as general human dignity. You could discuss such concepts as individual human consciousness, of course at an elementary level. The Greeks did not yet have the concept of human dignity. They did have the concepts of the *polis*, of a community to which individuals belonged, but they were divided into groups, the masters and the slaves. The Greeks did not have a fundamental conception of the human being, and you should discuss that with the students. You could also discuss the concept of what is human, a concept that is not very alive because we are not nearly Christian enough in modern times, but that can be very alive for the children through their studies of natural history.

You can awaken the concept of what is universally human in the following way. Describe Leonardo's *Last Supper* and what he wanted to achieve with that picture—it is actually there only in a sense, there are only some little specks of color left in Milan. Today, unless you can see clairvoyantly, you cannot understand what he wanted to achieve, but the thought of the picture still exists. You can enliven your presentation by placing the picture in front of the children. You can make clear to the children that there are twelve human beings, twelve people pictured by the artist as the twelve apostles surrounding the Lord in the middle, in their positions with various attitudes, from the devoted John to the traitorous Judas. In a certain sense, you can develop all human characters from these twelve pictures. You can show the children how different human characters are, and then indicate how the Lord in the middle relates to each of the individuals. You can then have the children imagine someone coming from another planet.

Of course, you do not need to say it that way, but say it in some way so it is clear to them. If you imagine someone from a foreign planet coming down to earth and looking at all the pictures on earth, that being would need to look only at these twelve people and the transfigured face in the middle to know that that face has something to do with what gives the earth its meaning.

You can explain to the children that there was once a time during which the earth underwent a developmental preparation, followed by another time that had been awaited and that, in contrast to the preparatory period, provided a kind of fulfillment. You can show them that all of earthly human development is connected with that event of Golgotha, and that the earth's development would have no meaning if that event had not occurred. That is something that is also alive today and that we can very easily enliven, at least to the extent that it has withered during our half-heathen times. In short, it is important that you explain this second age of humanity. It is an age that developed through the rise of Christianity, through the rise of what is universally human. In contrast, the central purpose of the previous period was the creation of concepts and artistic perception, which could be developed only by an aristocracy, and has remained in its entirety as our inheritance.

When you take up Roman history, you can show how it has a tendency toward something that has hardly any significance as such. It would be clear to an objective observer of Roman history how great the distance is between the Roman people and those of Greece. The Greeks gave both the Romans and us everything that has endured. The Romans were actually students of the Greeks in everything of importance to humanity, and as such were a people without imagination. They were a people who had prepared themselves for the Christian concept of humanity only through the concept of the citizen. At this age you can teach children about the effects of Christianity upon Roman culture. You can also show them how the old world declined piece by piece, and how Christianity spread piece by piece in the West. In that way, the first millennium of Christianity acquires a kind of unified character, namely, the spreading of the concept of universal humanity. When you teach the children such a living, intense concept as the importance of Christianity in human development, then you also have the possibility of describing the whole modern age for these young human beings.

After the first thousand years of Christian European development, something new slowly begins. Something I would call very prosaic for us clearly begins to enter the development of humanity. Things will look quite different for those who follow us in a thousand years, but today, of course, we need to teach history for our period. We look back at ancient Greece and at something that may be heathen, namely, art and the life of ideas, and so forth. Then we look at the first thousand years of Christian development and find that the feeling life of Europe had just developed. What we find when we then look at what occurred after the first thousand years of Christian development is the development of European will. We see primarily that the activities of economics become an object of human thinking as well as a source of difficulties. Earlier times took care of these activities in a much more naïve way. In connection with that, you can attempt to show how the earth has become a level stage for human beings due to the voyages of discovery and the invention of printed books. You can also attempt to show that this latter period is the one in which we still stand. You will no longer be able to give a broad overview in the same way that you did for the Greek and Christian Roman periods, and their effects upon life in Central Europe. You will need to more or less allow everything that occurred from the eleventh or twelfth century forward to fall into the disarray of details. However, in doing this you will be able to awaken in children the proper feeling for the rise of national will during that period of history.

What do we accomplish when we do this? We do not teach causal history or pragmatic history or any of the other wonderful things people have admired at various times. Causal history assumes that what follows is always the result of some event preceding it. However, if you have a surface of water and you look at the waves, one following the other, can you say that each wave is the result of the one preceding it? Would you instead not need to look into the depths of the water to find the reasons, the general cause of the series of waves? It is no different in history. People look past what is most important when they look only for cause and effect. They look past the depths of human developmental forces that bring individual events to the surface in the course of time. We simply cannot present those events from the perspective of cause and effect. What occurs in one century is not simply the result of what occurred in previous centuries. It is, in fact, independent and only secondarily an effect. In my opinion, what occurs is brought independently to the surface out of the depths of the stream of human development.

We can give children an impression of this, and we should do so at this stage of their development. If people do not develop an awareness for these patterns during childhood, they can remain obstinate in their belief of pragmatic or causal history. They remain fixed in their understanding of history and later have little tendency to accept anything that has a real future. In contrast to all other presentations of history, we could call our presentation symptomatological history. Those who try to view history symptomatologically do not believe it is necessary to look at each individual event and describe it for itself. Instead, they see such events as symptoms of deeper development. They might say to themselves that if Gutenberg[1] lived and invented the art of printing books during a particular historical time, that was connected with what existed in the depths of humanity at that time. The invention of printing is only an indication that humanity at that time was mature enough to move on from certain simple concrete ideas to more abstract ones. If we come into life during a time that is held together more through printing than through direct and basic content, then we live life in a much more abstract manner.

The way life became more abstract during the course of historical events is seldom taken into account. Think for a moment about a simple example. I can say that my coat is shabby. Everyone can understand it when I say that my coat is shabby, but no one actually knows what that really means. What it means was originally connected with moths, with small insects.[2] At that time people hung their coats in the closet and did not brush them properly. These little insects lived in them and ate the cloth. The coat then had holes in it, and the word *shabby* arose from the destruction of coats by moths. There you have the transition from the concrete to the abstract. Such transition continually takes place and is something we should take note of. In the area in Austria where I grew up, the farmers spoke about "sleep in their eyes." For them, the sleep in their eyes was not something abstract in the way we think of it today when we say the sleep is in our eyes. The farmer rubbed his eyes, and what he rubbed out of the corners of his eyes in the morning, that specific excretion, he called "sleep." Those farmers do not have any other concept of sleep; they must first be taught the abstract idea of sleep.

Of course, such things are now dying out. Those of us who are older can remember such things from our youth, if we did not grow up in the city. We can remember how everything was concrete, but with the close of the nineteenth century, such things more or less died out. I could give you a number of such examples, and you would hardly believe that people in the country thought in such a concrete way. You can experience many curious things in the country. There is an Austrian poet[3] who wrote in dialect and wrote a number of beautiful things that are admired by all the city people. But only city people admire them; country people do not understand them. He used words the way city people use them—abstractly. People in the country do not understand his poetry at all because they have specific things in mind, so everything has a very different meaning. I recall, for example, that one of his poems speaks about nature. It is completely incomprehensible for farmers, because a farmer does not have the same concept of nature as an educated person. A farmer understands the word *nature* to mean something very concrete. In the same way, I can find examples everywhere that would show how the transition from the concrete to the abstract occurs throughout human development, and how a whole wave moving toward abstraction crashed in upon humanity with the rise of book printing. In a way, people began to filter their concepts through the influence of book printing.

It would not be bad to teach children some concepts of modern history that would make them more objective about life. There would be, for example, much less discussion about battling capitalism and so forth if the people who said such things did not speak as though they had never heard anything about capitalism, and had no idea that to simply angrily attack capitalism has absolutely no meaning. It has nothing to do with what people today really want; it only shows that such people do not properly understand the significance of capitalism. My books such as *Social Renewal* seem so unintelligible to them because they were written about life and not about the fantastic ideas of modern agitators.

A truly living consideration of history requires that people understand external events as symptoms of something hidden within, and they need some idea of what considering those symptoms means. When you consider history from a symptomatological perspective, you will slowly realize that first there is an ascent, then the highest point of a certain event is reached, and then a descent follows. Take, for example, the event of Golgotha. If you look at that part of history and see the external events as symptoms of an inner process, you rise above the purely historical into the religious. The historical thus deepens into the religious. Then, you will find a way that will lead you through feeling into an understanding of what we can teach children at an early age, for instance, the Gospels or the Old Testament. However, we cannot give them an inner understanding of such things, nor is that necessary. You teach them in the form of stories, and when the children have a living, historical feeling for the stories, the material in the Bible takes on a new life. It is good when certain things gain their full liveliness only in stages. Primarily though, considering history symptomatologically deepens a desire for religion, a feeling for religion.

I said before that we should prepare children for learning history by teaching them about nature and that we should proceed in the way I characterized earlier. At the same time, we prepare children for life on earth by teaching them about botany in the way I described. We can then go on to geography at this stage of childhood. We should base geography upon stories describing various areas, including far distant places, for example, America or Africa. Through our descriptions of natural history, that have presented the plant realm as part of the entire earth, the children are prepared by about the age of twelve to understand geography. At this time it is important to show in geography that everything in history depends upon all the things that come from the earth —the climates, the formations, the structures of the earth in various places. After giving them an idea about the connection of land, sea, and climate to ancient Greece, you can move on to what we can portray as a symptom of the inner development of humanity in the characteristics of ancient Greece. It is possible to find an inner connection between our geographical picture of the earth and historical developments. Actually, we should always make inner connections between our descriptions of various parts of the earth and our descriptions of historical developments. We should not, for example, discuss

American geography before we have presented the discovery of America in history. We should certainly take into account the fact that the human horizon has extended in the course of development, and we should not try to bring human feelings to some firm absolute point.

Nor is it good in so-called mathematical geography to begin dogmatically with a drawing of the Copernican solar system. Instead we should begin by describing for the children, at least as a sketch, how people came to such a perspective. In that way children do not learn concepts that are beyond the level of their human development. Of course, people taught children the fixed Ptolemaic concepts when the Ptolemaic view of the world predominated. Now we teach them the Copernican perspective. It is certainly necessary to give children at least some idea about how people determined the positions of the stars in the sky and, from a summarization of those positions, came to some conclusion that then became a description of the planetary system. We do not want the children to believe, for example, that such a description of the planetary system came about by someone sitting in a chair outside of the universe and simply looking at the planets. When you draw the Copernican system on the blackboard as though it were a fact, how can a child imagine how people came to that view? Children need to have some living idea about how such things develop; otherwise they will go through their entire lives with confused ideas, which they believe are absolutely certain. That is how a false belief in authority develops, something that does not occur when you develop a proper feeling for authority between the ages of seven until fourteen or fifteen.

In the same way it is good to recognize that it is not only significant for the development of the children's souls to teach them the proper ideas at the proper moment, but that it also has a significance for the entire human being, including healthy physical functioning. Try to think for a moment what it means to teach a child between the ages of seven and twelve exactly the amount of material he or she can remember, or to not do that. Try to understand what it means when you misuse the so-called good memory of a child. You should not work to strengthen the memory of a child who has a good memory. Instead you should be careful to see that the child often receives new impressions that erase earlier impressions. If you emphasize memory too strongly, the child will grow stocky and not as tall as he or she would if you worked with memory in the proper way. The restrained growth you can see in people is due to an improper working with their memory. In the same way people who are incapable of controlling their facial expressions, or who have a certain fixed expression, did not receive sufficient artistic or aesthetic impressions around the age of nine.

Particularly during childhood, the effects upon the physical body of properly working with the soul are enormous. It is enormously important that you try to see that children speak clearly and with full tones and, as I described before, that they speak well-roundedly, in full sentences and with full syllables. In human beings, proper breathing depends upon proper speaking; thus the proper development of the human chest organs depends upon proper speaking. In this regard it would be interesting to take a survey about the currently common chest illnesses. We could ask to what extent tuberculosis is the result of too little attention to proper speaking while attending school or too little attention to proper breathing while speaking. We should remember that speaking does not begin with breathing, but the other way around. Children should therefore speak properly. They should acquire a feeling for proper speech, for long and short syllables and words, and their breathing will develop accordingly. It is pure nonsense to believe that we should first train breathing in order to then come to proper speaking. Breathing, proper breathing, results from a proper feeling for speech, which then brings about proper breathing. In just this way, we should look more thoroughly at the connections between the physical body and the development of the spirit-soul.

I would now like to turn to a question I have often been asked, which has some significance, the question of lefthandedness and ambidextrousness.

Righthandedness has become a general human habit that we use for writing and other tasks. It is appropriate to extend that by making the left hand more dexterous, in a sense. That has a certain justification. When we discuss such things, however, our discussion will bear fruit only if we have some deeper insight into the conditions of human life.

When we move into a period when the entire human being should be awakened; when, in addition to the capacities for abstraction that are so well developed today, developing the capacities for feeling as well as for doing plays a role, we will be able to speak quite differently about many questions than we can now.

If education continues as it is today and does not help us understand the material through the spiritual, so that people are always stuck in abstractions (materialism is precisely being stuck in abstractions), then after a time you will realize that teaching people to use both hands for writing traps them in a kind of mental weakness. This results in part from how we are as modern human beings, how we presently use the right hand to a much greater extent than the left. The fact that the whole human being is not completely symmetrical also plays a part, particularly in regard to certain organs. Using both hands to write, for example, has a deep effect upon the entire human organism.

I would not speak about such things had I not done considerable research in this area and had I not tried, for example, to understand what it means to use the left hand. When people develop a capacity for observing the human being, they will be able to see through experimenting what it means to use the left hand. When human beings reach a certain level of independence of the spirit and the soul from the physical body, it is good to use the left hand. But the dependence of modern people upon the physical body causes a tremendous revolution in the physical body when the left hand is used in the same manner as the right, for example, in writing. One of the most important points in this regard is that this stresses the right side of the body, the right side of the brain, beyond what modern people can normally tolerate. When people have been taught according to the methods and educational principles we have discussed here, then they may also be ambidextrous. In modern society, we may not simply go on to using both hands; however, these are things that can be said only from experience. Statistics would certainly support what I have said.

If you want an idea of how strongly the effects of the spirit-soul act in parallel with the physical body of the child, then we need to look to the spiritual world. That is why I find eurythmy so promising in educating children, because eurythmy is an ensouled movement and thus increases the activity of the will, in contrast to the normal passivity of the will, which is what normal gymnastics primarily trains.

13

CHILDREN'S PLAY

Basel, May 10, 1920

We have already seen that teaching history is beneficial only for developing children at about the age of twelve. Considering history is a kind of preparation for the period of life that begins with sexual maturity, that is, at about the age of fourteen or fifteen. Only at that time can human beings gain the capacity for independent reasoning. A capacity for reasoning, not simply intellectual reasoning, but a comprehensive reasoning in all directions, can only develop after puberty. With the passing of puberty, the supersensible aspect of human nature that carries the capacity of reason is born out of the remainder of human nature. You can call this what you like. In my books I have called it the *astral body*, but the name is unimportant. As I have said, it is not through intellectual judgment that this becomes noticeable, but through judgment in its broadest sense. You will perhaps be surprised that what I will now describe I also include in the realm of judgment. If we were to do a thorough study of psychology here, you would also see that what I have to say can also be proven psychologically.

When we attempt to have a child who is not yet past puberty recite something according to his or her own taste, we are harming the developmental forces within human nature. These forces will be harmed if an attempt is made to use them before the completion of puberty; they should only be used later. Independent judgments of taste are only possible after puberty. If a child before the age of fourteen or fifteen is to recite something, she should do so on the basis of what an accepted authority standing next to her has provided. This means she should find the way in which the authority has spoken pleasing. She should not be led astray to emphasize or not emphasize certain words, to form the rhythm out of what she thinks is pleasing, but instead she should be guided by the taste of the accepted authority. We should not attempt to guide that intimate area of the child's life away from accepted authority before the completion of puberty. Notice that I always say "accepted authority" because I certainly do not mean a forced or blind authority. What I am saying is based upon the objective observation that from the change of teeth until puberty, a child has a desire to have an authority standing alongside her. The child demands this, longs for it, and we need to support this longing, which arises out of her individuality.

When you look at such things in a comprehensive way, you will see that in my outline of education here I have always taken the entire development of the human being into account. For this reason I have said that between the ages of seven and fourteen, we should only teach children what can be used in a fruitful way throughout life. We need to see how one stage of life affects another. In a moment I will give an example that speaks to this point. When a child is long past school age, has perhaps long since reached adulthood, this is when we can see what school has made of the child and what it has not. This is visible not only in a general abstract way but also in a very concrete way.

Let us look at children's play from this perspective, particularly the kind of play that occurs in the youngest children from birth until the change of teeth. Of course, the play of such children is in one respect based upon their desire to imitate. Children do what they see adults doing, only they do it differently. They play in such a way that their activities lie far from the goals and utility that adults connect with certain activities. Children's play only imitates the form of adult activities, not the material content. The usefulness in and connection to everyday life are left out. Children perceive a kind of satisfaction in activities that are closely related to those of adults. We can look into this further and ask what is occurring here. If we want to study what is represented by play activities and through that study recognize true human nature so that we can have a practical effect upon it, then we must continuously review the individual activities of the child, including those that are transferred to the physical organs and, in a certain sense, form them. That is not so easy. Nevertheless the study of children's play in the widest sense is extraordinarily important for education.

We need only recall what a person who set the tone for culture once said: "A human being is only a human being so long as he or she plays; and a human being plays so long as he or she is a whole human being." Schiller[1] wrote these words in a letter after he had read some sections of Goethe's *Wilhelm Meister.* To Schiller, free play and the forces of the soul as they are artistically developed in *Wilhelm Meister* appeared to be something that could only be compared with an adult form of children's play. This formed the basis of Schiller's *Letters on the Aesthetic Education of Man.* He wrote them from the perspective that adults are never fully human when carrying out the activities of normal life. He believed that either we follow the necessities of what our senses require of us, in which case we are subject to a certain compulsion, or we follow logical necessity, in which case we are no longer free. Schiller thought that we are free only when we are artistically creative. This is certainly understandable from an artist such as Schiller; however, it is one-sided since in regard to freedom of the soul there is certainly much which occurs inwardly, in much the same way that Schiller understood freedom. Nevertheless the kind of life that Schiller imagined for the artist is arranged so that the human being experiences the spiritual as though it were natural and necessary, and the sense-perceptible as though it were spiritual. This is certainly the case when perceiving something artistic and in the creation of art.

When creating art, we create with the material world, but we do not create something that is useful. We create in the way the idea demands of us, if I may state it that way, but we do not create abstract ideas according to logical necessity. In the creation of art, we are in the same situation as we are when we are hungry or thirsty. We are subject to a very personal necessity. Schiller found that it is possible for people to achieve something of that sort in life, but children have this naturally through play. Here in a certain sense they live in the world of adults, through only to the extent that world satisfies the child's own individuality. The child lives in creation, but what is created serves nothing.

Schiller's perspective, from the end of the eighteenth and beginning of the nineteenth century, can be used as a basis for further development. The psychological significance of play is not so easy to find. We need to ask if the particular kind of play that children engage in before the change of teeth has some significance for the entirety of human life. We can, as I said, analyze it in the way that Schiller tried to do under the influence of Goethe's adult childishness. We could also, however, compare this kind of play with other human activities. We could, for example, compare children's play before the change of teeth with dreaming, where we most certainly will find some important analogies. However, those analogies are simply related to the course of the child's play, to the connection of the activities to one another in play. In just the same way that children put things together in play—whatever those might be—not with external things but with thoughts, we put pictures together in dreams.

This may not be true of all dreams, but it is certainly so in a very large class of them. In dreaming, we remain in a certain sense children throughout our entire lives.

Nevertheless we can only achieve a genuine understanding if we do not simply dwell upon this comparison of play with dreams. Instead we should also ask when in the life of the human being something occurs that allows those forces that are developed in early children's play until the change of teeth, which can be fruitful for the entirety of external human life. In other words, when do we actually reap the fruits of children's play? Usually people think we need to seek the fruits of young children's play in the period of life that immediately follows, but spiritual science shows how life passes in a rhythmical series of repetitions. In a plant, leaves develop from a seed; from the leaves, the bud and flower petals emerge, and so forth. Only afterwards do we have a seed again; that is, the repetition occurs only after an intervening development. It is the same in human life.

From many points of view we could understand human life as though each period were affected only by the one preceding, but this is not the case. If we observe without prejudice, we will find that the actual fruits of those activities that occur in early childhood play become apparent only at the age of twenty. What we gain in play from birth until the change of teeth, what children experience in a dreamy way, are forces of the still-unborn spirituality of the human being, which is still not yet absorbed into, or perhaps more properly said, *reabsorbed* into the human body.

We can state this differently. I have already discussed how the same forces that act organically upon the human being until the change of teeth become, when the teeth are born, an independent imaginative or thinking capacity, so that in a certain sense something is removed from the physical body. On the other hand, what is active within a child through play and has no connection with life and contains no usefulness is something that is not yet fully connected with the human body. Thus a child has an activity of the soul that is active within the body until the change of teeth and then becomes apparent as a capacity for forming concepts that can be remembered.

The child also has a spiritual-soul activity that in a certain sense still hovers in an etheric way over the child. It is active in play in much the same way that dreams are active throughout the child's entire life. In children, however, this activity occurs not simply in dreams, it occurs also in play, which develops in external reality. What thus develops in external reality subsides in a certain sense. In just the same way that the seed-forming forces of a plant subside in the leaf and flower petal and only reappear in the fruit, what a child uses in play also only reappears at about the age of twenty-one or twenty-two, as independent reasoning gathering experiences in life.

I would like to ask you to try to genuinely seek this connection. Look at children and try to understand what is individual in their play: try to understand the individuality of children playing freely until the change of teeth, and then form pictures of their individualities. Assume that what you notice in their play will become apparent in their independent reasoning after the age of twenty. This means the various kinds of human beings differ in their independent reasoning after the age of twenty in the just the same way that children differ in their play before the change of teeth.

If you recognize the full truth of this thought, you will be overcome by an unbounded feeling of responsibility in regard to teaching. You will realize that what you do with a child forms the human being beyond the age of twenty. You will see that you will need to understand the entirety of life, not simply the life of children, if you want to create a proper education.

Playing activity from the change of teeth until puberty is something else again. (Of course, things are not so rigidly separated, but if we want to understand something for use in practical life, we must separate things.) Those who observe without prejudice will find that the play activity of a child until the age of seven has an individual character. As a player, the child is, in a certain sense, a kind of hermit. The child plays for itself alone. Certainly children want some help, but they are terribly egotistical and want the help only for themselves. With the change of teeth, play takes on a more social aspect. With some individual exceptions, children now want to play more with one another. The child ceases to be a hermit in his play; he wants to play with other children and to be something in play. I am not sure if Switzerland can be included in this, but in more military countries the boys particularly like to play soldier. Mostly they want to be at least a general, and thus a social element is introduced to the children's play.

What occurs as the social element in play from the change of teeth until puberty is a preparation for the next period of life. In this next period, with the completion of puberty, independent reasoning arises. At that time human beings no longer subject themselves to authority; they form their own judgments and confront others as individuals. This same element appears in the previous period of life in play; it appears in something that is not connected with external social life, but in play. What occurs in the previous period of life, namely, social play, is the prelude to tearing yourself away from authority. We can therefore conclude that children's play until the age of seven actually enters the body only at the age of twenty-one or twenty-two, when we gain an independence in our understanding and ability to judge experiences. On the other hand, what is prepared through play between the ages of seven and puberty appears at an earlier developmental stage in life, namely, during the period from puberty until about the age of twenty-one. This is a direct continuation. It is very interesting to notice that we have properly guided play during our first childhood years to thank for the capacities that we later have for understanding and experiencing life. In contrast, for what appears during our lazy or rebellious years we can thank the period from the change of teeth until puberty. Thus the connections in the course of human life overlap.

These overlapping connections have a fundamental significance of which psychology is unaware. What we today call psychology has existed only since the eighteenth century. Previously, quite different concepts existed about human beings and the human soul. Psychology developed during the period in which materialistic spirit and thought arose. Thus in spite of all significant beginnings, psychology was unable to develop a proper science of the soul, a science that was in accord with reality and took into account the whole of human life. Although I have tried hard, I have to admit that I have been able to find some of these insights only in Herbart's psychology. Herbart's psychology is very penetrating; it attempts to discover a certain form of the soul by beginning with the basic elements of the soul's life. There are many beautiful things in Herbart's psychology. Nevertheless we need to look at the rather unusual views it has produced in his followers. I once knew a very good follower of Herbart, Robert Zimmermann,[2] an aesthete who also wrote a kind of educational philosophy in his book on psychology for high-school students. Herbart once referred to him as a Kantian from 1828. In his description of psychology as a student of Herbart, he discusses the following problem:

If I am hungry, I do not actually attempt to obtain the food that would satisfy my hunger. Instead, my goal is that the idea of hunger will cease and be replaced by the idea of being full. My concern is actually with ideas. There exists an idea that must arise contrary to inhibitions, and which must work against those inhibitions. Food is actually only a means of moving from the idea of hunger to the idea of being full.

Those who look at the reality of human nature, not simply in a materialistic sense, but also with an eye toward the spiritual, will see that this kind of view is somewhat one-sidedly rationalistic and intellectual. It is necessary to move beyond this one-sided intellectualism and comprehend the entire human being psychologically. In so doing, education can gain much from psychology that otherwise would not be apparent. We should consider what we do in teaching not simply to be the right thing for the child, but rather to be something living that can transform itself. As we have seen, there are many connections of the sort I have presented. We need to assume that what we teach children in elementary school until puberty will reappear in a quite different form from the age of fifteen until twenty-one or twenty-two.

The elementary-school teacher is extremely important for the high-school teacher or the university teacher—in a sense even more important, since the university teacher can achieve nothing if the elementary-school teacher has not sent the child forth with properly formed strengths. It is very important to work with these connected periods of life. If we do, we will see that real beginning points can be found only through spiritual science.

For instance, people define things too much. As far as possible, we should avoid giving children any definitions. Definitions take a firm grasp of the soul and remain static throughout life, thus making life into something dead. We should teach in such a way that what we provide to the child's soul remains alive. Suppose someone as a child of around nine or ten years of age learns a concept, for instance, at the age of nine, the concept of a lion, or, at the age of eleven or twelve, that of Greek culture. Very good; the child learns it. But these concepts should not remain as they are. A person at the age of thirty should not be able to say she has such-and-such a concept of lions and that is what she learned in school, or that she has such-and-such a concept of Greek culture and that was what she learned in school. This is something we need to overcome. Just as other parts of ourselves grow, the things we receive from the teacher should also grow; they should be something living. We should learn concepts about lions or Greek culture that will not be the same when we are in our thirties or forties as they were when we were in school.

We should learn concepts that are so living that they are transformed throughout our lives. To do so, we need to characterize rather than define. In connection with the formation of concepts, we need to imitate what we can do with painting or even photography. In such cases, we can place ourselves to one side and give one aspect, or we can move to another side and give a different aspect, and so forth. Only after we have photographed a tree from many sides do we have a proper picture of it. Through definitions, we gain too strong an idea that we have something.

We should attempt to work with thoughts and concepts as we would with a camera. We should bring forth the feeling within the child that we are only characterizing something from various perspectives; we are not defining it. Definitions exist only so that we can, in a sense, begin with them and so that the child can communicate understandably with the teacher. That is the basic reason for definitions. That may sound somewhat radical, but it is so. Life does not love definitions. In private, human beings should always have the feeling that, through incorrect definitions, they have arrived at dogmas. It is very important for teachers to know that. Instead of saying, for instance, that two objects cannot be in the same place at the same time, and that is what we call *impermeable*, the way we consciously define impermeability and then seek things to illustrate this concept, we should instead say that objects are impermeable because they cannot be at the same place at the same time. We should not make hypotheses into dogmas. We only have the right to say that we call objects impermeable when they cannot be at the same place at the same time. We need to remain conscious of the formative forces of our souls and should not awaken the concept of a triangle in the external world before the child has recognized a triangle inwardly.

That we should characterize and not define is connected with recognizing that the fruits of those things that occur during one period of human life will be recognized perhaps only very much later. Thus we should give children living concepts and feelings rather than dead ones. We should try to present geometry, for example, in as lively a way as possible. A few days ago I spoke about arithmetic. I want to speak before the end of the course tomorrow about working with fractions and so forth, but now I would like to add a few remarks about geometry. These remarks are connected with a question I was asked and also with what I have just presented.

Geometry can be seen as something that can slowly be brought from a static state into a living one. In actuality, we are speaking of something quite general when we say that the sum of the angles of a triangle is 180°. That is true for all triangles, but can we imagine a triangle? In our modern way of educating, we do not always attempt to teach children a flexible concept of a triangle. It would be good, however, if we teach our children a flexible concept of a triangle, not simply a dead concept. We should not have them simply draw a triangle, which is always a special case. Instead we could say that here I have a line. I can divide the angle of 180° into three parts. That can be done in an endless number of ways. Each time I have divided the angle, I can go on to form a triangle, so that I show the child how an angle that occurs here then occurs here in the triangle. When I transfer the angles in this way, I will have such a triangle. Thus in moving from three fan-shaped angles lying next to one another, I can form numerous triangles and those triangles thus become flexible in the imagination. Clearly these triangles have the characteristic that the sum of their angles is 180° since they arose by dividing a 180° angle. It is good to awaken the idea of a triangle of a child in this way, so that an inner flexibility remains and so that they do not gain the idea of a static triangle, but rather that of a flexible shape, one that could just as well be acute as obtuse, or it could be a right triangle (see diagram).

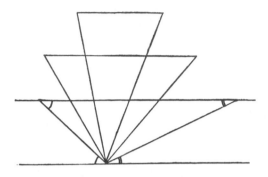

Imagine how transparent the whole concept of triangles would be if I began with such inwardly flexible concepts, then developed triangles from them. We can use the same method to develop a genuine and concrete feeling for space in children. If in this way we have taught children the concept of flexibility in figures on a plane, the entire mental configuration of the child will achieve such flexibility that it is then easy to go on to three-dimensional elements—for instance, how one object moves past another behind it, forward or backward. By presenting how an object moves forward or backward past another object, we present the first element that can be used in developing a feeling for space. If we, for example, present how it is in real life—namely how one person ceases to be visible when he or she moves behind an object or how the object becomes no longer visible when the person moves in front of it—we can go on to develop a feeling for space that has an inner liveliness to it. The feeling for three-dimensional space remains abstract and dead when it is presented only as per-spectives. The children can gain that lively feeling for space if, for instance, we tell a short story.

This morning at nine o'clock I came across two people.

They were sitting someplace on a bench. This afternoon at three, I came by again and the same two people were sitting on the same bench. Nothing had changed.

Certainly as long as I only consider the situation at nine in the morning and three in the afternoon, nothing had changed. However, if I go into it more and speak with these people, then perhaps I would discover that after I had left in the morning, one person remained, but the other stood up and went away. Though he was gone for three hours, he then returned and sat down again alongside the other. He had done something and was perhaps tired after six hours. I cannot recognize the actual situation only in connection with space, that is, if I think only of the external situation and do not look further into the inner, to the more important situation.

We cannot make judgments even about the spatial relationships between beings if we do not go into inner relationships. We can avoid bitter illusions in regard to cause and effect only if we go into those inner relationships. The following might occur: A man is walking along the bank of a river and comes across a stone. He stumbles over the stone and falls into the river. After a time he is pulled out. Suppose that nothing more is done than to report the objective facts: Mr. So-and-So has drowned. But perhaps that is not even true. Perhaps the man did not drown, but instead stumbled because at that point he had a heart attack and was already dead before he fell into the water. He fell into the water because he was dead. This is an actual case that was once looked into and shows how necessary it is to proceed from external circumstances into the more inner aspects.

In the same way if we are to make judgments about the spatial relationship of one being to another, we need to go into the inner aspects of those beings. When properly grasped in a living way, it enables us to develop a spatial feeling in children so that we can use movements for the development of a feeling for space. We can do that by having the children run in different figures, or having them observe how people move in front or behind when passing one another.

It is particularly important to make sure that what is observed in this way is also retained. This is especially significant for the development of a feeling for space. If I cast a shadow from different objects upon the surface of other objects, I can show how the shadow changes. If children are capable of understanding why, under specific circumstances, the shadow of a sphere has the shape of an ellipse—and this is certainly something that can be understood by a child at the age of nine—this capacity to place themselves in such spatial relationships has a tremendously important effect upon their capacity to imagine and upon the flexibility of their imaginations.

For that reason we should certainly see that it is necessary to develop a feeling for space in school. If we ask ourselves what children do when they are drawing up until the change of teeth, we will discover that they are in fact developing experience that then becomes mature understanding around the age of twenty. That understanding develops out of the changing forms, so the child plays by drawing; at the same time, however, that drawing tells something. We can understand children's drawings if we recognize that they reflect what the child wants to express.

Let us look at children's drawings. Before the ages of seven or eight or sometimes even nine, children do not have a proper feeling for space. That comes only later when other forces slowly begin to affect the child's development. Until the age of seven, what affects the child's functioning later becomes imagination. Until puberty, it is the will that mostly affects the child and which, as I mentioned earlier, is dammed up and becomes apparent through boys' change of voice. The will is capable of developing spatial feeling. Through everything that I have just said, that is, through the development of a spatial feeling through movement games and by observing what occurs when shadows are formed—namely, through what arises through movement and is then held fast—all such things that develop the will give people a much better understanding than simply through an intellectual presentation, even though that understanding may be somewhat playful, an understanding with a desire to tell a story.

Now, at the end of this lecture, I would like to show you the drawings of a six-year-old boy whose father, I should mention, is a painter so that you can see them in connection with what I just said. Please notice how extraordinarily talkative this six-year-old boy is through what he creates. I might even say that he has in fact created a very specific language here, a language that expresses just what he wants to tell. Many of these pictures, which we could refer to as expressionist, are simply his way of telling stories that were read to him, or which he heard in some other way. Many of the pictures are, as you can see, wonderfully expressive. Take a look at this king and queen. These are things that show how children at this age tell stories. If we understand how children speak at this age—something that is so wonderfully represented here because the boy is already drawing with colored pencils—and if we look at all the details, we will find that these drawings represent the child's being in much the way that I described to you earlier. We need to take the change that occurred with the change of teeth into consideration if we are to understand how we can develop a feeling for space.

14

FURTHER PERSPECTIVES AND ANSWERS TO QUESTIONS

Basel, May 11, 1920

I would be very sorry if anything I have said here were to be taken dogmatically or to become one-sided in some way. That spiritual science can be fruitful for education is the basis of everything I have said. Anthroposophy could help teaching and education to gain a more living character, and the general directions I have described here can be put into practice in many ways. It would be good if there were an exchange of opinions among the listeners as well as others who are interested in some way in the further development of education as it is conceived here. It is important to arrive at what is necessary in our time through a living comprehension of human development as a whole and of present developments in education. We are not concerned with developing a new formal basis for education, but rather with extending the circle of people who have an interest in the perspective presented with regard to human development.

What is the state of the development of humanity today? What must we teach children if we are to take into account the perspective of the present state of humanity today and of the near future? If we do not recognize what has recently occurred as a clear indication of the need of a renewal in education, we do not understand our present time.

Of course there are an uncountable number of details to mention. Consider for a moment how appropriate it would be to include my characterization of arithmetic—to place analytical methods alongside synthetic methods, and to work with the sum and products and not simply from adding and factoring—along with what is normally done. You can see how appropriate it would be to treat fractions and everything connected with them from this perspective. When we move from working with whole numbers to working with fractions, we move in a quite natural way into the analytical. Moving from whole numbers to fractions means just that: analyzing. It is therefore appropriate to bring in another element when working with fractions than we use when working with whole numbers.

We certainly cannot object to the fact that in the nineteenth century computing machines were introduced into schools. Nevertheless computing machines should not lead to an overly materialistic valuation of illustrative materials. While we should be clear about the value of examples, what is important is that human capacities be developed through teaching. The primary task of the period from the change of teeth until maturity is to develop memory. We should avoid underestimating the value of examples as a basis for forming memory as well as the value of memory when viewing examples. We should begin in a simple way—and here for those who are capable of teaching in a living way, the ten fingers on our hands are sufficient—by presenting the number ten in all kinds of ways that show the various arithmetic operations. In doing so, however, we should present arithmetic in a way that is appropriate to life, to the life of the soul in a human being.

There are certainly detailed discussions in philosophy, whole sections of philosophy, concerning what a number or fraction really is. This shows that as children, we may learn about numbers or fractions, but in later life, even if we were philosophers, we could say that we now need to research what a number signifies in reality, or what a fraction is in reality. It is not necessary to go into all kinds of minute details if we want to make this process clear to children. Instead we need to bring many other things to children that then become part of their memory and which only can be studied in more detail later, when they are mature enough. I have already spoken about such things from another perspective.

Working with fractions is another question. Since fractions are in a certain sense analytical, we need to take the need for analysis into account, as I mentioned in some of the previous lectures. For that reason, we would do well to make working with fractions as visual as possible. We could perhaps divide a large cube into smaller cubes, for example, taking a large cube and dividing it into sixteen smaller cubes. From that, we can go on to the concept of a quarter by dividing the large cube first into quarters, then each quarter again into a further quarter. In this way you can show the children all kinds of relationships between a sixteenth or an eighth and so forth. If, later, you give each of the portions a different color, you can then place the various fractions of the larger cube together again in different way, which then gives a very pretty picture.

I do not want to make the transition from normal fractions to decimal fractions in some irrational way, in a way that does not correspond to reality. From the very beginning, the children should gain a feeling that the use of decimal fractions is based upon human convention or convenience. They should also gain a feeling that the way we write decimal fractions is nothing more than a continuation of the way in which we write normal numbers: we first count to ten and then, when we go on to twenty, which is twice ten, the first series of ten is included in that so that by going to twenty, we have simply added a new series of ten, and so forth. If we work toward the left using the same principle that we used when working with decimal numbers to the right, the children will realize that all this is relative and that it would form a unity if I set the decimal point two places to the right.

From the very beginning, we should teach children about these conventions, which are hidden in the way we divide things. In this way many other kinds of conventions then fit into the social fabric. Many erroneous beliefs in authority would disappear if we show the children that everything that is based simply upon tradition is nothing more than social convention. Most important, however, is that through a spiritual-scientific permeation of education, we attempt to work with children during the period from the change of teeth until puberty by taking into account everything that I have said here about that period of life and how different capacities appear in different periods.

In addition, we need to give children an idea of the practicalities of life. Each topic in our teaching should be used to guide the children to a view of practical life. If we understand children properly, we will begin to teach them about physics and chemistry at around the age of twelve as well as teaching them about minerals in the way I have discussed here. At about the same time, or perhaps one year earlier, we might attempt to present arithmetic similarly to the way we would teach about minerals, physics, or chemistry, namely, by always taking the practical into account. In arithmetic, the children should gain an idea about how monetary exchange rates work—what a discount rate is, how financial accounts are held. They should learn about writing letters describing business and financial practices or relationships with another business. Instruction from the ages of twelve until about fourteen or fifteen needs to be arranged that by the time children are fifteen years old and leave grammar school to go on to a higher school or into life, they have a real and practical idea about the most important areas of life.

Some may object by saying, where are we to find the time for all this? How are we to find time to give children a real idea of how paper or soap or cigars or such things are manufactured? If we are well-organized, we can take typical examples, such as typical industries or typical methods of transportation. We can enable children to go out into the world with an understanding of all the major areas in the environment that confront them. We can certainly see how children from the city have not the slightest idea of the difference between rye and wheat. We can also see how children who do not live near a soap factory do not have the slightest idea of how soap is made. But even children who live near a soap factory still have no idea how soap is manufactured because they have been taught nothing about what is in their neighborhood.

Consider how many people today step onto or leave a streetcar without having even the dimmest idea of how a streetcar is made or how it moves and so forth. Generally speaking, today we use the products of our culture without having the slightest idea of what these products actually are.[1] For this reason we have become anxious. If we are continuously surrounded by things we do not understand, we become confused, and that confusion has an effect upon our subconscious. Of course it is not possible for people to understand everything in modern life in all details. But everything that is not directly connected with our own jobs or professions should not remain a mystery. If a person is not a bookkeeper, generally accounting is a mystery. Or if a person is not a teacher, how school is held is a mystery. All those things that fragment our modern society need to be overcome. We need to understand one another again.

We should not allow children's capacities to understand practical life to lie fallow. During the period beginning at the age of twelve, when the capacities for human reason develop, it is possi-

234

ble to teach children about the most important aspects of practical life. I do not know what the subjects for essays are here in Switzerland (though I have read the school curriculum), but in the former monarchical countries, instead of writing essays about frivolous subjects such as the monarch's birthday, essays should be written that somehow involve business life, sales practices, or industrial questions.

This is certainly not an area that should be based upon idealism or some intellectual perspective. A spiritual perspective does not need to continuously emphasize ideals and how they should be taught. Instead a spiritual attitude can be held by having the students work out of a spiritual impulse, that is, by allowing that which desires to arise out of the spirit from year to year to rise to the surface. In that way the overall perspective is connected with the individual details.

I have been asked whether it is possible to explain the late eruption of the wisdom teeth from a spiritual-scientific perspective. Is the growth of wisdom teeth connected with the freeing of certain cognitive forces in the same way as the regular change of teeth?

The change of teeth indicates that certain forces, which previously permeated the entire organism and gave it strength, have now become free and have become, as I have explained to you earlier, the forces of independent thinking. We certainly cannot strictly encapsulate everything that occurs in the organism, as that would certainly be contrary to the way things develop. The things that are primary during one period of human development continue to exist, but to a much lesser extent. We grow wisdom teeth much later because at a later time in the life of our organism there is something that continues to work that was particularly active up to the age of seven. Some small amount must still remain. If everything were suddenly completed, then people would experience a very strong jolt every time they would want to begin thinking of something. When we begin to think about something, we voluntarily activate those forces that were involuntarily active in the organism before the age of seven. Those things must exist as a bridge between the separated realms of the spirit soul. What was organic at that time must continue to exist to a certain extent. For imaginative thinking we need to become independent, but at the same time we still need to be connected to our organism. That is what is expressed by the late eruption of the wisdom teeth. Some of the strength that is freed for imaginative thinking still remains in organic development. We could discover all kinds of things in human development that are similar to the situation with wisdom teeth.

Another interesting question was posed: to what extent is it possible for teachers working out of a spiritual-scientific pedagogy to help children recognize their capacities and find their right place in social life?

From the perspective of spiritual science, such questions are of little importance, since they are based upon rationalistic and materialistic thinking. In fact we have to protect children from situations where they might pose such abstract questions as, how can I find my proper place in life based upon my own capacities? Children need to slowly come to such decisions through all the stages associated with feeling. If some day the abstract question of how can we utilize our capacities in the service of humanity should arise in our soul, that is actually an illness of the soul. We need to grow slowly into our relationship to the development of humanity and to other human beings. We will do that if we have been brought up in the way I described here. In that case, we would never fall into the unwholesome situation of asking, how can I be of social service with my specific capacities? We would have a healthy, practical understanding by the time we leave grammar school, so we would recognize that life itself will present us with our position in it. The fact that such questions arise and are seriously discussed shows how much we have fallen into an intellectual and materialistic way of thinking in our time.

For that reason, I would like to mention how concrete general rules can always be developed into practical action if we have the will to do so. I would therefore like to answer in detail a question given to me about what we should do about those who are weak in spelling where the weakness arises in words where what is written is not clearly indicated, for example, whether an *h* or an *e* is in the word to form a longer sound.

As I already mentioned, training in clear listening is the basis of proper spelling. Training in proper hearing will support proper spelling. Clear hearing, if trained properly, will also train precise seeing. The different capacities support one another. If one capacity is developed in the proper way, the others will also have to develop properly. If we accustom ourselves to exact listening, we will tend to retain the appearance of the word as such, that is, its inner appearance. Exact listening supports exact seeing. For words that appear to have an arbitrary spelling, such as those that have silent letters that make the preceding vowel long, we can support the child's proper spelling by having the child repeat the syllables of the word clearly and with varying emphasis.

I would ask you not to take what I have just said in a dogmatic way. Instead you should take it so that it can be used in many various ways. For example, someone may view the position of the Greeks in the general course of Western culture differently than I did in my discussion of teaching history a few days ago. Someone could have a very different perspective but could nonetheless present it with the same methods I used. For me, it is not important to say something dogmatic about the Greeks. I wanted to show how a particular perspective about one topic or another could be taught through a symptomatological understanding of history. I believe that it is particularly necessary for teachers today to be aware of how much we need to allow the spirit and the influences of the spiritual upon the totality of human activity to flow into teaching. We need to look without prejudice at what children bring with them if we are to raise them as they need to be raised so that the next generation will move past the social ills that have such a terrible effect upon us at present.

If you objectively observe human life, you will see that by developing the intellect in children, something that is so terribly characteristic of human nature arises: the desire for comfort, even laziness. What is necessary in order to develop intellect is—and you may laugh at this paradox—the development of will. Children will have a healthy intellect if we develop a healthy will in them through the methods I previously discussed; that is, through an introduction to art at the earliest possible time in elementary school, since art strengthens the will. We develop the will and thus in a quite particular way take care of the intellect. The reverse is also true. If we widen the view of the child by presenting broad and noble pictures, as it is possible to do in teaching history and religion, we will also have an effect upon the will.

Strangely, the proper development of intellect activates the will, and the proper development of will activates the intellect. Because of the terrible materialism of the last few centuries, an enormous dark cloud has spread over such things. Today we hardly notice how in the depths of human nature there is a certain kind of inner laziness in the soul that acts against the development of thinking. We should study egotism because it has such a subtle yet strong effect on the development of feeling today. That is something we always need to be aware of. People can develop a strong will in the proper way only if we continue to enlarge their perspective and direct them toward those things that act spiritually in the world, those things coming from the stars that have a spiritual effect upon world history and upon the depths of the human heart. It is only when people's worldview includes the spiritual that they can properly activate their wills.

We need to move beyond certain things. In the attitudes that we have toward teaching, there is still much too much Robinson Crusoe.[2] Robinson Crusoe and everything connected with him is characteristic of all the narrowmindedness, all the pedantry of life. Robinson Crusoe was created for the hard-hearted middle class worldview of the eighteenth century and was then imitated everywhere else afterward. The English Robinson was barely there and then came the Czech, Polish, German, even a Croatian Robinson? There are Robinsons in every European language. Robinson Crusoe is a person who is not actually a person, because in a certain way he is a person who was mechanically placed in a situation of need and left alone so that out of his own inner activity and out of his external circumstances only those things necessary for healthy human development could develop piece by piece.

We could go through page by page of the Robinson Crusoe story and show the narrowmindedness that is expressed through his character. We could show the weakness of a rationalistic religious worldview, which says that God is a unity and that human beings are good only when they are not spoiled through one thing or another. This unimaginative view completely puts aside the fact that human beings need a living spirit, one that permeates their souls, one that can be found everywhere in history and which has an effect right up to the stars. This Robinson Crusoe view lives even where the book is not read as the general attitude. This narrowminded attitude must be removed from humanity, as it has subtly formed life as it is today, so that we find everywhere only a sense for what is mediocre, and people today can no longer rise above a certain level. It is Robinson Crusoe who has brought about this feeling for only the average, for nothing that is special or spectacular.

By pointing to Robinson Crusoe and his imitators and by making people aware of the intellectual adventures of the European-American civilization that overvalues the Robinson Crusoe ideal, I realize I am going against the feelings of many people. We need to leave people with that feeling a little bit, the feeling that they have moved into a little bit of the realm in which they grew up. People grew up with a Robinson Crusoe attitude and now need to think about it a little, in order to rid themselves of that part of this attitude that has permeated modern humanity.

In one sense Robinson Crusoe was a kind of protest against something that has developed more and more in Christianity. Although this is not the original Christian impulse, Christianity has developed in such a way that it assumes human nature is spoiled. Rationalism and the eighteenth-century Enlightenment out of which Robinson was conceived and written assume that human nature is still good and that all that is needed is for its evil enemies to be removed so that that goodness can come forth. Both of these positions are terribly one-sided. It is certainly understandable that a prejudice toward the basic goodness of human nature arose to oppose the prejudice of the basic evil of human nature. Basically, it is nothing more than the last remains of narrowmindedness, but a very severe form of narrowmindedness in which Jean-Jacques Rousseau[3] lives. It is essentially the opinion that if we allow people to grow as some child of nature, they will do everything just as Robinson Crusoe did in the best and most conscientious way (even though they may be under the influence of some French Baptist minister). That is about what people think.

From the present point of cultural development, we cannot progress if we allow ourselves to fall into either of these one-sided perspectives. This one-sidedness needs to be resolved through a normal synthesis. Human beings are certainly naturally good; human nature is good. Children as they enter the world as imitative beings certainly show that they unconsciously believe in the goodness of the world that has accepted them. Nevertheless, although it is true that human beings in their nature are good, it is just as true that human beings are a product of living. Fresh meat is good, but after eight days it is no longer good. It is bad because it then stinks, and something must be done to improve it if we are still to enjoy eating it after a week. Human beings are in their nature basically good. However, if they remain as they are when they entered the physical world from their pre-earthly existence, they become bad if the strength is not awakened in them to improve themselves.

There you have both: human beings are in their original nature good, but strengths must be awakened in them in order to retain the good. They are not bad in their origins, but can be spoiled if we do not awaken the forces in them that can enable them to retain their original strengths. It is just as erroneous to say that the good would shine through if we allowed people to be as they like as it is erroneous to say that people are basically not good. What is correct to say is that human beings by their nature are good, but the forces must be reawakened in them that enable what is good within to develop. If it is not supported with guidance toward the good, human nature will spoil.

We should always carry this attitude within us in regard to human development. It will be transferred to children when we tell a fairy tale or describe a ladybug or a star in such a way that it is possible to perceive, either in the details or in the general context, that we are convinced that human beings have something which is good. However, this goodness must be continuously cared for; the goodness of the world depends upon our care for human beings. It is the responsibility of human beings to participate in the formative development of the world.

In this regard we have moved away from the wisdom of our ancestors. This kind of wisdom genuinely exists in humanity. It is curious how even in ancient Greece, not to mention Egypt, it was common practice for all instruction, all activities of the priests or other religious people with the general population, to be connected with healing. In ancient times, providing knowledge was closely connected with healing. I could even say that in essence a physician was just another kind of priest and a priest another kind of physician. (Even today we find a deep-seated feeling among people that being a doctor is somehow connected with making better. "Dr. Mammon" is, of course, simply a product of the present.) All things connected with learning or understanding and providing it to others, such as being a teacher or a physician, were one in the original instincts of humanity, and the concept of healing was connected with all of them. Why is that? It was based upon a particular perspective, a perspective that we today in our materialistic times unfortunately no longer have, but one toward which we must turn again. It is the perspective that to the extent that natural forces play a role in the historical development of humanity, there is an element of demise, an element that leads toward decadence, and human beings are called upon out of their own strength to transform that decline continuously into ascent.

Culture continually threatens to become ill. Through teaching and activity, humans continually need to heal what tends to become ill in culture. History contains forces of decline, and we cannot expect these forces of decline to support humanity. The fact that Marxism today lives from the idea that everything is based upon economic forces and that which is spiritual is only a superstructure is fundamentally based upon the materialism of the past centuries. What would occur if these purely economic forces were left to themselves, if people did not continuously attempt to improve? Those forces would only make social life ill. Trotskyism and Leninism only mean to make the entire cultural development of Europe ill. If Marxism is realized, if Marxism permeates schools, then the East will become an artificial illness of European culture. It assumes that culture can develop only out of those things lying outside of human beings. But culture can only develop when human beings continuously heal what exists outside of humanity and which tends to decline.

We must revive the idea that a teacher, when he or she enters the school, acts as a kind of physician for the development of the human spirit and provides the medicine for cultural development to developing children. It is neither vanity nor arrogance when a teacher feels herself to be a physician for culture. If this is felt in the proper way, it gives us a feeling, particularly if we are teachers, to look toward those things that have always been of greatest interest to humanity. The teacher's view cannot be broad enough. The teacher's importance cannot be high enough. If we are aware of what education should achieve for humanity, the high-mindedness of the educator's view will always bring with it the necessary sense of responsibility and humility.

During these lectures, you will have seen that I have attempted to make true for a spiritual-scientific foundation of education something Herbart said: he could not imagine instruction that was not at the same time upbringing, nor could he think of any upbringing without instruction. It is important to permeate ourselves with enough spirit that is sufficiently alive that we bring all the material available to us about the progressing development of humanity into school, so that in our hands it becomes an upbringing for the children. Humanity as a whole has given us a very high task. We need to recognize what humanity has achieved and transform it so that it is appropriate for even the youngest child. We can do this if we comprehend the spirit with such liveliness as it is presented in spiritual science, and as it should be perceived here when we speak of a fructification of education through spiritual science.

I do not want to bring these lectures to a conclusion with some kind of summary. Rather I prefer to let them resound with something that I say without sentimentality, but which arises out of what I have attempted to present to you. Education can only be properly practiced if it is understood as healing and when educators are aware that they are also healers. If these lectures have provided some insight toward deepening an awareness of education so that we can all again feel how we are healers; and how we must become physicians of the spirit if we are to teach and educate in the highest sense, then these lectures will have at least achieved a hint of their goal. I hope only for what the chairman of this conference has already spoken of, namely, for a working through of the material of these lectures. I am, of course, always ready to do what you wish so that what I have presented in an incomplete form in these fourteen lectures, and which I wish so much to enter into the awareness of humanity, can be realized so that it continues to pervade our consciousness.

Appendix 1

INTRODUCTION TO A EURYTHMY PERFORMANCE[1]

Dornach, May 15, 1920

Today we offer you a performance of eurythmy. Through this art we want to place something into the spiritual development of humanity. We can view eurythmy from three perspectives: from the purely artistic, the educational, and the hygienic.

As an art, eurythmy represents a kind of voiceless, visible speech. Although it takes the form of gestures and movements, either in groups or individually, you should not confuse it with mime or pantomime[2] or with some form of artistic dance. Eurythmy uses the entire human being as its language; this visible unvoiced speech is developed through a study of the laws of voiced speech.

Voiced speech is a way of expressing what lies within the human being. Schiller was right when he said, "When the soul speaks, then, sadly, the soul no longer speaks." Language carries the human soul to the external world—or at least it should. It is also the means of communication between one person and another, and is therefore subject to convention. In a certain sense language is a social artifact. The more language must serve as a means of communication and of expressing thoughts, the less it can serve as a means of artistic expression, since art must arise out of the whole person.

Language has two sides. The first is the social side. The person must bow to the social world when speaking. Only in that way does language retain something that is intimately connected with the entirety of the human being. Young children do not learn language from their dreams. They learn it during that time when they need to adjust their entire being to their surroundings. This natural adjustment protects language from being just a means of communication.

When a poet—that is, an artist with words—wants to express something, he or she needs everything that hovers behind language. A poet needs pictures and, above all, musicality. True poetry, that is, the artistic aspect of a poem, is not at all found in the direct content of the words; rather it is in the way the content is formed. In poetry we need most of all to take into account what Goethe said in *Faust*: "Consider the what, but even more so, the how." The way the poet shapes the poem is what is most important in poetry.

You can see this much more clearly if, when you express yourself artistically, you do not use a means of expression that is too strongly permeated by thoughts but instead use your entire being. For this reason we have used both sensory and supersensory observation to study the way the human larynx, tongue, and other organs of speech move when people express themselves through voiced speech. We studied the movements that are transformed into sounds, into vibrations in the air through normal speaking. We transferred those movements to other human organs, particularly those that are most comparable to primitive organs of speech: the arms and hands.

When people first see eurythmy, they are often surprised that the performers use their hands and arms more than their other limbs. You can see this as an obvious outcome if you consider that even in normal speech, when someone wants to express more than simple conventions, if someone wants to express his or her own individuality or perception or feelings through speech, that person finds it necessary to move into these more agile, more spiritual organs. Of course eurythmy takes the entire human being into account, not just the arms and hands. Eurythmy uses the expressiveness of movements in space, whether of groups or of individuals.

The most important thing to remember is that those movements, whether they are done by individuals or groups, are not at all arbitrary. They are the same movements that are the underlying foundation of what we express through voiced speech, transferred to the entire human being.

I need to emphasize once again that what we see on stage is essentially the entire larynx, represented through the whole person. What we present is the function, rhythm, and tempo of the larynx. It represents the musical and the pictorial aspects, as well as what is poetic when poetry is genuine art. The entire group reveals it all.

What is presented in eurythmy as voiceless and visible speech is also accompanied by music or recitation. Since music and speech are just other forms of expression for what lives in the human soul, we need to use that good old-fashioned form of recitation that Goethe had in mind when he was working with actors. He kept a conductor's baton in his hand so that they would not only understand the content of the words but would also learn their rhythms. In our case, we need to avoid precisely the things that our inartistic age sees as important in recitation, namely, the emphasis upon the literal content of the words. We need to go back to what was artistic in more primitive recitations. This is rarely seen today, particularly if you live in a city. However, much of it is still alive in people my age, who can remember the traveling speakers of their childhood who recited their street ballads.[3] They drew pictures on a blackboard and then spoke the text. They never spoke without keeping time with their foot, and at an exciting point in the story, they marched up and down or did other things to indicate that the tempo of the verse and its inner form were as important as the inner content. They wanted the listener to be aware of that.

You will see that we attempt at every turn to emphasize this deeper aspect of art. Even on those occasions where we attempt to present poetry in humorous or fantastic ways through eurythmy, we do not present the literal content through such things as facial gestures or pantomime. We do not present the content of the poem through musical or poetic forms expressed solely in space but not in time. Instead we present what the poet or artist has shaped from the content.

These are a few things I wanted to mention about the artistic aspect of eurythmy. Since the human being is the instrument, not a violin or piano, not colors and shapes, eurythmy is particularly able to portray what exists within the microcosm of the human being of the ebb and flow of cosmic forces.

The second aspect of eurythmy is that of education. I am convinced that ordinary gymnastics, which developed during a materialistic period, focuses too much on anatomical and physiological aspects. In addition to physical development, there is also a development of the life of the soul and the will. We very much need these things, but mere gymnastics does not develop them in the growing human being. In the future, when people can look at such things more objectively, they will recognize that such gymnastics can strengthen human beings in a certain way, but that this strengthening does not at the same time strengthen the soul and will.

From a pedagogical perspective, we can see eurythmy as ensouled gymnastics, ensouled movement. In the small example we will present to you today with the children, you will see how those movements are carried by their souls.

We also need to say that although we are presenting some children's exercises here, the children can study eurythmy only during those few hours available during school time. However, that is not really right. The education lying at the basis of our efforts in Dornach—which the Waldorf School in Stuttgart has realized to a certain extent—has the goal of not requiring children to attend any lessons outside of regular school time.

For that reason, it is especially important that we clearly understand the educational significance of eurythmy and completely integrate it into the school curriculum. Then the children will have everything that can serve them for normal spiritual, soul, and physical development, particularly the content of eurythmy.

Third is the hygienic element. The human being is a little world, a microcosm. All ill health essentially stems from the fact that human beings tear themselves away from the great laws of the cosmos. We could represent ill health by saying that if I removed my finger from my organism as a whole, it would no longer be a finger; it would wither away. My finger retains its inner function only in connection with my organism as a whole. In the same way, the human being realizes its inner nature only in connection with the universe as a whole. What happens in human beings really is connected with the entirety of the universe. People are not merely enclosed within the boundaries of their skin. Just a moment ago the air you now have within you was outside of you. After you have inhaled it, it becomes part of your organism, and what you now have within you will be exhaled. As soon as you have exhaled it, it will be outside you. Even if we only lived within our skin, we could not prove we are only that which is enclosed by our skin. We are not just a part of the air but of the entire cosmos.

We can therefore see that everything unhealthy results from things that people do that are not appropriate, that are not befitting of the entirety of human nature or the age in which we live, and that do not support the harmony and fulfillment that must exist between human beings and all creation. However, since every movement in eurythmy naturally comes forth out of the entire human organism, just as the movements of the larynx and its associated organs do for normal speech, everything done in eurythmy can bring the human being into harmony with the entire universe.

We can certainly say that what a person, even as a child, can gain from the movements of eurythmy has a healing element. Of course, it must be performed properly and not clumsily. This is something we can certainly consider as an aspect of soul, spirit, and physical hygiene.

These are, then, the three perspectives from which we should see eurythmy and from which we have placed it in our spiritual movement.

Even though many visitors may have been here often and may have seen our recent attempts to move forward in our forms and utilization of space in the groups, we still need to appeal to your understanding for today's presentation. Eurythmy is at its very beginnings. This is an attempt at a beginning, but it is an attempt that we are convinced will improve and become more perfect. Perhaps others will need to join in and take up what we can accomplish with our weak forces and develop it further. Nevertheless it is certainly possible to see our intent from what will be shown today. Eurythmy opens the artistic wellsprings at their source, because it uses the entire human being as its means of expression, because it pedagogically develops the soul, spiritual, and physical aspects of the child, and also because it places human beings into movements that have a health-giving effect. Therefore it is an art that can be justifiably placed alongside the other, older arts, especially when our contemporaries turn their interest toward it.

INTRODUCTION TO A EURYTHMY PERFORMANCE

Dornach, May 16, 1920

Today, as in the past, I would like to say a few introductory words before this performance of eurythmy. I do this not in order to explain what will be presented since, of course, what is artistic will need to have its effect through direct experience, and it would be inartistic to give some theoretical explanation before such a performance. Nevertheless I might say that the art of eurythmy is an attempt to reach down into a source of art that exists in human beings. That wellspring seeks expression in artistic forms that are particularly well-suited for revealing the needs of all art, namely, to bring what is artistic into the realm of the sense and super-sense-perceptible.

Goethe coined the expression "sensible and supersensible viewing"[1] out of the depths of his world perspective and his feeling for art. The form of the art of eurythmy is completely based upon this sense and supersensible perception.

On the stage you will see all kinds of movements performed by individuals and groups. At first you might have the impression that the eurythmy presentation should be accompanied by poetic or musical performance and that the eurythmy is simply another expression of that. You might have the impression that eurythmy is simply gestures invented to mimic what is presented through the poetry or music. That is not the case. Eurythmy is based upon movements exercised by the organs of speech themselves and which have been revealed through a careful sensory and supersensible study of human speech.

In normal speech, the movements of the lips and gums and so forth directly affect the air. They are transformed into subtle vibrations that form the basis of what we hear. It is, of course, not these vibrations that are important here in eurythmy; rather what is important lies at the basis of an entire system of such vibrations.

This has been studied and was transferred from the organs of speech to the entire human being according to the Goethean principle of metamorphosis,[2] according to which, for instance, the entire plant is only a leaf that is more complicated in form.

What you will see on the stage are not simply random movements. Instead they are movements that strictly follow certain laws. They follow the same laws and occur in the same order as do the movements of the organs of speech when giving tone while speaking or sounds while singing. Within these forms resides an inner necessity of the same sort as is created by music in forming a series of tones. What we are concerned with here is, in fact, a kind of visible speech that closely follows certain rules.

Modern culture will need to find its way into this visible speech, as modern culture contains something quite inartistic within it. Things that were quite common during the Romantic period are much less so today—for example, people intently listened to poems when they did not actually understand the words; they listened more to the rhythm and the inner form of the sounds.

We will see this in the recitations that accompany the eurythmy presentations in much the same way as does music, that there is nothing other that we could emphasize in this element of artistic eurythmy than the actual artistic element of the poetry itself. It is not the word-for-word content of the poem that is important; rather, it is the formal form that the artist has created which is important. Thus you will see that we attempt to present forms and spatial forms created by groups. They are not simply mimicking the content of the poetry; rather something follows from the character of the poem that the poet developed into the words. Even when the presentation is concerned with something surreal, something affected, such as we will attempt to present in the second part of the presentation today, you will see that it is concerned not with some imitative presentation of the content, but rather with forming connections of such a nature that the individual movements have little effect; the effect is formed through the harmonious forms acting together.

In general, we can say that through eurythmy we return to the sources of art because eurythmy is an art that should not affect us solely through our thoughts. When our concern is with science in our modern materialistic sense, it is only thoughts that affect us, and for that reason, we can penetrate only into the sense-perceptible content of the world. In the art of eurythmy, our concern is more that the sense and supersensible character should be expressed than the fact that the entire human being or groups of human beings are the means of expressing it.

We can thus say that the human being, the ensouled human being, the human being permeated by spirit, places soul and spirit into each movement, namely, that soul and spirit that we can hear through the truths sounding from the poetry. All this shows how the sense-perceptible, which we can see through the limbs of the human being, at the same time carries the spirit on its wings. It is, therefore, genuinely sensory and supersensibly perceptible. Eurythmy thus expresses what Goethe demanded of all art when he said, "Those to whom nature begins to reveal its secret will have a deep desire for nature's highest level of expression, namely, art."[3]

For Goethe, art is in a certain sense a way of experiencing nature through feeling. How would it be possible to better correspond to nature than to bring to expression those capacities that enable human beings to move based upon their will, so that a kind of visible speech is therefore expressed? Thinking, which in general ignores art, is thus shut out. It is only will that is expressed in the movements. The personality of human beings is transferred to these movements in an impersonal way, so something that is highly artistic and represents something sense- and super-sense-perceptible is expressed through these presentations.

Eurythmy also has a significant educational effect in that it is at the same time a kind of ensouled gymnastics. If you think about these things objectively, then you will see that what has long been treasured as gymnastics and something which we certainly do not wish to eliminate is something that experiences a particular kind of growth when we place alongside it this ensouled form of gymnastics as we have done for the children at the Waldorf School in Stuttgart. You will see some of this children's eurythmy during the second part of our presentation today.

Normal gymnastics strengthens the body, of course, and for that reason we certainly do not want to go without it. However, ensouled gymnastics, which has an effect not simply upon the physical body but the spirit and soul as well, is particularly effective in developing the will. Future generations, who will have an increasingly difficult life, will need stronger will energies.

Eurythmy also has an important hygienic side. The movements of eurythmy are those movements through which individuals can best place themselves into the rhythm and harmony of the world. All unhealthy things are essentially based upon people separating themselves from that rhythm. We are certainly not doing anything reactionary, and I would ask therefore that you do not consider me to be rejecting the aspects of modern culture. There are many things today that are necessary, things we need, things we cannot eliminate. We must also admit there are many reasons modern human beings would want to separate themselves from the rhythm and harmony of the world. Each time we sit in a railway car or an automobile, and when we do many other such things at the same time, we undertake actions that separate us from universal rhythms. This separation sneaks slowly into human health and undermines it in a way that is not even noticed. These things can be seen only by those who have an intimate understanding of the relationship of human beings with the universe. However, the universe seeks today to give something that will return human beings to health.

Where do people today seek health? I know that with the following I am saying something contrary to what is commonly held today, but in the future people will think more objectively of this. Prior to this terrible world catastrophe that crashed in upon us, there was an attempt to achieve health through such things as the Olympic Games. That is a terrible thought that lies entirely outside of any genuine understanding. The Olympic Games were appropriate for the Greek body. When undertaking such things, people do not at all realize that each cultural period has its particular requirements.

That is something, however, that we attempt to do through the art of eurythmy. We do not attempt to provide humanity with something based upon some abstract theory or something from the past. Instead we try to do what is necessary for modern civilization, something that we can find within human nature and which is appropriate for the structure of modern humanity.

Such things certainly cannot be proven anatomically or physiologically, because we cannot dissect the ancient Greeks. Those who can look into cultural development through spiritual science recognize that modern human beings in their physical form and especially in their soul and spiritual structure require something else.

Eurythmy is a beginning toward finding those requirements placed before us by our cultural period itself. Eurythmy attempts to correspond to our culture.

As you know, what we will present here today is at its very beginnings, and therefore remains simply an attempt. We are nevertheless convinced that because we are serious about working based upon the requirements of our cultural period, others will further develop what we can present here today, so that a mature art form will arise that is worthy of being placed alongside its older sisters.

NOTES

1. SPIRITUAL SCIENCE AND MODERN EDUCATION

1. Johann Friedrich Herbart (1776–1841), a philosopher and educator who taught in Göttingen and Bern. He is considered the founder of the science of pedagogy that is closely connected with practical philosophy, ethics, and psychology. His works include *General Pedagogy* (1806); *Textbook of Psychology* (1816); and *An Outline of Pedagogical Lectures* (1835).

2. Franz Exner (1802–1853), philosopher and professor in Prague and Vienna. Beginning in 1840, he was a minister in the Austrian Ministry of Culture, and together with Bonitz he was able to place his *Draft for the Organization of the Upper Schools in Austria* into effect in 1840. Among other things, he wrote *The Psychology of the Hegelian School*, 1842–1844, in two volumes. In previous German editions of *The Renewal of Education*, Exner was referred to as Oetzler. This appears to be a stenographic error, as there is no other mention of a person named Oetzler in Steiner's works.

3. These schools were formed by Hermann Lietz (1868–1919). The goal of these schools was to raise the children entrusted to them "to be harmonious and independent people, to be German youths who are strong and healthy in body and soul, who are industrious physically, practically, scientifically, artistically; who can think clearly, feel warmly, and will with strength and courage." This was to be achieved by creating educational institutions far from the chaos of the cities in a country environment. The first such country boarding school was founded by Lietz in 1898 in Illsenburg in the Harz, and other schools then followed in Haubinda, Thüringen, in 1901 (which Steiner visited once), and in Schloss Bieberstein in the Rhone. Later, some of Lietz's colleagues founded their own schools. See Hermann Lietz, *German Country Boarding Schools: Educational Principles and Organization* (1906).

4. In 1920 Europe, the then widely used term "social relationships" did not mean "interpersonal relationships," but was used to indicate a proposed societal

257

organization that was less hierarchical and more cooperative and had as goals meeting the economic needs of its members and seeking for a system of rights based on a recognition of the value of contributions to the whole made by people at all levels of society. The term "socialism" sprang from this understanding, but quickly became a very one-sided technical term that was much more limited than its origins would imply. Despite the fact that "social relationships" is no longer used in its 1920 meaning, we have chosen to retain it throughout this translation. —*Trans.*

5. Tuiskon Ziller (1817–1882), professor and head of the Pedagogical Seminar in Leipzig and founder of the Herbart-Ziller School. He wanted to concentrate instruction around those subjects that formed attitudes and developed the formal stages of lectures, namely, analysis, synthesis, association, symptom, and method. Among his works are *Introduction to General Pedagogy* (1901); *Foundation for Educative Instruction* (1884); and *General Ethics* (1886).

6. Friedrich Adolf Wilhelm Diesterweg (1790–1866), private tutor and then high-school teacher; after 1820 was the head of the Teaching Seminar in Mörs and after 1832, in Berlin. He was a champion of elementary schools and worked to develop them in the direction indicated by Pestalozzi (see below). He developed the ideas of the Enlightenment and was a defender of democratic liberalism. He wrote numerous teaching books, among them *On Teaching* (1820); *German Pedagogy* (1835).

7. Johann Heinrich Pestalozzi (1746–1827). Early in his career he had an orphanage in Switzerland, where he taught and raised children and where they also worked in agricultural and commercial jobs. Beginning in 1780, he began to write and turned his attention toward describing the inhumane conditions of his time. In 1798, he undertook to help children orphaned during the war in Stans. In 1799, he taught in Burgdorf and, beginning in 1805, in Yverdon where he became famous worldwide for his work. In particular, he attempted to connect schools, teacher training, retirement homes, and orphanages. He had an enormous effect upon pedagogy and the school system through his writings, which include *The Evening of a Hermit* (1780); *Lienhard and Gertrude* (1781–87); *My Research into the Course of Nature in the Development of the Human Race* (1797); and *How Gertrude Teaches Her Children* (1801).

8. Jean Paul: Jean Paul Friedrich Richter (1763–1825), poet, pedagogue, and publisher. He wrote a number of novels, among them *The Invisible Lodge* (1796); *Titan* (1800–03); and *Levana* (1807).

DISCUSSION FOLLOWING LECTURE ONE

1. An important family of mathematicians living in Basel during the seventeenth and eighteenth centuries.

2. The first musician of the family was Hans Bach, who immigrated to Thüringen in 1590 and who died in 1626. His great-grandson, Johann Sebastian Bach

(1685–1750), was the most important of the more than fifty musicians in the Bach family.

2. THREE ASPECTS OF THE HUMAN BEING

1. Rudolf Steiner, *Riddles of the Soul*, trans. William Lindeman (Spring Valley, N.Y.: Mercury Press, 1996); see in particular chapter six, "The Physical and Spiritual Dependencies of Man's Being." The original work, *Von Seelenrätseln*, was originally published in Berlin in 1917.

2. Edward Hanslick (1825–1904) discusses Wagner's compositions in detail in his *On What Is Musically Beautiful* (1854). See also Steiner's discussion in his lecture of December 29, 1910, in *Occult History: Historical Perspectives and Events in the Light of Spiritual Science*, trans. D.S. Osmond and Charles Davy (London: Rudolf Steiner Press, 1957).

3. UNDERSTANDING THE HUMAN BEING:
A Foundation for Education

1. Vladimir Ilyich Lenin (Ulyanov; 1870-1924), social revolutionary and theoretician of dialectical materialism. He was the son of a Russian landowner. He led the Bolsheviks and during the November Revolution of 1917 became chairman of the People's Committees. He was the founder of the Soviet Union in 1922 and remained its leader until his death.

2. Leon Trotsky (Lev Davidovich Bronstein; 1879–1940), a close colleague of Lenin who played a significant role in the development of military power in the Soviet Union. He was exiled by Stalin in 1929 and emigrated to Mexico, where he was murdered in 1940.

3. Richard Avenarius (1843–1896), philosopher who founded the school of critical empiricism and an opponent of Lenin. His main work is *Criticism of Pure Experience* (1888–90).

4. Karl Vogt (1817–95), zoologist and geologist, who was one of the main proponents of materialism and Darwinism. Steiner often quotes from his article "Belief of the Charcoal Burner and Science" (1855).

5. Ernst Mach (1838–1916), physicist and philosopher and one of the founders of the school of critical empiricism. He upheld the views of Berkeley and Hume in his epistemology, which had a major influence upon theoretical physics. Among other things he wrote *The Development of Mechanics* (1883) and *Knowledge and Error: Sketches of a Psychology of Research* (1905).

6. Friedrich Adler (1879–1960), philosopher and leader of the Austrian Social Democrats as well as a theoretician of Austrian Marxism. He attempted to extend Marxism with Mach's philosophy. On October 21, 1916, he shot the Austrian President Graf Stürgkh and was sentenced to death. He was freed, however, in

1918. Later he became a leader of the Socialist Workers' International.

7. Karl Graf von Stürgkh (1859–1916), Austrian politician. From 1909 to 1911, he was the Minister of Education and then became President of Austria. He was shot by Friedrich Adler.

8. Steiner is referring here to an essay by Nikolai Berdyaev, "Political and Philosophical Truth," which was published in a book edited by Elias Hurwicz, *Russia's Political Soul* (1918). This essay had appeared in Russia in 1919. The essay states that "[Russian intelligence] went on to the thoughts of Avenarius, since his most abstract or pure philosophy without his knowledge went on to suddenly become the philosophy of Bolshevism."

9. See Johann Wolfgang von Goethe, *Theory of Colors*, trans. Charles Lock Eastlake (Cambridge, Mass.: M.I.T. Press, 1978 [1940]).

10. Karl Schmid, "Heartbeat and Pulse," in *The Viennese Medical Journal*, nos. 15–17 (1892).

11. Moritz Benedikt (1835–1920), criminologist. See his book, *Biomechanical Thinking in Medicine and Biology* (1903).

12. Carl Georg Lange (1834–1900). See his book *The Nature of Feelings and Their Influence upon the Physical Body, Particularly upon Events That Cause Illness* (1910).

4. THE TEACHER AS SCULPTOR OF THE HUMAN SOUL

1. During the weeks prior to the opening of the Waldorf School in Stuttgart, Steiner held a pedagogical course to prepare the teachers he had selected. The lectures in this course, which went from August 21 to September 6, 1919, have been published under the titles *The Foundations of Human Experience,* trans. Robert F. Lathe and Nancy Parsons Whittaker (Hudson, N.Y.: Anthroposophic Press, 1996); *Practical Advice to Teachers,* trans. Johanna Collis (Hudson, N.Y.: Anthroposophic Press, 2000); and *Discussions with Teachers,* trans. Helen Fox et al. (Hudson, N.Y.: Anthroposophic Press, 1997). Steiner's notes for the course have been published in *Beiträge zur Rudolf Steiner Gesamtausgabe,* no. 31, Michaelmas 1970. A chronology of the school foundation is available in the double issue of the *Beiträge,* nos. 27–28, Michaelmas 1969.

2. Steiner is referring here to Ernst Haeckel's basic biogenetic law. In an essay Steiner wrote in 1900, "Haeckel and His Opponents," he makes the following remark: "Haeckel showed the general validity and wide-ranging significance of the biogenetic law in a series of works. The most important conclusions and proofs can be found in his *The Biology of Chalk Sponges* (1872), and in his *Studies of Gastraea* (1873–84). Since then, other zoologists have further developed and confirmed this theory. In his most recent book, *The Riddle of the World* (1899), Haeckel says, referring to the theory, 'Although at the beginning this did not find general acceptance and was opposed by numerous authorities for over a decade, it has been in the past

fifteen years accepted by most people familiar with the subject.'" In his essay, Steiner quotes Haeckel's biogenetic law as follows: "The short ontology or development of the individual is a compressed repetition or recapitulation of the long physiological development of the species."

3. Friedrich August Wolf (1759–1824). Steiner quotes Wolf directly in his lecture "Education and Spiritual Science," in *The Education of the Child and Early Lectures on Education,* trans. George and Mary Adams et al. (Hudson, N.Y.: Anthroposophic Press, 1997), p. 65.

DISCUSSION FOLLOWING LECTURE FOUR

1. Lao Tsu, a Chinese theologian of the sixth century B.C. He wrote the *Tao Te Ching,* in which the *Tao,* the "way," is the foundation of the universe.

5. SOME REMARKS ABOUT CURRICULUM

1. Emil Molt (1876–1936), director of the Waldorf-Astoria Cigarette Company in Stuttgart. He created continuing education courses for the workers at the Waldorf-Astoria factory. The idea of a school for the workers' children arose from those courses. Molt called upon Steiner to organize and lead the Waldorf School. In 1919, Molt was one of the most enthusiastic advocates of Steiner's "threefolding" idea. See Molt's autobiography, *Emil Molt.* Some of his essays have been published in *Beiträge zur Rudolf Steiner Gesamtausgabe,* no. 103, Michaelmas 1989.

2. For the content of this compromise, see the translators' introduction to *The Spirit of the Waldorf School,* trans. Robert F. Lathe and Nancy Parsons Whittaker (Hudson, N.Y.: Anthroposophic Press, 1994), pp. xi–xv.

3. The so-called Bow-Wow Theory is based upon the assumption that through our organs of speech what we externally hear, like the sound of some animals, is then imitated. The linguist Max Müller belittled this theory because he saw how unsatisfactory and speculative it was, and thus named it the Bow-Wow Theory. Instead he developed another theory, which his opponents regarded as mystical. Müller believed that all objects had within them something like a tone. Müller's opponents in turn belittled his views by referring to them as the Ding-Dong Theory. Steiner discusses this in his lecture of January 20, 1910, "Spiritual Science and Language," in *Metamorphosis of the Soul,* part 2, GA 59. Max Müller (1823–1900) was one of the most important scholars of the Orient in his time as well as being a linguist. He taught at Oxford and wrote *The Science of Language* (1892).

6. TEACHING EURYTHMY, MUSIC, DRAWING, AND LANGUAGE

1. Beginning in 1911, Steiner developed an art of movement, known as eurythmy, that was also used pedagogically and therapeutically. Many of his introductions to eurythmy performances are contained in *An Introduction to Eurythmy.*

2. See Goethe's *Metamorphosis of the Plant.*

3. Hermann Grimm (1828–1911), professor of art history in Berlin. Steiner mentions Grimm in his *Autobiography: Chapters in the Course of My Life, 1861–1907,* trans. Rita Stebbing (Hudson, N.Y.: Anthroposophic Press, 1999), pp. 102, 137. See also Steiner's essays about Grimm in *Methodische Grundlagen der Anthroposophie, 1884–1901. Gesammelte Aufsätze zur Philosophie, Naturwissenschaft, Ästhetick, und Seelenkunde,* GA 30 (not translated). Grimm says about his despair concerning students in the upper grades, "I am always astonished by the incapacity of young people to recognize things such as copperplate engravings done as copies of Raphael's works. When I ask them to say something about the picture in general, or about individual figures, they don't know what to say. They see the things without any understanding of what is in front of them. I do not believe that art history should be taught in the upper grades. I ask myself, however, how it is possible that such a deficiency in seeing has arisen in university students."

4. Raphael Sanzio (1483–1520), Italian painter of the Renaissance. A chronological overview of Steiner's lectures in which he discusses Raphael and his work is published in *Beiträge zur Rudolf Steiner Gesamtausgabe,* no. 82, Christmas 1983.

DISCUSSION FOLLOWING LECTURE SIX

1. René Descartes (1596–1650) is considered the founder of modern philosophy. See Steiner's *Riddles of Philosophy* (Spring Valley, N.Y.: Anthroposophic Press, 1973), pp. 67–70.

2. Sigmund Freud (1856–1939), psychiatrist and, after 1902, professor in Vienna. He is considered the founder of psychoanalysis. For Steiner's views on Freud, see his lectures from November 10 and 11, 1917, in *Freud, Jung, and Spiritual Psychology,* trans. May Laird Brown (Great Barrington, Mass.: Anthroposophic Press, 2001), pp. 31–56.

3. See Goethe's poem "Eins wie's andere."

4. Gustav Theodor Fechner (1801–87), a physicist and professor in Leipzig. He was also the founder of psychophysics.

5. Carl Gustav Jung (1875–1961), psychologist and professor in Zurich and Basel.

7. THE PROBLEM OF TEACHER TRAINING

1. The boy's father was the philosopher Franz Brentano.

8. TEACHING ZOOLOGY AND BOTANY TO CHILDREN NINE THROUGH TWELVE

1. Friedrich Nietzsche (1844–1900), philosopher. His book *The Birth of Tragedy from the Spirit of Music* was published in 1872.

2. Lorenz Oken (1779–1851), zoologist and professor of medicine.

3. This reference was never found.

9. DIALECT AND STANDARD LANGUAGE

1. "Es regnet," "Es blitzt," "Es wetterleuchtet" are subjectless forms like the English "It is raining," "It is snowing," etc. The form is not subjectless in the grammatical sense, but in the connotative sense: strictly speaking, there is no "it" that is the referent.

2. Substantiated verbs are verbs that have been modified to become nouns. In English the gerund has the same role.

10. SYNTHESIS AND ANALYSIS IN HUMAN NATURE AND EDUCATION

1. "The German noun *Kraft*, 'force, strength,' has only its corresponding adjective *kräftig*, 'strong, robust.' Rudolf Steiner invented the corresponding verb *kraften*, 'to work actively, forcefully,' and the verbal noun *das Kraften*, 'actively working force or strength'": Rudolf Steiner, *The Genius of Language*, trans. Gertrude Teutsch and Ruth Pusch (Hudson, N.Y.: Anthroposophic Press, 1995), p. 16n.

2. Friedrich Theodore Vischer (1807–1887), writer and philosopher often quoted by Steiner. Regarding cynicism, see Vischer's book *Mode und Zynismus* (1878).

12. TEACHING HISTORY AND GEOGRAPHY

1. Johannes Gutenberg (Johannes Gensfleisch, 1400–1468) invented movable type around 1445. See Steiner's "Gutenbergs Tat als Markstein der Kulturentwicklung" ("Gutenberg's Deed as a Milestone in Cultural Development" in *Gesammelte Aufsätze zur Kultur- und Zeitgeschichte, 1887–1901*, GA 31, not translated), given at a celebration of the 500th anniversary of the invention of movable type.

2. In German the word for "shabby" is "*schäbig*." A southern German/Austrian word for *moth* is *Schabe*.

3. Josef Misson (1803–1875), priest and writer of poetry in dialect. Steiner speaks about him in detail in *The Riddle of Man* (Spring Valley, N.Y.: Mercury Press, 1990).

13. CHILDREN'S PLAY

1. Friedrich Schiller (1759–1805). The reference here is to Schiller's *Letters on the Aesthetic Education of Man*, where he says, "Human beings play only when they are human beings in the complete sense of the word, and they are completely human only when they play." See also Steiner's lectures on Schiller in *Über Philosophie, Geschichte, und Literatur: Darstellungen an der Arbeiterbildungsschule und der Freien Hochschule in Berlin 1901 bis 1905 (*GA 51).

2. Robert Zimmermann (1824–1898), philosopher and professor of philosophy at

the University of Vienna from 1861 to 1895. He was one of the most important representatives of the Herbartian school and wrote *Anthroposophie im Umriss: Entwurf eines Systems idealer Weltansicht auf monistischer Grundlage* (Vienna, 1882). His book *Philosophische Propädeutik* was published in 1852. Zimmermann treats the problem discussed by Steiner in the chapter "Empirische Psychologie."

14. FURTHER PERSPECTIVES AND ANSWERS TO QUESTIONS

1. See Steiner's lecture of September 3, 1919, in *Practical Advice to Teachers*, pp. 154–64.

2. Daniel Defoe, *The Life and Strange Surprising Adventures of Robinson Crusoe of York, Mariner*, published in 1719. The archetypal situation of the marooned sailor was imitated in numerous other works.

3. Jean-Jacques Rousseau (1712–1778), cultural philosopher. Here Steiner is referring to Rousseau's book *Emile*.

Appendix 1
INTRODUCTION TO A EURYTHMY PERFORMANCE

1. The participants of the education course had been invited to this as well as to a eurythmy performance on May 16.

2. Mime is wordless acting; pantomime is wordless acting through dance.

3. Steiner is referring to *Moritaten*, a popular form of nineteenth-century entertainment in which a sensational event, such as a murder, was described in prose or verse with some songs interspersed, often with the accompaniment of a barrel organ.

Appendix 2
INTRODUCTION TO A EURYTHMY PERFORMANCE

1. In his autobiography, *Dichtung und Wahrheit*, Goethe says, "I did not see with the eyes of the body, rather with those of the spirit riding along the same path to meet myself." See also Steiner's Introduction to Goethe in *Kürschner's Deutsche National–Litteratur,* in which he states, "We learn to see with the eyes of the spirit without which we would particularly in understanding nature stumble around blindly." He also states in the same volume, "Regardless of how successful this method was, that he (Wolff) used to achieve so much, he did not believe there is a difference between seeing and *seeing*, that the spiritual eyes exist in a constant connection with the eyes of the body, as otherwise we would be in danger of seeing and at the same time looking past."

2. See Goethe's *Metamorphosis of Plants*.

3. See Goethe's *Sprüche in Prosa* ("Sayings in Prose").

INDEX

THE FOUNDATIONS
OF WALDORF EDUCATION

THE FIRST FREE WALDORF SCHOOL opened its doors in Stuttgart, Germany, in September 1919, under the auspices of Emil Molt, director of the Waldorf Astoria Cigarette Company and a student of Rudolf Steiner's spiritual science and particularly of Steiner's call for social renewal.

It was only the previous year—amid the social chaos following the end of World War I—that Molt, responding to Steiner's prognosis that truly human change would not be possible unless a sufficient number of people received an education that developed the whole human being, decided to create a school for his workers' children. Conversations with the minister of education and with Rudolf Steiner, in early 1919, then led rapidly to the forming of the first school.

Since that time, more than 600 schools have opened around the globe—from Italy, France, Portugal, Spain, Holland, Belgium, Great Britain, Norway, Finland, and Sweden to Russia, Georgia, Poland, Hungary, Romania, Israel, South Africa, Australia, Brazil, Chile, Peru, Argentina, Japan, and others—making the Waldorf school movement the largest independent school movement in the world. The United States, Canada, and Mexico alone now have more than 120 schools.

Although each Waldorf school is independent, and although there is a healthy oral tradition going back to the first Waldorf teachers and to Steiner himself, as well as a growing body of secondary literature, the true foundations of the Waldorf method and spirit remain the many lectures that Rudolf Steiner gave on the subject. For five years (1919–24), Rudolf Steiner, while simultaneously working on many other fronts, tirelessly dedicated himself to the dissemination of the idea of Waldorf education. He gave manifold lectures to teachers, parents, the general public, and even the children themselves. New schools were founded. The movement grew.

While many of Steiner's foundational lectures have been translated and published in the past, some have never appeared in English, and many have been virtually unobtainable for years. To remedy this situation and to establish a coherent basis for Waldorf education, Anthroposophic Press has decided to publish the complete series of Steiner lectures and writings on education in a uniform series. This series will thus constitute an authoritative foundation for work in educational renewal, for Waldorf teachers, parents, and educators generally.

RUDOLF STEINER'S
LECTURES AND WRITINGS
ON EDUCATION

I. *Allgemeine Menschenkunde als Grundlage der Pädagogik. Pädagogischer Grundkurs,* 14 Lectures, Stuttgart, 1919 (GA 293). Previously *Study of Man. The Foundations of Human Experience* (Anthroposophic Press, 1996).

II. *Erziehungskunst Methodische-Didaktisches,* 14 Lectures, Stuttgart, 1919 (GA 294). *Practical Advice to Teachers* (Rudolf Steiner Press, 1988).

III. *Erziehungskunst,* 15 Discussions, Stuttgart, 1919 (GA 295). *Discussions with Teachers* (Anthroposophic Press, 1997).

IV. *Die Erziehungsfrage als soziale Frage,* 6 Lectures, Dornach, 1919 (GA 296). *Education as a Force for Social Change* (previously *Education as a Social Problem*) (Anthroposophic Press, 1997).

V. *Die Waldorf Schule und ihr Geist,* 6 Lectures, Stuttgart and Basel, 1919 (GA 297). *The Spirit of the Waldorf School* (Anthroposophic Press, 1995).

VI. *Rudolf Steiner in der Waldorfschule, Vorträge und Ansprachen,* Stuttgart, 1919–1924 (GA 298). *Rudolf Steiner in the Waldorf School: Lectures and Conversations* (Anthroposophic Press, 1996).

VII. *Geisteswissenschaftliche Sprachbetrachtungen,* 6 Lectures, Stuttgart, 1919 (GA 299). *The Genius of Language* (Anthroposophic Press, 1995).

VIII. *Konferenzen mit den Lehren der Freien Waldorfschule 1919–1924,* 3 Volumes (GA 300a–c). *Faculty Meetings with Rudolf Steiner,* 2 Volumes (Anthroposophic Press, 1998).

IX. *Die Erneuerung der Pädagogisch-didaktischen Kunst durch Geisteswissenschaft,* 14 Lectures, Basel, 1920 (GA 301). *The Renewal of Education* (Anthroposophic Press, 2001).

X. *Menschenerkenntnis und Unterrichtsgestaltung,* 8 Lectures, Stuttgart, 1921 (GA 302). Previously *The Supplementary Course—Upper School* and *Waldorf Education for Adolescence. Education for Adolescents* (Anthroposophic Press, 1996).

XI. *Erziehung und Unterricht aus Menschenerkenntnis,* 9 Lectures, Stuttgart, 1920, 1922, 1923 (GA 302a). The first four lectures available as *Balance in Teaching* (Mercury Press, 1982); last three lectures as *Deeper Insights into Education* (Anthroposophic Press, 1988).

XII. *Die Gesunder Entwicklung des Menschenwesens,* 16 Lectures, Dornach, 1921–22 (GA 303). *Soul Economy and Waldorf Education* (Anthroposophic Press, 1986).

XIII. *Erziehungs- und Unterrichtsmethoden auf Anthroposophischer* Grundlage, 9 Public Lectures, various cities, 1921–22 (GA 304). *Waldorf Education and Anthroposophy 1* (Anthroposophic Press, 1995).

XIV. *Anthroposophische Menschenkunde und Pädagogik,* 9 Public Lectures, various cities, 1923–24 (GA 304a). *Waldorf Education and Anthroposophy 2* (Anthroposophic Press, 1996).

XV. *Die geistig-seelischen Grundkräfte der Erziehungskunst,* 12 Lectures, 1 Special Lecture, Oxford 1922 (GA 305). *The Spiritual Ground of Education* (Garber Publications, 1989).

XVI. *Die pädagogisch Praxis vom Gesichtspunkte geisteswissenschaftlicher Menschenerkenntnis,* 8 Lectures, Dornach, 1923 (GA 306). *The Child's Changing Consciousness As the Basis of Pedagogical Practice* (Anthroposophic Press, 1996).

XVII. *Gegenwärtiges Geistesleben und Erziehung,* 4 Lectures, Ilkeley, 1923 (GA 307). *A Modern Art of Education* (Rudolf Steiner Press, 1981) and *Education and Modern Spiritual Life* (Garber Publications, 1989).

XVIII. *Die Methodik des Lehrens und die Lebensbedingungen des Erziehens,* 5 Lectures, Stuttgart, 1924 (GA 308). *The Essentials of Education* (Anthroposophic Press, 1997).

XIX. *Anthroposophische Pädagogik und ihre Voraussetzungen,* 5 Lectures, Bern, 1924 (GA 309). *The Roots of Education* (Anthroposophic Press, 1997).

XX. *Der pädagogische Wert der Menschenerkenntnis und der Kulturwert der Pädagogik,* 10 Public Lectures, Arnheim, 1924 (GA 310). *Human Values in Education* (Rudolf Steiner Press, 1971).

XXI. *Die Kunst des Erziehens aus dem Erfassen der Menschenwesenheit,* 7 Lectures, Torquay, 1924 (GA 311). *The Kingdom of Childhood* (Anthroposophic Press, 1995).

XXII. *Geisteswissenschaftliche Impulse zur Entwicklung der Physik. Erster naturwissenschaftliche Kurs: Licht, Farbe, Ton—Masse, Elektrizität, Magnetismus,* 10 Lectures,

Stuttgart, 1919–20 (GA 320). *The Light Course* (Anthroposophic Press, 2002).

XXIII. *Geisteswissenschaftliche Impulse zur Entwicklung der Physik. Zweiter naturwissenschaftliche Kurs: die Wärme auf der Grenze positiver und negativer Materialität,* 14 Lectures, Stuttgart, 1920 (GA 321). *The Warmth Course* (Mercury Press, 1988).

XXIV. *Das Verhältnis der verschiedenen naturwissenschaftlichen Gebiete zur Astronomie. Dritter naturwissenschaftliche Kurs: Himmelskunde in Beziehung zum Menschen und zur Menschenkunde,* 18 Lectures, Stuttgart, 1921 (GA 323). Available in typescript only as "*The Relation of the Diverse Branches of Natural Science to Astronomy."*

XXV. *The Education of the Child and Early Lectures on Education* (A collection) (Anthroposophic Press, 1996).

XXVI. Miscellaneous.

During the last two decades of the nineteenth century, the Austrian-born Rudolf Steiner (1861–1925) became a respected and well-published scientific, literary, and philosophical scholar, particularly known for his work on Goethe's scientific writings. After the turn of the century he began to develop his earlier philosophical principles into an approach to methodical research of psychological and spiritual phenomena.

His multifaceted genius has led to innovative and holistic approaches in medicine, philosophy, religion, education (Waldorf schools), special education, science, economics, agriculture (Biodynamic method), architecture, drama, the new arts of speech and eurythmy, and other fields of activity. In 1924 he founded the General Anthroposophical Society, which today has branches throughout the world.